SHWY

Design, photography, and layout: C. Smith Ladd

Published by: Lasmi Enterprises

ISBN: 978-0-9904075-1-5 (First Edition, June 2014)

~ To all who yearn to embrace the gift of life, each and every day, with a smile of liberation from negatives such as fear, frustration, and worry... this book is for you. ~

{In loving memory of Bj}

Acknowledgement

To my dearest "sisters," Darlene Mitchell and Julie Gaines Doss, thank you for trusting me to help you along your way and for your prodding of me to publish a book with "Charmainisms" at its core. The very thought of my words being held and read by any and all who've encouraged me to write this book, gives me great pleasure.

To all my wonderful, dear friends and family members who have, over the decades, allowed me to enter their worlds by asking my opinion and advice: thank you for the pallet on which my skills were honed into a philosophical art form. Thank you for your love, as well as your continued faith and trust in me. And thank you for always being there—through thick and thin, and everything in between. My love for you all is immeasurable.

This rings especially true for one of my dearest and most enduring friendships; that with Stephen William Price, Ph.D. Stephen, thank you for accepting my advice and opinions for nearly four decades ("lovingly/hatingly," as you've affectionately deemed it), as well as being a most trusted confidant. Love you!

To the memory of my wonderful and incredibly dear friend, Diamonda Tobias, I so wish you were here to help me celebrate the completion and publication of this book. You are forever cherished in my heart and mind. I love and miss you tremendously.

To my biggest fans, my children, Bj (William Dean Ladd II, 1974-2005) and Breighan (Michele Breighan Ladd Long), you are my Beacons of Light forever and a day. To my cherished and adored grandchildren, William Dean (Ladd III), Diana Jean (Lienemann), and Stace William (Long), may this book help guide you throughout your lives in your times of need.

And a tremendous thank you to my very best friend (and one-in-a-million husband of over forty years) who's always felt my outlook and philosophies on life should be shared with all who love to learn new ways to live life to the fullest: Bill Ladd, thank you for always being there by my side and for being the greatest father any mother could want for her children. As we embark on this newest chapter in our lives, from seafaring sailors back to landscaping landlubbers, the timing was perfect as it served as an irresistible encouragement for me to write this book.

No one else could have been as helpful and dedicated in assisting with the final editing; as no one else knows firsthand quite as much of the back story and what this book means to me as you do. Thank you for your unwavering encouragement, patience, and intense love. My father was always indebted to you for carrying on what he'd started. Daddy noticed it about you right off, and genuinely admired your deep and passionate love for me. There's no question as to why, to this very day, I'm still so very, very much in love with you. You, my darling, are oh, so very easy to love.

C~

Dedication

My father will forever remain the most positive influence in my life. He was quite the man of confidence, incredibly comfortable with people from all walks of life, and owned a charisma that few have witnessed up close and personal. Exceedingly generous with his optimistic disposition, sound wisdom, and savvy advice, my father was my greatest mentor. In that declaration, I am not alone. Daddy mentored a plethora of adolescents and young adults who became the better for knowing him. He introduced and taught many a youngster a trade upon which they could build their skills of expertise and earn a living. He also taught them self-respect, consideration and respect of others, and the importance of good character.

During WWII, my mother was completely swept off her feet by a strikingly handsome man in Naval uniform with a suave demeanor and charming words. Her country girl roots failed to prepare her for someone as worldly as the dapper and eloquent young man from Springfield, Illinois who would become my father.

It wasn't long before my mother realized she was in way over her head. During my entire childhood, Father made promises and Mother cried every time those pledges were broken. Sometimes she would cry from sunup to sundown and back around again. Insecurity and worry about the welfare of her family had her teetering in and out of depression.

Mother soon found a great source of comfort and hope in the promises made by a new-to-her religion that held meetings at the Kingdom Hall; while Daddy found his comfort and hope in the libations and gambling offered at the local *Pool* Hall. You could say it was a household of entirely mixed signals. It was a never-ending tango of my parents' internal wars: positive energy doing negative things, and negative energy doing positive things.

For me, I was going to make some sense out of the nonsense that was my household. While others were worried, I'd shake my head a lot and laugh it off with incredulousness. Just thinking about the futility of it all was funny to me.

Watching my parents fight about every little thing under the sun was much like an episode of "Ma and Pa Kettle." It really was somewhat like living in a sitcom (except it wasn't very funny to those living it that didn't see the humor in it). That was a big difference between my siblings and me.

The reality of it was that the arguments between my parents would disrupt the entire household and the younger children were understandably concerned and frightened. The smaller children felt very insecure. It became my role to keep the younger children at peace during the turbulent times of flaring tempers. My peacemaking role kept their minds in a better place and let them know that there was nothing to worry about. That role came easily to me. Father was blamed for everything that went wrong within the household and Mother made sure all the children knew where to place that blame. But I was a total "Daddy's Girl," and that unique closeness and love for my father gave me a vastly different perspective and complete faith in him. It was second nature for me to keep everyone calm and collected until things settled down. All the while, I would quietly defend my father's honor. Daddy would always be there with food and money whenever we needed it. And he always found a way to do just that.

My father taught me to be highly optimistic and to have a happy disposition at all times. He would often tell me, "Every day's a holiday!" and he meant it. It was his mantra. And I believed his every word. My father had his faults, but his philosophies on living life to the fullest stuck with me throughout my life.

The choice as to which of my parents' behaviors to emulate was easy for me to make. When comparing the negativity, frustration, and constant worry that became the mindset consuming my mother's every waking moment, to that of the positive disposition and seemingly far more controlled emotions of my father; I chose to become a positive person like my father. His calmness, peacefulness, and highly positive nature allowed him to enjoy his life no matter what his shortcomings where. Meaning, he could rage on during a weekend-long alcoholic binge; forgive himself, and move right on back into the 40-hour workweek grind. At the end of the day, he'd be there for his wife and children. No time to whine about a regretful binge or torment himself with self-loathing—as life was far too short for such things! Daddy loved himself as much as he loved others. Being objective, positive, and optimistic allowed him that possibility. Therefore, the choice was obvious to me early on: emulate my father.

My earliest lessons in life were not solely developed just by observing and desiring to emulate my father; but also from observing the plights of my mother and understanding how frustration can negate most all the enjoyment a person could have in life. Her plight taught me about the value of being able to understand the human beings we love and how very important it is to learn how to communicate effectively with them. From the ongoing battles of my parents, I saw that the total lack of compromise and the ability to adapt on the part of my mother, left my father in a constant, "damned if I do, damned if I don't" dilemma. Therefore, if he was going to be ultimately damned, then he'd make damn sure he'd be happy doing *all* he wanted to do throughout the entire ordeal.

Bridging the gap by way of translating between those who talk and those who don't listen became a natural knack for me. Being objective, even though I was more beholden to my father, also became a natural skill for me. I wanted to be understanding of my mother, but also wanted to help her understand my father better. Sometimes it actually worked to calm her.

My skills as a peacemaker, I therefore owe to *both* my parents. The enormously valuable lessons gained while being exposed to viewpoints from the far sides of each of their individual perspectives, has made me…well, *me*.

It's therefore with great love and the utmost in respect, that I dedicate this book in honor of my two greatest teachers.

Thank you Daddy, and thank you Mom.

Loving you both forever and a day,

Daughter #3

Table of Contents

Chapter One: Lighting the Path

The Making of a Peacemaker

I am, in a word, a peacemaker.

Everything I share here is in the quest to help bring out the peacemaker in you. That's because I truly believe everyone deserves the chance at attaining happiness and inner peace, and those are the benefits of being a peacemaker. All you have to do is have the desire to understand yourself better, and to open your mind to doing the things that are in your best interest. This is what will allow happiness and inner peace to find you.

We've all gone through many challenges in our lives; and for as long as we live, there will certainly be difficult challenges on the horizon. But how you think you'll handle those challenges is what'll make your present reality either one filled with the fear of failure, or one filled with the freedom of happiness and inner peace.

With that in mind, it's my hope that my experiences and philosophy will raise your confidence in knowing that your becoming a peacemaker will give you the tools needed to better handle life's trials and tribulations with grace, dignity, and a positive spirit.

The lessons learned from being a peacemaker in the household of my childhood became the foundation of my peacemaker philosophy. Throughout this book, I'll be sharing personal experiences that have helped solidify and strengthen that philosophy into what it is today. Several of my experiences have been some of life's rudest awakenings that needed taming in order for me to overcome them. I could have either died from a broken heart, or I could choose to live. My philosophy as a peacemaker proved to be a lifesaver. Being a peacemaker has helped me live a lifetime of happiness and inner peace, even when the clouds of darkness and despair rolled in to test my resolve and inner strengths.

There are lessons in everything, if we look closely enough.

From my earliest memories, the role of being peacemaker in my household belonged to me. It began as being the defender of my father, who was a most charismatic, caring, and highly optimistic man. However, he still would have his battles with his demons, as many before him and after would do. Daddy's alcoholism caused great insecurities for my mother and siblings. It led to his gambling, which did put food on the table most of the time; but sometimes it would get totally out of control and he'd lose a car or a house. My father ultimately lost three houses to gambling before he swore off it forever.

As a young child, I believed with all my heart that being able to see the light of day was a miracle in itself, and that anything that transpired after that...well, that too was indeed a miracle. I learned that way of thinking from my father. Daddy taught me very early on to enjoy every miracle of life. From my earliest memories I recall him singing to me, in that Elvis Presley style, the song, I Believe. "I believe from every drop of rain that falls, a flower grows." Elvis recorded that song in 1957 and it was one of Daddy's favorites. It was a lullaby for me. And on those nights when I'd close my eyes, I believed every single word of that song. Life was glorious!

Worry was never a part of my being because the incredible brilliance of life's light kept negative energy completely invisible to me. Everything wonderful was possible! Worry was not an option. Worry was what my mother did and she was totally miserable.

Mother would sit and talk about how awful the world was becoming as supposedly God-fearing people actually played Bingo! Bingo was gambling to her. To me, it was just a game. But then again, I loved games--all kinds of games. When I think about it, I don't recall my mother ever playing a game of any kind. Perhaps it was that she didn't have the time, but it seemed to me she didn't have any interest. Mother could be sort of a prude, you know. When in public, she was prim, polished, and quite proper in every respect; but in private, she was miserable and terribly unhappy.

That meant she and her "Scamp," that was my father, made quite an interesting pair. Mother was gorgeous, and even after a night of carousing; Daddy could clean up remarkably well. One minute he'd remind you of the bad boy roles of Jimmy Cagney--the scruffy-around-the-edges scrapper who's ready to box and take you down with one quick left hook; and the next minute, Daddy would appear debonair and charismatic, the likes of a Cary Grant! Daddy was funny, witty, and incredibly charming. So much so, that those redeeming qualities served to completely neutralize any remnants of the scruffy "Scamp" scrapper by producing a vision more akin to that of an angel – handsome as all get out! It was, no doubt, a combination of both scamp and angel that was attractive to my mother and swept her off her feet. But I'm sure she was praying the angelic side of this captivating young man was his dominant side. Oops!

My mother was born and raised in the country on her family's land in Roanoke Rapids, North Carolina. Her Grace Kelly-esque qualities of naturally radiant, stunningly good looks, combined with her refined diction and etiquette, made her humble country roots spread out quite comfortably whether she was in the company of sharecroppers or millionaires. Everyone who came in contact with her knew that one day the world would become her oyster.

Born to a father of Black African and Cherokee heritage, and a mother of European, Black African, and Cherokee heritage; the physical characteristics of my mother were quite exotic. With long, raven hair, incredibly high cheekbones, big doe-like eyes with long llama lashes to match, and smooth, flawless, caramel-hued skin; she was a jaw-dropping beauty. Her elegant manner was a perfect complement to her overall physical beauty and ever-impeccable taste in attire. She was the kind of beauty who'd look gorgeous wrapped in a burlap bag.

This beautiful country girl who would become my mother, was only nineteen years old when she met a most handsome and charming young sailor. He was stationed at the Naval base in nearby Newport News, Virginia. She fell so hard for him that she failed to heed the advice of her very wise father. He'd told her not to become hypnotized by the smooth talking, handsome city fellow in uniform. Little did she know how soon that charming young sailor would turn her world upside down, and all her dreams of the world becoming her oyster…into oyster *shells*.

With the dreams of my mother quickly being crushed, and two daughters to care for, Mother was ready to make the sacrifices necessary to own up to her responsibilities as a caregiver for her family. Though Father felt the same way, he didn't quite see things the same as my mother. He wasn't quite ready to sacrifice his love of life and zest for all that life offered, by being forced into a life of total dedication to his family. At least not to the point where doing so would end his ability to live a life of his own. Their inability to compromise on their differences continued to divide them. I also think it proved to my father that my mother could be, especially on this particular subject, quite unreasonable at times. Daddy wanted to compromise, but he felt that what Mother was asking of him was just too much! His position was that he would not be manipulated into changing into someone he was not. Not by anyone and not for any reason. This soon led to a long-term separation. Mother and the children stayed in New York while Father returned alone to Springfield, Illinois where he was born and raised.

Having been in a depressed state during the time of the multi-year separation from my father, Mother came to the Midwest and tried to take better care of herself after reconciling with Daddy and learning she was pregnant with me. She was determined to do better than the diet that had caused her to lose so much weight (known to a myriad of New Yorkers caught up in the pressures and stresses of a fast-pace, worrisome and depressing lifestyle at the time, as "C & C's": Coffee and Cigarettes). Unhealthy eating habits during the separation had caused her to become very underweight. While carrying me, Mother worked hard to get her health back in line. Regardless of her efforts to improve her health, I was born premature and remarkably underweight with a number of physical ailments (the most debilitating of those, which would be diagnosed later, being that of congenital spinal stenosis).

But the reward at the time was that three little beautiful girls inhabited the Smith household and life for Mom was again worth living! Daddy had promised to clean up his act and do better to provide for her and the needs of his girls. And this time Mom would do a much better job of handling her frustrations and communicating better with Daddy. And she went about doing just that.

Mother commanded respect and admiration wherever she went. With a dry wit and good sense of humor, some weren't sure how to take her at times. Her being a stickler for spot-on enunciation, diction, grammar, and choice of using just the right word for the occasion; seemed more fitting to someone far more serious in nature. Mother was also humble, caring, and God-fearing. Even though it was obvious she cared about her looks, her vanity came off as being more of that as completely natural and refreshingly down-to-earth. Mother really did have a "Grace Kelly-esque" way about her – as if she were meant for royalty.

It didn't take long before it appeared to Mother that Daddy didn't miss her as much as she thought. She felt that once again she had been lied to and promised things that her Scamp could not deliver. He merely played her. Played up to her love for him and her desire to provide a solid and loving family environment for her children. Since their reconciliation, there were now several more children in tow, and it was impossible for her to even think about how to get away and try to begin anew. She had tried that before and now she sat, once again, longing for her homeland of Roanoke Rapids where all her family lived. Mother began to talk of "going home" constantly. It was like a broken record. She wore it out day in and day out…and though I felt for her, I often wished she'd just leave rather than bicker about it. The life my father had in mind for my princess of a mother was a very rude and crude awakening for her. He wasn't going to change, even though he made promises that made it sound like he would try to do so. Mother, though, knew that *something* had to change!

Coming to the realization that the never-ending promises made by my father would settle like dust bunnies in the same "no can do" corner as all of his previous promises, Mother found solace in a religion that promised her hope. The Kingdom Hall and its fellowship became Mother's place of salvation and a way to teach her daughters how not to be charmed or fooled by garden snakes who pass themselves off as handsome and sincere human beings. The congregation became her refuge of comfort and escape from what was otherwise uncertainty, insecurity, and seemingly no hope for change. At first, Daddy said he'd go with her to the meetings, and he tried for a time; but soon Mother was on her own to get herself and we children to the meetings, which convened three times a week.

My father also found his place of comfort and solace by which to temporarily escape his entrapment of a constantly nagging wife -- and that was the local Pool Hall. Daddy was an accomplished pool shooter and that mastery no doubt subsidized his income and helped him acquire the finances to eventually raise seven children. But this was also where his demons would be conjured up from the bottom of a whiskey bottle, allowing his gambling to often get out of control. He was a truly high-functioning alcoholic, always working a full-time job at the same place for over thirty years. He was forever happy and upbeat, regardless of his woes, and instilled in me the value of having an eternally positive and optimistic disposition.

Knowing what my father was capable of falling prey to (the gambling that caused their first separation), my mother often sat and cried with the tears of angst and frustration when he was gone. The children became worried too and blamed our father for Mother's constant suffering. But the little girl who was her third daughter, the one who saw her daddy as her Hero, worried not. For you see, unlike all my other siblings, I happened to be very much like him. It was my nature to assure the household that no matter what might happen, or where Daddy might be, he would always be home in time when we needed him. My father had my complete faith and understanding.

Therefore, our household was one of intense polarization. My mother and father were polar opposites in more ways than I can count, which put the children in the middle to choose sides. For everyone else, their sympathies went to my mother as she sat and cried out of frustration and despair day and night. Would he show up in time with food for breakfast before her children had to be off to school in the morning? Would the gas, electricity, or water suddenly be turned off? To me, my father could do no wrong. If the gas, electric, or water were turned off, Daddy would just turn it back on. He could perform magic tricks all day and all nightlong. He had every tool known to mankind and he knew how to use them! Daddy was my Hero!

My Mother felt trapped by the popular and well-liked Scamp who performed magic tricks for those in need throughout the neighborhood; yet failed to keep an extra rabbit in his hat for his own family. She would get no sympathy from the neighborhood at all. This is where he'd been born and raised. He knew everyone and they all knew him. She was the outsider. Their first years together were in New York with Daddy's brothers, that's where my two older sisters were born. But now Mom was in Daddy's home territory and she had no family and very few friends.

The turmoil between my parents, and the financial difficulties that came along with raising a larger family, began to affect my eldest sister, Sylvia. Being over eight years my senior, her world was entirely different than mine. She saw herself as the eldest, but of just two sisters who were just three years apart. I came along five-and-a-half years after my sister, Cheyenne. My birth created quite a large gap in ages between my older siblings and me. Following my birth, the gap closed incredibly as my sister, Antoinette came along in 18 months; and then another 18 months brought my brother Maurice. It's my recollection, that by the time my little brother Maurice was born, Sylvia had become very bitter and resentful to what she probably saw as yet another mouth to feed and less of the finer things in life for her. I've a feeling La's resentment began prior to my recollections; it's just that at that time I wasn't old enough to properly interpret her actions. (I called Sylvia "La," because as a toddler, I couldn't pronounce her name. So what came out was, "Syl-la-la." That soon became "La-la;" and later turned into simply, "La." I affectionately call her "La" to this very day.)

To me, my sister Sylvia was "the Ogre who lived in my house." I was the protector of my two younger siblings (as well as standing up for my soft-spoken, older sister, Cheyenne). I'd take the brunt of my Ogre-sister's anger and physical abuse for any of my siblings. I was the one who was just as outspoken as Sylvia, and even though about a third her size, always stood up to her bullying of others. This infuriated her. She inflicted physical punishment my way each and every day. It was a routine. When things would sometimes get really bad, my "good" sisters would tell on her and what she'd done to me, but I don't think my parents ever thought it could've been as bad as the reports told, because I never complained about it at all. I never once went running to Mother or Daddy about her. But I do recall, a couple of times, dreaming about ways of killing her. LOL

Seriously, I thought, the only way to get through to my sister would be to break <u>her</u>! My only real way of attempting to do that would be by making sure the-Ogre-that-was-my-sister would never, ever break <u>me</u>, <u>or my happy-go-lucky spirit</u>! That conclusion came from recalling boxing strategies told to me by my former Golden Gloves pugilist father. I remember asking him about the "cruelty of boxing," as that's what my mother called it. And Daddy said to me, "Boxing is like a chess match. For good position, you move your hands and feet instead of your pieces. You capture your opponent's pieces by connecting with punches that go all the way *through* him. And when you finally wear him down, you've captured his King and won the match."

So to me, I didn't have to physically hit my sister back, as I could beat her down with my mind by being defiantly happy! I'd never, ever give in to her demands. My happiness was what weakened her evil spirit (or so it seemed to me at the time, that she must have some entity of evil residing in her). She could beat me up each and every day, and she often did just that – but I'd never give in to her and thus allow her to make *me* unhappy. And I <u>never</u> did.

That reminds me of a prizefight scene between Sugar Ray Robinson and Jake LaMotta in Martin Scorsese's film, "Raging Bull." The scene picks up as LaMotta (portrayed by one of my all-time favorite actors, Robert Deniro), eggs on Sugar Ray to give him his best shot and stands against the ropes inviting the punishment. Sugar Ray is more than happy to oblige the seemingly sadistic pugilist. Robinson pummels LaMotta with what seemed like a five-minute beating, bludgeoning him ruthlessly, so much so that ropes nearby were dripping with LaMotta's blood. When the fight is finally stopped by the referee, and LaMotta can't even stand on his own, with the help of his cornermen holding him up, he gets way up into Sugar Ray's face and defiantly exclaims, "But you never got me down, Ray, you never got me *down*."

No one was ever going to get me down. No one. Not even if I were to be beat to a bloody pulp. *And* I wasn't ever going to cry about any of it. Never. I was never going to whine or cry and blame anything that happened to me on anybody else. To me, as a young child, it seemed that only self-centered, selfish people sat around crying about their miseries. Because, to me, what exactly was the point of being miserable and then drawing everyone else around you into that misery? Smart people knew how to roll with the punches and move on. Smart people didn't get miserable. So what was wrong with those who did? That question intrigued me. But more than that, I truly wanted my mother to find a way to be happy. To me, everyone deserved to be happy. I used to think, if Daddy were my husband, I'd be happy.

My absolute love for movies...I got that from my mother. With my ailments, I never slept very well and was a night owl. I had what's now known as Restless Leg Syndrome, so I had my own bed, because my "all night running legs" would keep my little sister Antoinette (her childhood nickname was "Toni") from being able to sleep. After the other kids were sound asleep, and I'd still be there wide-awake in my bed, I'd get up and go halfway downstairs. I'd sit on the staircase until noticed and invited to come down.

"Mainie, come on down," my mother, in a medium whisper, would then say.

Mother and Daddy would be on the living room couch with their tray of cheese and crackers and libation of Gin and Squirt nearby. Daddy would be passed out by that time, and Mother would pat the sofa to let me know it was okay to come on in and get comfy next to her. She'd then catch me up on the movie as if talking to a close girlfriend; explaining every actor in it (and their sister who starred in another movie that we saw last week). I'm sure my father was grateful because it spared him having to deal with romantic, tear-jerker movies the ilk of, "Imitation of Life," "An Affair to Remember," "Madam X," and "Backstreet." I loved them all and got a great education watching every minute of such sentimental and film noire movies, learning and reciting every line.

And those movies also helped me deal with my problems with Sylvia. Movies showed me that my eldest sister wasn't the *only* evil entity on the planet...meaning my life could actually be worse! There also was Rhoda Penmar! LOL!! Young Patty McCormack's portrayal of Rhoda, the little girl with the fake sunshiny attitude and ever-swinging blonde braids was "The Bad Seed" (1956). This became one of my all-time favorite movies because it explained a *lot* to me. If you haven't seen it, you should. I think everybody should see it. Realness. To this day, every now and again, I have to remind my eldest sister to forget about the past, as she's often disturbed and even distraught over her behaviors back then. But I understand it all and have made total peace with it. It's all okay!

Sylvia was a frustrated youngster, just as my mother was a frustrated adult. Mother often took out her frustrations on La, and she in turn, took her frustrations out on her siblings. It was just that it was my nature to stand up to her and that pushed her anger even further. I don't blame her or regret any of it, for it all played an integral part in the shaping of the peacemaker that I am. And yes, I do love my sister – yes, the one who *used* to be an ogre! I truly hope she knows I really do love her. Because I do!

My constantly sunny disposition livened up the household and helped keep the younger children from being worried or insecure in all the turmoil. It soon became my pleasure to calm the storm for them by making up stories that would end on a cliffhanger each night and then resume the following night. Yes, just like the old serials at the movies. That tradition carried on through after the birth of my youngest sister, Tempi; followed by the birth of Mother's last child, my youngest brother, Caleb. Throughout my life, it was my place to keep the younger children emotionally safe in a better place where they wouldn't feel so insecure. I was their peacemaker.

I never realized just how much they loved my stories until they became adults and continued to relay to me their great memories of my stories. My heart leaps with joy whenever they talk about it. Even to this day, their eyes light up with enthusiasm and warm recollection as they talk about those great times listening to my stories. I had no idea how much those stories meant to them.

Throughout the following years and decades, my role as a peacemaker continued nonstop. Schoolmates, friends, relatives, and co-workers would oft come to me for advice about difficulties they were having. It became my calling to help others with my ability to assist them to gain a better perspective over that, which seemed overwhelming to them.

Sometimes that's exactly what it took: a different set of eyes to hand over a new and fresh angle by which to remove the film and get down to a clearer, more realistic and less daunting picture of what was really happening. Such is much akin to the difference of an unremarkable photo taken by someone, and then seeing a photo taken of the same subject by someone who has a keen eye for detail and artistic flair. In comparison, the result is mesmerizing when you compare how the subject interpreted by a skilled photographer was turned into a genuinely beautiful work of art.

I had developed the keen eye of a wise and highly skilled peacemaker.

No matter where you are along the path of this journey called life, the fact is that you beat the odds and were born. The moment you took your first breath, you became a winner. When the chips are down; remember you have already won the greatest prize known to mankind: Life. Embrace it, in good times and bad. Life is the greatest gift and you are a winner! – Charmainism

Finding the Peacemaker Within You

When grateful for another day to breathe air and seize the day…we can handle just about anything. But most days, our gratitude doesn't come to the surface unless we encourage it to do so. We can bring that thankfulness to the surface each day by waking up and first remembering to make peace with ourselves. Making peace means yesterday has come and gone, and today we are tremendously thankful for the incredible blessing of having another day to enjoy. Doing so will immediately put all other concerns, petty in comparison, in a new light of perspective. This will give you more positive energy to tackle the things you need to do in order to change your life course for the better.

By making peace with oneself first, the act of making peace with everyone and everything else becomes much simpler to do. When at peace, each day is seen as a miracle; and each moment is cherished with the contentment of knowing the simple satisfaction of genuine gratitude. Genuine gratitude means that whatever happens will simply *be*. And you'll *be* good with it.

We have to remind ourselves that life isn't something that's "happening" *to* us. Rather, it's akin to an incredible, once-in-a-lifetime invitation to attend the greatest and most exclusive party on earth! We're definitely going to attend, oh yes! But are we *guaranteed* to have a great time? No. It's up to each of us to decide that we'll have a fabulous time while attending this soiree called life. From then on, it should become our mission to go about finding ways to ensure that each and every day we do exactly that! We find our way to happiness and greatness so that the party of life is a blast each and every day!

If we make the mistake to allow ourselves the option of wondering whether or not we should go to the party as we over think our insecurities or self-conscious feelings about the way we look or whether or not we'll see this person or that person at the party…well, then, you're off to a very rocky start! Second-guessing is a party pooper! It really is. Who cares "if the guy who used to date so-and-so might show up because Evelyn will be there," or if your "busybody Auntie will make an appearance" as well, and you "just can't stand her!"

Instead of worrying over such possibilities, you *should* be having so much fun just knowing you *have* that invitation to the party of a lifetime in your hand! You *should* be so content in that fact alone that none of those other things should be any concern at all to you. A positive person armed with the skills of a peacemaker, is never intimidated by the presence of negative-minded people. Why should your life be "on hold" because of others? It shouldn't! So that type of thinking has to stop.

Being positive is the neutralizer to those types of individuals who otherwise make you uncomfortable. Why would anyone give other people such power over their own life? Especially people they don't really care about much at all. I've never understood that. So tell yourself right here and now, that you are re-accepting that once-in-a-lifetime invitation and you are going to par-*tay* this time with that golden opportunity. Yes, PAR-TAY!!! You're going to enjoy each and every precious moment of this journey called life. As my father would often exclaim, "Every day's a holiday!" He meant it and I believed it. It was his mantra and it became mine!

How we expect to feel about something is often how we think we *should* feel, so we're forever apt to unknowingly fall into the habit of acting the part. If we think we won't have fun at the party because of what could happen, then we've set ourselves up for not going...all based on what ifs. That makes little sense! However, if we embrace the concept that "Every day really *IS* a holiday," then we're upbeat and making the best of everything that comes our way that day. We're happy to be on this earth to breathe air into our lungs and feel the light of day! We're immensely grateful! This is the thought process we need in order to carry on a positive disposition about us each and every succeeding day.

Let a positive disposition eliminate those "worrywart" exercises in futilities that are wholly counterproductive to positive thinking. Worrywarts worry about things that haven't yet occurred! They fabricate scenarios and then hash them over time and time again. The result isn't only a total waste of time, but also a frustration level that can consume one's entire well-being, and ultimately, take over their once sane lives.

Countless people worry needlessly day in and day out over things that are completely out of their control. They do so because they live in fear of many things – things they haven't faced, neutralized, and thus overcome. Add to that the responsibilities of day-to-day living and dealing with other real hardships and tragedies in life, and feelings can spiral down into those becoming ever more despondent, overwhelming, and ultimately hopeless. It doesn't have to be this way. Not ever.

No matter what we do, we cannot delay the march of time.
Enjoy every beat! – Charmainism

The "SHWY" Philosophy

I truly believe that happiness is dependent on learning how to control one's negative emotions and thus remain positive and optimistic throughout times of stress and strife. When emotions suddenly go from traversing the high peaks of elation and drop down like a rock to the valleys low with grief and sadness…if we don't have something to fall back on to help us regain altitude, then we surrender what could be our bright and emotionally healthy life to one of despair in the darkness of melancholia. When we're low, the first inclination can be to forget about being grateful of the opportunity to even *have* the light of a new and glorious day. Instead, doubts, fears and regrets begin to fuel negative and destructive thinking. Worry and frustration set in to cloud any hope of clear and constructive thought.

Becoming a peacemaker, like myself, is the answer to the end of worry, frustration, anger, bitterness, resentment, self-doubt, self-loathing, and other types of wholly negative and self-destructive thinking. Most need reminders to help keep them on the right track when their viewpoint becomes negative and thus slips from its proper perspective. For me, those reminders are a natural instinct. As a lifelong peacemaker, I've developed a philosophy that will teach you the way to what I call the Lighthouse of Inner Peace.

Such is a testament as to why everyone needs an effective philosophy in place – one that can be counted on to help change the darker moods into brighter, healthier ones. The philosophy should be able to make quick work of neutralizing negativity by offering simple ways to recall and put into motion, positive practices that will put you back onto the high road of happiness and inner peace. Philosophies like this are often used as accents of inspiration to one's spirituality.

My philosophy, "Shake Hands with Yourself" ("Shwy"), does just that. It's based on neutralizers I've used throughout my life in order to make peace with some of the most stressful challenges and situations thrown my way. We all have our stresses, but before we opt to stay too long down in the pit of inner hell…we need to know that it's in our best interest to find a way to meet such devastatingly crushing challenges with grace and dignity…and the proper perspective to see us through it. Such is the key to fire up the engine of strength to carry on and find the vigor of living life to its fullest once again -- no matter what comes our way. And it teaches how to completely let go of the past so you can move on to embrace your bright present and radiant future.

It's not required that you be unhappy or searching for happiness in order to enjoy reading this book. What this book can do for those who are searching, it can also do for those who are currently quite content -- in the sense that it will always be there to serve as a fallback, or go-to guide, whenever a boost is needed to lift your step! It can also be of help to someone you care about who is having trouble making sense of the nonsense in their life.

Many of those I've helped through the years have implored me to put some of my philosophies and inspirational sayings for a happier life in book form so they can carry "me" with them. My tidbits of wit and wisdom were coined "Charmainisms" over ten years ago when used on my boating website and other boating forums. (Note: A dear friend and tennis buddy of mine, Todd Johnson, actually was the first to coin the term about twenty-five years ago. He used to say my way of thinking was unique and thought provoking, often proclaiming during our conversations, "Now that's a classic Charmainism!" The moniker stuck among close friends and family.)

With the advent of Facebook and statuses, "Charmainisms" graduated into something much more prominent when posted as my daily Facebook musings. They would often stick with people and give them something for which to live up to as they read them as a source of inspiration. "Charmainisms" are therefore sprinkled throughout for emphasis, inspiration, and as a tribute to how this book came to be.

This book is about soul searching to discover the happiness and inner peace you so desire. Whether contentment is near you or far away, the inspirations herein will help you throughout your journey. Sharing some of the things that have happened throughout my life and allowing you to see how I dealt with them, will let us go hand-in-hand on this journey. Though I've reached my status as a peacemaker, I felt it prudent to let you see exactly what has shaped who I am throughout the years. It's my intention that my life stories will become an inspiration and motivation for you to continue your journey of self-discovery on the road to happiness and inner peace. It should assure you that no matter what you're going through or where you've been…happiness and inner peace await you. You need only be a peacemaker at heart.

We can't stop terrible things from happening on this spinning orb, but we can learn to accept whatever *does* happen, choose to make peace with it, and move on while enjoying our lives. My philosophy has carried me through the heartaches and immense challenges that began in my early youth and throughout my life. I've not only *survived* each test, but have *thrived,* as I've never lost my genuine gratitude and zest for life.

Losing my only son and my mother quite suddenly on the very same day, though they were over a thousand miles apart, was a blow for which I could've never been prepared. It's my belief that had it not been for a lifetime of honing my skills as a peacemaker, I would've never been able to make peace with myself in the midst of this tragic situation. I've no doubt that otherwise I would've surely died of a broken heart.

Whatever stresses and strife you struggle with, or if you're one of those constantly feeling the pressure of what "might" be lurking on the horizon; we all are in this together. Life is a <u>challenge</u>. We *all* must find a way to effectively deal with our times of grief, frustrations, fears, and doubts. The philosophy I offer to you will take you through a journey of self-discovery, real awakening, and guide you to the enlightenment of inner peace. Your happiness depends on it.

My philosophy is simple. It all starts when you decide to "shake hands with yourself" and make amends, as you learn to understand yourself better. Then you can prepare your mind for truly positive change. That means forgiving yourself and the world for being imperfect and then doing the same for all others. This is how all negativity can be totally eliminated from your life. Once you forgive yourself, extending that same courtesy to others becomes natural because you'll realize that doing so is actually what's best for you. By embracing this premise, attaining inner peace isn't only possible; it's highly likely you'll do so. After you've attained inner peace, this book will become your "Go to" maintenance guide to keep you ever on the path of light, truth, and remaining positive.

My philosophy's effectiveness is partially due to its being easily understood. Thus, you retain it because you're inspired by its foundation and simple logic. Becoming a peaceful person will change your life in a manner so positive you'll think it your miracle. The key to unlocking your miracle is achieved by following three steps:

1. Shake hands with yourself – rid all negative energy towards yourself and others.

2. Neutralize fear and frustration to gain complete control over your emotions.

3. Learn the art of unobtrusive, Positive Indifference to finesse the art of letting go.

You'll learn about yourself and develop a new appreciation and understanding about how having control of your emotions gives you control of your life. That control will free you from becoming a victim of your own frustrations. You'll dissect your fears and frustrations until only tiny little pieces are left -- palatable and easy to swallow once and for all. And then you simply let them go.

*Make peace with yourself, and you
make peace with the world.* – Charmainism

It's much to do about choices. What we choose to do in order to dilute the times of hardship and reduce them down to mere blips on the radar of our flight in life, rather than seeing them as insurmountable obstacles, is key. This is what makes all the difference between those who give up and those who choose to give it another go! Regardless of the hurt or pain you may think you've a right to feel and act out on, it's still your choice whether or not to do any of those things. You don't have to let it overtake you. There are ways to keep your emotions calm and your mind sane during such times of high stress and heavy burdens. You can be happy through it *all*. Yes! You can be happy enough to *be* happy for life itself... even when the going gets *really* tough. Now that's something for which to strive!

Each day as we arise, we are physically up. The challenge throughout the day is to be emotionally up. Rationalize and neutralize to stay up when anything starts to wear you down. You can do it! Because life is what we make it...and we can make it pretty darn GOOD! It's up to you! So despite anything...have a wonderful day! – Charmainism

Those who are happy despite all else that occurs in this world are so because they've made their happiness a priority. Despite all else, they know that by doing so they can awake happily to each new day as yet another dawn to continue their quest for positive and progressive change. They awake each day to continue to unwrap the gift of life!

People really do tend to fear change. When we procrastinate out of fear of failure, we become stagnant and get nowhere. Our mood becomes more and more intensely dour and angry. When we're angry with ourselves, we're angry at the world. Deep down, our anger easily becomes self-loathing. As we fail each time to climb up the ladder of self-esteem, we not only flog ourselves, but others around us as well.

When the flogging begins, we tend to stop taking care of ourselves. It happens bit by bit, overtime, until we're completely out of the routine of proper hygiene and caring about our appearance or what we eat, how much exercise we're getting, and staying hydrated, etc. etc. etc. We find it hard to muster up the strength to *care*. This, we all know, is something we do to ourselves. Therefore, we have to be on guard for the first signs of any negligence towards our well-being. It's like this: If the bananas don't smell too good, throw them out and get new ones, or make banana bread – but, above all else, don't just let them sit there and rot!

Water is the greatest natural healer of mankind.
Hydrate! - Charmainism

We tend to treat ourselves badly when we're down and somewhat depressed; but we usually *start* it off with the subtle ill treatment of ourselves. But there are things we can do to help counteract that negative energy against ourselves! We can do an about-face on it and turn it into something positive. At the very first inkling that you're feeling a bit low, <u>make yourself</u> grab a tall glass of water. It will do your mind and body a world of good! Even better, add a few squeezes of lemon to it! Refreshing! If nothing else, you've thought about your need to make a quick and positive change…and that's *always* a good thing…and you did it! Before long, it will become a fabulously wonderful routine that will change your health and life for the better. It's a habit you want to have!

Just a tall glass of water can help curtail those blips as they surface on your emotional radar. It's amazing that something so natural, simple, and *free* can help us deal with that which rears its ugly head and then branches out to whip all those within reach. We can keep the anger from boiling to the top, as we so badly want to stop the pain of being angry, bitter, and helpless to end the cycle of self-loathing. It's gotten out of our control and has lasted far too long.

Whether due to great personal loss, health issues, financial woes, tiring of trying to please others, and/or any number of other catalysts, nothing will change one's demeanor and improve self-worth unless the decision is made to make a progressive and positive change for oneself. Until that "go-to" is found, our lives tend to be one of action and reaction. No longer can another moment be wasted sitting and waiting for some miracle to fall from the sky and fix everything. *You* have to take the lead. I'm here to help you along your way.

Mind you, this isn't about faith in a higher power. This is other than that: this is about using your brain to help your mind and body get in tune with what's best for you. We all must make the effort to help ourselves by owning up to the fact that we want to make life more positive. We want to become positive people doing positive things. By doing so, we can evoke positive change not only in ourselves but in others as well. We then know we can make a difference on this planet with our own lives being in balance. We can empower ourselves by bringing up to the surface the very best mindset that now sits dormant and unused deep within us. We've forgotten it's always been there within us. . . or perhaps you think you didn't know it was there. Well, I'm here to prove to you that it really is there.

Situations and circumstances are constantly changing, but our minds can always make sense of any turmoil and allow us to think clearly enough to know how to counteract it—we just need a way to help us do just that. There's no "undo" button in life when we need it most. But what you do have in your hands right now is a philosophy that will help you make peace with the things you wish you could "undo." One of the basic fundamentals of my philosophy is that what we do to ourselves we can also undo! And what we learn to undo we can learn to avoid in the future. Negative thinking is truly our own doing *and* undoing. We can therefore learn to rely on positive thinking as the neutralizer and gain control over our emotions. My philosophy's methods work to do just that.

What we do to ourselves...
we can also undo! – Charmainism

Doing such is how one can go about changing what's seen as a perpetually dark winter of one's emotions back into the brightness of a spring of youthful exuberance for life! It's never too late to do so.

My style is that it can all be done with a smile and a lilt in one's step all the while, because when one decides to make this enormously positive change; one's life changes for the better. You win the very moment you decide to direct your life onto the path of happiness and inner peace.

Showing others the way to a happier life is what I love to do. I love people, and helping them understand themselves better so they can find their way to happiness is what I've been doing all my life. My entire being has a great love for people and this world. Even so, it's important to keep expectations of others marginal; otherwise the possibility of deep disappointment emerges. Humans set themselves up by being unrealistic about their expectations, thus turning into their own saboteurs in the process. It doesn't have to be so. People are not perfect, as we all make mistakes. We must forgive and move on.

Take that negative energy and reroute it to become a positive force as you become a champion for yourself! Let the things beyond your control not be a bother. Control only that which is within your control and most important to you. That means placing an emphasis on attaining and maintaining inner peace and happiness! *That* is the foundation for your path to happiness and inner peace. It means becoming a Peacemaker! Being a peacemaker comforts your soul with a blanket of solace and fulfillment. Inner peace and happiness go hand in hand.

When you learn that inner peace is totally under your control, then learning the methods by which to attain it brings forth an eagerness you may have thought was left behind years ago. You're now sitting at the helm of a beautiful yacht called life. Get ready for the wind to lift your sails! Your journey to inner peace and happiness awaits you.

One reader at a time can affect hundreds of others just by sharing what they learn here and by becoming a person who exemplifies peace that others strive to emulate. Peacemakers unite! Let it begin with you!

The miracle of life...to breathe it is to know it. Whether we realize it or not, our energy radiates. It is an energy that not only makes a difference in our lives but also in the lives of those around us. There's only one you, and the energy you've been given is yours to use to empower yourself and others. As living miracles it is on us to make the most of the precious gift we've been given. – Charmainism

So let's continue with gaining a better understanding of who we are. Yes, "we." We're all in this together. As positive as I am, I still have to hone and finesse my neutralizing skills from time to time. LOL Well yeah...I am a peacemaker, but I'm also only human. And I truly believe that change is good! It's good for our well-being.

Stay atop the peaks of life and let the valleys roll beneath your feet. – Charmainism

Due to my mother's religious beliefs, I was taught at a very young age that the world would soon end -- in nineteen seventy-five, to be exact. The Elders at the Kingdom Hall preached what the Organization interpreted as gospel: in that year would come the day of reckoning, Armageddon. The world, as we knew it, would end. When I look back on it, it amazes me that such a little one, as myself at the time, could still be as happy as I was while living under the darkest clouds of doom and gloom. I remember the terrifying depictions in their literature of people running in panic with the look of horror on their faces as earthquakes, volcanic eruptions, and total carnage and mayhem wreaked havoc to swallow the earth, the trees, and the people! I thought to myself that someone doesn't know God at all if they think He'd do that. God is LOVE. There was nothing loving about such destruction as that!

Of course there was always a full explanation that included sunshine, rainbows, and a Skittles-like future! The world wouldn't really end…just those who were wicked. After that, the earth would return to its naturally intended, paradisiacal state. And mankind, in favor with Jehovah God, would live for all eternity upon it.

That was too much for a little girl. To get to the good part one had to endure the hell of it all. I was having none of it. So it was easy for me to neutralize the thoughts of impending doom by watching old movies and also by allowing the written word to come to my rescue.

By first grade, I was walking to the local library and spending so much time there that my mother would call and ask one of the librarians to send me home. She knew all the librarians by their first names even though she'd never been there, as they all knew me and I them. The window seat on the first floor should have had my name on it, as it certainly had the imprint of my backside all over it. Ha! Well, even if no one else saw it…I sure did. It was "My place." Curled up in that nook, I'd read everything I could get my hands on and then some. Soon, there I was, chatting up a storm to the librarian as she checked out for me all the books I could possibly carry back home.

The librarians would show off my reading skills to others. While still in first grade, my sister, Cheyenne, took me to her sixth grade class as her "Show and Tell." I read from her textbooks as her teacher, Mr. Trail, looked on incredulously. Cheyenne says she was known from then on as, "One of those smart Smith girls." And to think that after all these years, I still so vividly remember being preschool age and asking Cheyenne how to pronounce the first three-syllable word I ever saw. The word was: "favorite." She was so patient and proud of me. She and I've always had a most special bond even though there's a 5-1/2 year age difference.

My sister Cheyenne helped nurture my affection and skills for reading, but it was my father who gave me my voracious appetite for knowledge. My mother would ask me what was the point in reading about things that would no longer matter (since the world as we knew it would be ending soon and replaced by the New Order [which was also a "signifying" way of reminding me that I should be paying more attention to my bible studies rather than works of fiction!]). It is a pronounced understatement to say mine was a household of entirely mixed signals, but then again, all of the above has made me who I am today. I'm a person quite comfortable in the midst of ambiguity.

But then there came on the horizon another shining dimension of positive influence into my life. She was my first grade school teacher, Miss ("Kitty") Kittell. At some point during that school year, Miss Kittell asked for permission to come over to my house and administer a standardized test to me, as I was sick an unable to attend school at that time. She had explained to my parents how important it was and that she thought I was a very special little girl. Thus began the blossoming of a very special and dear friendship with "Kitty" and my family. My sister Antoinette and I were like her children, as she never had any of her own; and to Kitty's parents, since Kitty was an only child who came along much later in their lives, my sister and I were like the grandchildren they never had.

Being with Miss Kittell opened my world to a third dimension: one that further developed my love for reading and teaching. It also opened my world to the finer things in life. Kitty had exquisite tastes and had been a high-fashion model in Chicago and New York City before becoming a schoolteacher. I used to sit with Mrs. Kittell (Kitty's mother), and we'd go through all of Kitty's incredible portfolios over and over again. I almost knew every picture by heart and the order they were in the albums. And then, while still in middle age, Kitty lost her life to breast cancer.

Kitty's death was a harsh blow to me. I'll never forget her kindness, encouragement, and love. She too, most definitely had a large hand in shaping the peacemaker I became. She gave me a dignity and grace when it came to handling situations. Melding her teachings of refinement, with those of my father's, created a powerful sword of peace that was resilient to negativity and taught me that taking the high road could be very persuasive to others.

I hadn't really thought about my reading as being "escaping," or "neutralizing" my ambiguous household, but perhaps that was exactly what I was doing. My household was also quite turbulent, and I was a person full of peace, joy, and happiness. If others around me weren't in a peaceful and joyous mood that was not going to put a damper on my positive outlook and passion for adventure.

My earliest reading adventure memories were to places far away while walking in the shoes of Louisa May Alcott's "Little Women." Alice Danni, a woman who worked with my father at Taxpayer's Federation, a watchdog group headed up by Maurice Scott (my little brother Maurice Scott Smith was named after him), presented me with Alcott's beautiful tale in a lovely robin egg blue covering with gold leaf lettering, when I won an award for reading when in the second grade. I still have the letter she mailed to me. It was in a blue envelope to match the book covering, and even had a 2-cent George Washington stamp in a very close shade of blue on the envelope!

I'll never forget her kindness. She could've given it to me when I came to the office every Friday when Dad had mail to drop off at the post office, but she mailed it...the letter and the book. I felt very important that day when Mother told me a package had arrived for me. And a letter!

Books conveyed to me that the whole world was only a library away from me. All I had to do to see the other side of the mountain was to walk to the library and find a new place to visit. I loved reading.

Reading was traveling! I read everything and then some. Reading was so wonderful. I'd read to my little siblings, and Daddy was always having me read for a crowd. I didn't mind. It was amazing to those watching and listening, how this tiny little girl could have so much feeling and inflection in her voice when she was reading. And how could she possibly be so familiar with such a large and advanced vocabulary!

Both inflection and my love for words probably came from my love for acting out skits. I was always making up games and challenges for the kids of the house and our neighborhood to enjoy. Remember, I was a very young movie aficionado! LOL With Bette Davis and Barbara Stanwyck as two of my best guides, at a very young age, I learned to put my back into my reading! If you're going to do it…then put your back into it!

Granddad and Nana, my paternal grandparents, were also very important to me during my childhood. Granddad was a carbon copy of my father, just older. He was so funny! His sense of humor could have me howling for days! My father was the same way. Incredibly funny and could make anyone laugh until their sides felt like they were going to split open. I loved my grandparents so much. Granddad passed away when I was only nine years old. It was my first real experience with a broken heart. It was also the very first time I ever saw my father cry.

My maternal grandparents, I never got to really know for Mother's mom died when she was younger. Mother's dad, Collossie Byrd, was a fascinatingly gorgeous and tall man with the presence of Paul Bunyan (or at least to me!) He didn't look like a normal person; I certainly recall that when we visited the family farm around 1963. He was far more than "normal." He was the most beautiful man I'd ever seen. His face was a deep but brilliant reddish-brown, a strikingly lovely color that made him seem far more American Indian than anything else. His hair, at that time, was white as snow, and his coal black moustache was a contrast so startling that it was simultaneously so uniquely beautiful.

While there, in Roanoke Rapids, I remember thinking how wonderfully happy my mother was. We all were happy and were having fun as a family while there.

Do not fear dysfunction. Families are comprised of individuals. Everyone is different; therefore so is their function! Dysfunction is normal. – Charmainism

There's no better time to come to grips with the things of your past that have haunted you or held you back from being the very best you can be. You'll learn how to make simple changes that will bring you face-to-face with our often-fabricated shadows that lurk over us and need to be neutralized and dismissed into oblivion. At the same time, we'll bring forth the good things that should be out front and center, and exercised in the light of day – the things that are real and worthy of your attention. You'll also discover how to keep that which isn't worthy of your attention in the background and far away from impeding your progress to happiness and inner peace.

There's no better time than now to face your fears. So, in fact, that's exactly where our journey of self-discovery will take us next.

Let's do this thing!

Chapter Two: Facing Our Fears

The fears we put upon ourselves because that which we aren't familiar with scares us, causes more damage to mankind than anything else. Such fears tend to conjure up demons that otherwise wouldn't exist. Knowledge is the answer, for it will help you face and control your fears. – Charmainism

In the simplest of terms, we come unglued due to our lack of finding a way to make peace with that which scares us. By putting off learning how to face our fears, we stand in the way of why we've yet to overcome this dilemma. We do it to ourselves. If we'd only face our fears, most times, we'd find them completely unfounded. In fact, we'd find that it's really more of our worrying that's so troubling. Not that there aren't real fears of which to be concerned, but that many times we continue to succumb to that ever-present feeling of being suffocated by out-of-control emotions that render us helpless. That's when we become even more helpless to stop the pattern from repeating itself! And once again, we find ourselves giving in to being overwhelmed by the thought of facing that which we *think* we should fear…whether it's real or not!

Yes! We drive ourselves nuts with this type of stuff. Running around in loops and circles of utter nonsense. Scared of what's going to or *not* going to happen next! It's like being Rick Moranis' zany character, Louis Tully, the always-trying-to-fit-in-nerd-accountant neighbor of Sigourney Weaver in <u>Ghostbusters</u>. Once he manifests as "The Gatekeeper," his nerdy and obsessive characteristics are on steroids and for the remainder of the movie he's hysterical as he's forever running around sniffing up butts and conjuring up demons.

But we're not in a movie. We're just trying to survive LIFE. Even so, fear and frustration engulf us much the same as we frantically search for a neutral zone in which to retreat and just get back to where we were at a happier, and less stressful, time. We know we were happy once upon a time – weren't we? But even those thoughts seem more like a fairytale as we envision ourselves struggling to climb up atop any ledge saner than the one we find ourselves currently on. As we idly sit, we become even more convinced we might never win this internal battle that rages within us. Then comes the panic of anxiousness and we're out of breath at the thought of making a move in any direction! So we do nothing. We're too stressed and tired to engage!

And it's therefore no surprise that we're right back again facing the same panicky problems and bouts of anxiousness we had yesterday and the day before that. You see, we're spinning our wheels and getting nowhere while joy is passing us by at the speed of life!

Life is wasting away at great speed and we're helplessly watching it happen. Even so, we're often convinced there must be a magic pill somewhere that can solve our issues. But have we first made any real attempt at becoming the master of our own solution? Perhaps by understanding our patterns and shortcomings, then coming to grips with them by facing and conquering our fears, we might be able to actually help ourselves!

Stop asking yourself how or why
and tell yourself you can. – Charmainism

It's highly possible to end the suffering we put on ourselves. To overcome our fears, we need only to gain the proper motivation and courage to face and understand them. We must cease the habit of holding our breath when in turmoil and remember that our brains need all the oxygen possible in order to think clearly. Don't fear and remember to breathe! Serious business! We are often bracing for a gut punch that never hits. That's what happens when negative thinking sits in the driver's seat of one's inner control panel. BREATHE. THINK. Take back the reins and drive your horses the way you want them to run!

Remember that a fresh breath of life follows every sigh of exasperation. Breathe in, breathe out, and ENJOY every moment. It is how everything begins and ends. – Charmainism

When we begin to see things as they are and understand the pitfalls, we can avoid the trapdoors that open beneath our feet and whisk away all the fresh air of life -- the trapdoors that are exasperation and frustration. Without an ample supply of fresh air, we grow stale. Before we know it, we can't breathe. As the clock ticks faster and we grow older, we come to the realization that we're running out of time to get it right. We become even more exasperated and frustrated as we hear the ticking clock of Father Time getting louder and closer. Life, unless we change it, will become one giant panic attack. With not enough fresh air to breathe a new vigor for life each day, we begin to feel that we may be on our way to a dark depression.

Panic and anxiety paralyze us. One of the first symptoms is the seemingly inability to breathe. The chest tightens up, the throat swells into a big lump...we're out of our depth with no place lower to fall and not enough air to reach higher ground. That's when we have to use our minds to realize what we're doing to ourselves. It's our mind in total fear, paralyzed by the thought that we shall die from the pangs of enduring one more moment of unrelenting uncertainty. We do this to ourselves.

Fear won't be over until you deal with it. It must be faced, understood, and controlled. And that, my friend, is very doable. You need to understand more about the frailty of human nature, which is at the core of why we do the things we do! Whatever the reason for your dilemma, be it from hardship, heartache, or anything else, fear can be overcome. It will take understanding yourself better, methods to neutralize your fears, and the embracing of a philosophy that will bring your positive and optimistic inner-self to the surface for all to see.

Understanding Fear

Fear is a killer of happiness. It puts a chokehold on DOING. One wants to withdraw into a dark corner, or get in bed and gather the sheets over their head...and just forget there are problems. Somehow, it seems like in bed there are no problems. With not knowing what to confront or face up to, we attempt to hide from facing our feelings and therefore hide from ourselves. It can't be done. You follow yourself everywhere you go -- including in bed! The entire ordeal is so frustrating, but yet one knows not how to overcome it and get back on track towards a productive and satisfying existence.

Fear can be completely disabling. When we decide that whatever happens we can and will be able to handle it, there's no more fear. Not only is there a lack of fear, there emerges, in its place, an abundance of self-confidence and self-respect that seems to have come out of nowhere. It's within us all; we just need to bring it forth. We can watch our lives whither away as we're strapped and bound by fear, or we can learn to control our fear and thoroughly enjoy our lives. If we choose the latter, we must learn to be fearless.

Irrationality surfaces as you try to face your fears but you don't really know where to start. When you give it more thought, you sometimes imagine that perhaps the real problem is that everyone else has lost their minds! Because it seems that no one is easy to get along with anymore. Everyone is argumentative and combative. Is it possible that it just seems this way to you? But then why, you ask yourself, why do you also feel so down when others aren't even around you? There's something going on with you and you know it. You can't imagine why, deep down inside, you're so angry. You just want it to stop so you can get on with what's supposed to be the enjoyment of living. But what is it? What, exactly, is the problem? Why are you so mad?!

The problem is probably that you're in a pattern of being totally overwhelmed and distraught at the very *thought* of attempting to counteract the hold fear has on you. You're beat down. So much so, that part of you thinks inaction might be better than facing the feeling that you've failed again. This is where irrationality plays its role best: it tells you that no action is better than a possible wrong action. So you then decide to do nothing to change your course. The rational truth is that the fear of failure has you paralyzed to act against it.

Overcoming fears can be as simple as facing them. When faced, fears are stripped of their dark false power (irrationality) by being exposed to the light of truth (rationality). Facing your fears empowers you to heights of self-confidence and self-respect you may have never thought possible. It's my goal to help you get there: one word, one page; one chapter at a time.

We have to be open to the notion that failure is what we decide it is. Therefore, decide that the only real failure occurs when no effort is put forth. We then free ourselves to try. – Charmainism

When each day is the same dull routine and one's mental state immediately puts a damper on anything and everything throughout one's day, well, there's seemingly nothing at all to break the mold of stagnation. Instead, it's just another round in the battle to stave off the impending doom of what could become a deep depression. You feel it coming for you and you're bound and determined to hold it off, but you feel your life force weakening.

You can't think clearly enough for the length of time it takes to make the change you so desperately desire. You simply don't know what to do. You tell yourself that there has to be a way to get hold of your plot in life and shake the dust and dirt away to reveal that brightly shining sun beneath. In your heart, you know there has to be a happy life under there somewhere. If only you could find it and pull it to the surface. Believe me, it's there. However, you may not recognize it because you're too overwhelmed by the weight of worry, pain, and self-torture. No wonder you can't see the shine that awaits you.

So what can be done about gaining the motivation and courage to face fear? We can learn how much of a hostage we are inside the shadows of our own life when we're fearful, and we can learn to understand the futility of it. Think about it. What can one do to change the habit of waking to yet another day where the sun rises in the same place and shines just as brightly, yet the day continues on as dull in all the wrong places and as confusing as it was the day prior? Conflict, grief, worry, and frustration have shrouded any semblance of peacefulness and lasting sunshine. On a day-to-day basis, the variances from shine to shadow and shadow to shine are what make our lives so wonderful -- but only when we know how to navigate through it all with a smile and an exhilaration for all the challenges and joys of life!

When in harmony with yourself, life dances to the rhythm of your soul. Be content even through stressful times by being appreciative for the gift of life that allows you to experience challenge. - Charmainism

Many say that they can't get excited or motivated in a world gone mad. They worry about the state of affairs and the climate of what seems to be more hatred and less tolerance than ever. These things aren't new nor are they necessarily any more in abundance than ever.

It's far more reasonable to rationalize that there are simply more people than ever and with technological advances, more venues by which those who are negative have a voice! It certainly seems clear to me that those who are wholly negative have a way of demanding to be heard. Their ignorance is matched only by their arrogance. Let's face it: expecting the world to change is simply not reasonable. The world isn't going to change to our satisfaction unless every person needing change actually changes! The chances of that happening are, well, ridiculously outside of the realm of rational thinking.

Since we know that will never come to pass anytime soon, we need to realize what must be done is to change that which we are able to change: Change our own personal world to accept the things we can't change and carry forth being a better, new and improved model of ourselves.

Waste not a precious moment in frustration about the things you cannot change. Instead, focus on changing into a more tolerant and peaceful you! – Charmainism

Frustration is what evolves from not being able to face our fears. As there are a myriad of peoples on this earth, there are a myriad of fears. Some of those fears come in the most unassuming packages. Some fears are traced back to wants and the feeling that one needs to have certain things in order to proceed happily through this life. If one feels they can't obtain those things, then the fear of failure to get to that level overtakes them. Frustration then again rears its ugly head.

We live in a world where there are far too many adults who have the mindset that becoming highly frustrated when things aren't perfect is acceptable behavior. Even if society learns to accept it, negative behaviors should never be acceptable to us. It doesn't matter why we're upset or frustrated, we certainly have the capacity to make sense of it while remaining calm and able to produce productive thought processes to counteract it. We don't have to scream and shout! Sometimes this comes from watching others and thinking such outbursts are the way adults handle things.

Not all frustration is of the kind that results in temper tantrums. Much depends on the person behind the emotions. Some people are more the quiet and seething kind, rather than prone to emotional displays of outbursts. Emotions such as jealousy are often held close to the chest and not shared as openly with others.

Maybe we saw our mother looking across the street at the proverbial Joneses and she muttered something about how wonderful their lives must be to have all the material things they do. As a child, you heard her daydream but never saw the reality of paying the bills and owning up to all the other obligations of the Joneses! Your mother probably didn't see that either. Daydreams are like that. However, now we're all grown up and have to learn to keep it real. We have to realize that self-pity will take us to the Twilight Zone of irrational thinking. Not a good thing!

Jealousy is for small children who don't know better. Adults who have an affinity to be jealous or envious will never be totally happy. Because as long as anyone in their life seemingly has more than they do, they will never be top dog. So they bark incessantly like a spoiled Chihuahua depressed with "Little Dog Syndrome." – Charmainism

If it isn't jealousy, it's some other negative emotion that's forever crossing your path and making you doubt yourself. When a person thinks they only need this or that in order to find happiness, they're kidding themselves. Worse, deep down they actually <u>know</u> that.

We may have inherent fear as part of mankind's DNA, but even the most blockheaded person of all knows when they're being downright foolish – they just don't admit it because they are, well, they're being a blockhead! It doesn't take a genius to know that truly, happiness begins from within! That's where the seed is placed and cultivated. Deep within you is an Eden of the mind and soul; a paradise of peacefulness just waiting for you to become its Master Gardener. It's in that Eden within you where that small seed of hope for happiness begins to blossom into a flourishing habitat full of nutrients to make peace with all the frustrations that arise in the garden of life.

No gloves required.

Ah, speaking of gloves. That reminds me of my mother's gardening gloves. Yeah, we may not have had much, but mother was pleasantly vain about her looks -- and that included her lovely hands. She always had gardening gloves. She loved plants and taught me how to care for them. Her green thumb was incredible, so we always had nice green plants and flowers to liven up our living spaces.

Dad always had so much stuff out in the backyard; there was little room for much else. Daddy would collect all sorts of items to keep for use later. And, truth be told, he most always either found a way to use it or made some money on it by selling it to someone else. Or someone would come by to see if Daddy had this or that, and after a few minutes hunting, he would give him the extra whatever it is. Daddy usually had at least five of any one tool.

And sometimes he would find out someone was in need of something and he'd find an extra one and present it to them without charge. Through most of my life, a maximum of half of the backyard was clean enough to play in and make forts or sections for a tree house. The corner lot in the neighborhood where we lived when I was in late elementary and later Jr. High school was empty. That's where all the neighborhood children played baseball and ate pears from the pear tree on the lot. It was pretty cool...like having our own park! But that also meant that gave Dad free reign to eventually junk up the entire backyard with his "materials."

Mother was the opposite, of course. She was the model of cleanliness and neatness. Mom always provided a sparkling clean, lovely home for us. Mom was a master at wallpapering and painting. Daddy did small contracting jobs on the side, even though he worked full-time as a printer throughout my childhood. So he taught Mother many skills. She would reupholster couches with linens to match our drapes, and come up with very creative uses for things that others would discard. She had a way of finessing the look of inexpensive furniture by adding one or two nicer pieces and using accents of smaller, bargain-priced items that made the whole room look lovely.

Mom and Dad were much like "Lady and the Tramp." The funny thing is that I thought that the first time I saw the movie! I believe I was about nine years old. To me, it was adorable. There were my parents as these dogs in love and starring in their own movie! Preciousness!

As the years marched on, all my siblings were in school full-time or grown and out on their own. Mother then began to work as a nurses' aide at a nursing home a block from our house. It was a perfect set up for her. She didn't have to drive to work and she was literally in ear and eyeshot of hearing and seeing what was going on at the homestead.

Mom had a lot of experience with caring for others, specifically hands-on experience for nearly twenty years with seven children as a 24/7 job. Mother was making good money and was very good at her job. To the delight of her supervisor and the nursing home administrator, my mother excelled at every challenge set before her. Her superiors took a liking to her and were her biggest fans for mother to pursue a career in nursing at a higher level. But it was the administrator who began to do research and inform Mother of what scholarships were available. My mother thought she must be too old for such dreams. She had no idea that her dreams were about to become reality!

The Inherent Need to Fear

We're often our own worst enemy, becoming the stoic, hard-hearted judge of our every move and decision -- if and when we finally make a decision! The affinity to be indecisive is a big bull's eye when it comes to honing in on whether or not one is lacking emotional control. When one second guesses every move, one is going to discover inner peace even more difficult to find. But you can, and will find it! You need only have the desire to do so.

Whatever it takes is what must be done. So clear your mind and let happiness enter your heart! Most people are trapped within a defeatist mindset and have done it for so long they simply haven't thought about real change. Open the doors to that closed (and seemingly comfortable, i.e. "I've always thought that way.") mindset and your wings will allow flight to inner peace.

It's amazing to me those who think the way they have done things forever is so difficult to change. It's not at all a difficulty when you realize that the old ways haven't gained you that which you desire. We live in a society that, for the most part, is afraid of change. Change makes people think that perhaps they have wasted years or even decades of time when they could've made the change long ago. That type of hindsight thinking is totally counterproductive.

The way to think is for the here and now – the present and the future. The past is simply what it is: the PAST. The past is always running LAST. It's behind and has lost out to the NOW. Now is always FIRST.

Living in the past makes you sluggish for the present and dead for the future. It's time to move on and love every moment as you learn and put into practice the changes that will transform you from being fearfully frustrated into fabulously fantastic.

Until one let's go of all anger, resentment, and bitterness; happiness cannot be achieved. It is totally within you. Forgive, forget, and move on to a life that is positive. When positive-minded, your joy will help you skip right over turbulence and land onto clouds of contentment. – Charmainism

Imagine all the horrible crimes against humanity in this world. If it weren't for the unhappiness of someone else, such atrocities would, in all likelihood, never come to pass. People often think themselves into a frenzied lather of total frustration of which they can't emerge. At that

point, for some, there's nothing left to do but lash out at anything and anyone. This often leads to fear, loathing, and the taking of lives. We have to help change this pattern of self-destruction. And we can!

Can we honestly be happy knowing the seemingly dire situations of the world as a whole? The answer is yes. We merely have to retrain our minds to relax more and worry not over that which isn't under our control. Which means that even though we can't change the world, we most certainly can change our way of thinking and thus make great, positive changes for ourselves!

Agreed, this world is in turmoil, and there are a lot of unhappy, confused people in this world. Truth be told, however, this has always been the case. Mankind has been the personification of the word conqueror from day one. Survive and conqueror was the rule. If you don't make the first move, someone else will. Get it or be got! Well, we no longer have to live that way. We don't have to feel we're in a world that demands we fight for everything lest we be overtaken. That's the 'conquer first or be conquered' frame of mind of the past. Agreed, it is alive and well on this planet, but it will be the death of mankind if things don't change. We must learn to make peace and actively promote it. Peacemakers are the future! With peace, no one will ever need to live in fear. As each of us finds our own inner peace, the world begins to change into a more positive and loving place.

Life is never 'lived' in fear.
Truly, life is 'stifled' in fear. – Charmainism

That past was provoked by fear and fear alone of what *could* happen if we didn't act first. And, at times in history, that fear was most definitely warranted. Since that time we've progressed from that wholly self-preservationist, "strike first or be struck" way of thinking. However, it's a heritage that's very difficult to put into submission, even in our modern era.

Though we've learned that people who are different than ourselves aren't necessarily to be feared, there's still much of that fear running in the veins of people today. They fear the unknown. That includes people they don't know, whether those people are from another neighborhood, State, or Country different from themselves. It's ignorance, yes, and knowledge is indeed the antidote to the poison of ignorance. However, let's not ignore the undeniable innateness of fear:

As human beings, we have an inherent need for fear and are therefore somewhat predisposed to being fearful. It runs though our veins as if liquid self-preservation. Even through all the changing times of history, the need for fear has always been deeply ingrained in the beings we are. – Charmainism

We can become fearful of that which we aren't familiar, be it people, places, situations, or the thought of what the future may hold. Since we no longer have to look over our shoulders lest be thumped by a club and dragged off to another village not our own, we still have an innate need for fear. If there's nothing much to fear, our minds will conjure up something to satisfy that innate desire. This means that even when things are going well, if we aren't on guard against it, we tend to manifest some dark possibility of losing all that we've gained.

We then become trapped once again not only by being frustrated with our seemingly inability to be truly happy, but also by the fear of what tomorrow may bring—even if we're able to get our frustrations in check today. This isn't truly living, but indicative of merely existing.

Forgive the world and forgive yourself for using the turmoil of the world as an excuse for your unhappiness. – Charmainism

Existing, that is, just as uncivilized man of so long ago. He knew not of why he made choices, to him they weren't choices but necessities that would ensure the survival of he and his family. He had no thought of what tomorrow might bring and never worried about it. He lived each day at a time with no thought of what might happen tomorrow. He knew nothing of planning and tomorrow. Today was the Alpha and the Omega of it all.

In my father's day, once a man had a family, a man had to provide! No man worth his salt would be caught shirking his responsibilities by drowning them out sucking on a bottle. My father was not quite that kind of alcoholic. Rather, he was the highly functioning type that was convinced my mother was trying to suck all the life out of him by whittling him down to the role of solely that of being a provider. For Mother, Daddy's partying days must get behind him and quickly. There was no money for his drinking, gambling, and carousing. Mother thought that was more than fair, for she certainly never got time off from being a mother! I truly believe that my mother thought she could tame my father. But whether before or after children, with my father's genuinely free spirit, "taming" was not part of the deal for him and he was going to have a ball, just as he'd always done before meeting the woman who'd become my mother.

Though, quite admittedly, there were times when Dad's drinking was literally over-the-top in excess. Those times could become quite frightening for those who one minute saw their loving and kind father, turn the very next minute into someone unrecognizable. He looked something like our father, but the resemblance completely ended there.

This man was much like Robert Louis Stevenson's character, "Mr. Hyde," from the <u>Strange Case of Dr. Jekyll and Mr. Hyde</u>. It didn't happen *every* time he drank, but there was ever a distinct possibility of seeing Mr. Hyde when Daddy imbibed in certain liquors. Hard liquors. Beer or wine was fine, but hard liquor was my father's Achilles Heel (just as that concoction that Dr. Jekyll drank). He was never violent with Mother, or us, at anytime. Instead, this Mr. Hyde inside my father expressed himself as an overbearing and incessant philosopher. Once my father's Mr. Hyde came out, he would ramble on and on and on for hours or even days. For those who didn't know him, they could think it possible that Daddy's escalation in volume could be a precursor to violence.

Daddy's intense soliloquizing could be about the sun, the moon, or merely the passing thought of the glistening of morning dew that could provoke deep thought and thus stir my father's passion to serenade his ode for life and living to the fullest. He so loved life and all those in it. He would whistle when he was happy or sad. His whistling and singing were tools of communication to Daddy. Few people could whistle as piercingly as my father. He had a whistle that could make the world stand up and take notice! He whistled like a new species of bird. The sounds were hauntingly beautiful. Whether by words or whistle, when Daddy was philosophizing -- he was completely lost in it. Under the influences of grain alcohol, he was blind to everything and everyone as the pangs of frustration fed his flowing rhetoric as if it were literally a way to produce mourning with words. I truly felt for my father during those times. And many times I was right there, the twelve-year-old who'd get help to put him in the car...and I'd then faithfully drive him home. All the while, being quite responsible and honored to complete my task.

But we were happy. Or, I should say, at least I certainly was. Yes, even when waiting for Daddy outside of taverns and being able to hear him go on and on to eternity with, "Theoretically speaking on the theological point...if thus is so, and so is thus, then why fore do we so thus ignore? Is it not for the prognostication of man that we're here and that 'thus *is* so' becomes 'thus *and* so?'" And then he'd roar. Yes.

Like the lion he was. ROAR! I'd laugh and think about how tough it was going to be to get him in the car that night. He was far on the other side of drunkenness. But it was my duty and I was proud to be entrusted to the task of getting him home.

So whether he was home or not home, the main thing was that when he wasn't at home, he didn't have to hear the endless nagging pick right back up again. And if he were home, he'd make sure that he was nearly passed out drunk before he got there so as to not hear the barrage of disdain soaked words being flung at him by my mother.

My father may have been the head caveman in the family, but mother owned the club and she knew how to use it! Ha! Mercy! Their dance was one of bickering and bantering, usually slowly building as Daddy kept trying to make light of it and Mom having none of it. It would then escalate to the point where Daddy knew it was time to take off for a couple of days and then maybe Mom would appreciate him when he got back. I called them "Ma and Pa Kettle" to their faces. It was said with love and much affection, but all the while I was shaking my head with the mystery of it all.

Later in life, it became clear to me that had mother not nagged my father, I'm sure we wouldn't have had the necessities when we needed them. Daddy needed a regular jolt of reality to hit him every now and again in order to own up and not put off what he should be doing. Daddy was easily distracted. Being a very handsome and fit specimen of a man's man, Daddy was a great dresser who knew how to wear his clothes. Most of his distractions, however, knew how to wear perfume.

Mother had to let Daddy know that he had to own up to his duties as a father and a provider. If he didn't have time left over for her, she would wait...and she made that clear, even with an exclamation of, "...*if* I haven't forgotten by then that I actually give a damn."

My mother always got in the last word. *Always.*

Water your heart with kindness

and love will continue to grow. – Charmainism

Understanding Fear & Frustration

When we begin to understand why we react the way we do at times, it becomes easier for us to succeed in changing that negative behavior. Frustration is a reaction brought on by impatience and culminates with intolerance. Our reactions to situations or circumstances are evoked mostly by interpretation. Every person interprets somewhat differently. If you find yourself short-tempered and upset over the slightest things, it could be that your Tolerance Gauge is stuck on 'low-tolerance' instead of 'high-tolerance.'

We weren't born with a frustration setting etched in stone, and we're all well aware of that because we know how some people can set us off doing the same thing that others do and we're not bothered by the latter. In other words, what we become impatient with, and how much so, is of our own doing. Impatience more often is indicative of unhappiness with ourselves; or it can be that we're still frustrated with that particular person over something that happened another time but we still can't let it go. Or, perhaps it's a bit of both because we're still angry with ourselves for letting them get away with whatever it was they did!

Impatience hasn't one ounce of positive energy to it. It only arises to up one's blood pressure and evoke increasing frustration, which leads to anger. What's the sense of that when the choice is yours to make? You <u>can</u> choose to be patient. You <u>can</u> also choose to be tolerant. You <u>can</u> also choose to let things go! While you're at it, go ahead and choose to not be angry with yourself and you'll find you're no longer angry with anyone else. It's over and done with when *you* choose to end it!

45

What this means is that in <u>any</u> situation you always have the choice to select a reaction that's best for you and <u>your</u> peace of mind. You choose to let it go and harbor no ill feelings afterward. Instead, you're empowered to remain totally positive and upbeat to enjoy the rest of your day! Such is my premise of a philosophy I call unobtrusive, Positive Indifference. We'll talk more about that later.

Some people have never grown up emotionally. They are as an immature young child, reactionary and dramatic. It is a learned behavior that can be unlearned! – Charmainism

It's amazing when we realize how both impatience and frustration are at the heart of so many sources of conflict. One of the first lessons a young child *should* learn is that no one or thing is upsetting them or <u>making</u> them angry. Emotions are choices. Therefore, it's a choice as to whether or not to give in to any emotion. It's our own doing and so we can learn to gain control over them.

Teaching children how to entertain a different way of looking at things is key to their learning how not to allow their feelings to be hurt. It's about Perspective! Perspective is all about making sense of irrational emotions that hold us hostage when dealing with difficult times in our lives. Unchecked emotions can rob us of our peace of mind and another beautiful day in which to rejoice the gift of life and embrace it with everything we have. We lose the vigor for life when we no longer see the possibility of getting over the things that bother us to no end. So much so, that we can't take a step into the present without the mud of the past bogging us down and keeping us away from any chance at being happy ever again.

Understanding Fear & Self-Pity

Sometimes there's the feeling that something keeps whispering in your ear that you're not deserving of happiness so why bother. The real truth is that some are living in the past and that past isn't only killing the present, but the future as well. Many things can hold us there. Guilt is one of those things.

Forgive yourself for not being kind when you could have. Do not ever harbor guilt. The constant nagging of guilt is wholly negative and self-destructive. It keeps us from moving forward by holding us back while we're locked in a time warp of deep regret. – Charmainism

So is trying to be superhuman in a world of imperfect and fragile people. So is self-pity and thinking you should be unhappy because of great loss or hardship. We often expect too much and disappoint ourselves to no end when we think this way. In short, we set ourselves up for failure by wanting that which cannot be realistically attained. It's time to forgive our weaknesses and move on to the challenge of becoming strong.

Self-pity is a pit of your own digging.
Fill it in with the courage of change. – Charmainism

It's the reluctance to embrace change due to our own personal fears that holds us in the clutches of the past. The past will stifle any chance we have of being happy today or in the future. Until we choose to let go of such fears we'll continue to live a life that's far less than optimal. Our fears constantly get in the way and keep us adversely affecting many of our relationships. We make problems when there were none.

We're not sure how we do it, but we do it. We can't seem to get out of the way of others, and we most certainly are having a huge problem getting out of our own way!

And as if that's not bad enough, there are those who sometimes make the mistake of thinking we don't have to fear others if we control every situation. We then become truly self-insulating against any possibility of ever feeling the cold briskness of rejection, the heartache of loss, and the harsh reality of disappointment. But none of that is truth. We simply have found a fake comfort in our own foolishness.

Once again, it all comes down to basic fear. Fear, when engaged into high gear, brings out the self-destructive habit of harboring anger, resentment, guilt, and hate; which all relate back to that which we're uncertain about and are therefore compelled to assign blame for the way we feel. Sometimes we blame ourselves for being foolish and allowing others to take advantage of our feelings. We can be very hard on ourselves when others mistake our compassion for weakness. It's much easier to blame others rather than face our own shortcomings. Either way, we're angry nonetheless.

People happy in their own skin rarely have issues with much of anything. When happy, there is little time to sit and ponder over that, which is a waste of time and energy. Worry is not an issue. However, when things aren't what one expected, that is when the self-serving convenience to find fault with most anything and anybody tends to surface. Scapegoats can take the most intriguing forms. As the adage states, 'necessity is the mother of invention.' Need someone or something to blame for your problems? Go find one. It's all the rage, you know. But it is definitely not in your best interest to do so! – Charmainism

Growing up, we kids never really knew we were actually poor until Dad took us to a place to pick up commodities. It was a convent outside of town. There, they gave us large industrial-sized cans of foods; including tapioca, chop suey, and, oh yes, what we called "Commodity Milk." It was a dry powder that came in a large box and, of course, had to be mixed with water. Try with all your artistic skills and you'd never get all the lumps out of that milk! For years longer than I'd care to admit, I thought *all* milk had lumps in it. Ha!

We all used the term, "artistic skills," at a very young age, as our entire family was pretty artistic. Daddy was a wonderful artist who did portraits in his spare time for added revenue. My father had won numerous awards for his portraits at the Illinois State Fair over many, many years. Born left-handed, Daddy became semi-ambidextrous when forced to use his right hand in elementary school. There were times I'd stand and watch him draw in awe, as he would use his right hand as deftly as his left. We were very proud of Daddy and his talents.

My eldest sister, Sly, to me, is an artist of a magnitude that few will ever even know exists. She really is in a league of her own. She would draw characters that would make anybody drool…they were so perfect in their own way, yet with a magnetism of pain and despair at the same time. Her characters were mesmerizing! They could do anything, or so I always thought when I'd peruse her drawings.

My sister Antoinette also is an extremely talented artist. So much so that an article was written about her and her drawing talents when she was only five years old. She won backstage passes to spend some time with the singing group "The Fifth Dimension" when they were hotter than the hot air balloon of their shows. Antoinette took me as her guest to meet them. It was really interesting since they shared the same religion we did. Anyway, Antoinette has recently taken back to drawing and hasn't skipped a beat. Her skills may have sat dormant for years, but her works are even more remarkable than ever. She is an amazing artist!

And then some of us are singers and musicians, etc. etc. I know, "The Smith Five" we could've called ourselves. Yeah, right! Talented, yes. But all *that*? Uh, probably not...and *definitely* not if Mom had *her* say. It would be a definite "No Go!" LOL

So okay, back to those lumps...nothing artistic about them! We could laugh about being poorer than others. Not because we thought it was funny, but because it was our life. We were happy with life and had the sense of humor to exploit it to the nth degree with long, laboring belly laughs that would rock the whole house. Our house could be filled with the best laughter when we all got going. I found that through humor, life could be as funny as it was glorious. It wasn't really a conscious thought; it really was just the way I naturally thought. Life was funny! And that made everything okay and doable.

I'll never forget driving through what must have been a really nice neighborhood when my eldest sister, Sylvia (later called "Sly"), pointed and exclaimed, "Now you *know* that house got **groceries**." Hahahaaaa!! The whole car erupted in laughter, even though that's when it dawned on me that there were other people who lived better than we did. Up until that time, I'd no clue that some people didn't have lumps in their milk! Hey, I was only five or six years old, but it wasn't long after that when my little voice would chime in to offer up, "Bet *they* don't have to stir their milk!" And we'd all laugh again, even my parents.

I suppose they felt it hard for their children to get a bad disposition from a good sense of humor. From my perspective, it wasn't said as if we envied those more well-to-do people or wanted to be them, it was simply an observation that it was rather obvious the people in that house had more than we did. Besides, all the doors on their cars were exactly the same color as the rest of the car! LOL And I bet they had keys to start their cars. Our station wagon, "Big Red," had two wires that had to be intertwined by hand to start the car. And surely you know how it had to shut off. Ha!

The other side of that coin is remembering that many, many years later, talking to someone about that story and noticing an acquaintance of mine who was within earshot began to cry. I was living down in the Florida Keys at the time, and perhaps the woman had too much to drink, but she began to get very upset at the conversation. When I asked her what was wrong, she began to tell me how painfully poor she and her siblings were growing up and it left many scars for her. She became distraught.

That's such a shame. This woman was over sixty years old and still had not come to grips with the torture she wrestles with because she grew up literally dirt poor. Everything in this life is relative to something else. There are those who'd love to have a floor of any kind, even dirt, as long as they had the upgrade of a roof over their head! We have to keep things in the perspective of being grateful for that which we *do* have. Nothing can hold us back more from loving life and relishing every moment than the destructive habit of looking back at the movies in life we can't change. Just shut the projector off and move on.

In the big picture, we still have to know when to turn the movie off and go to bed. – Charmainism

You know, it's good to sometimes go back and revisit times gone by. Memories are like movies – pick the good ones to watch; the ones that make you feel really good. Just be careful to stay honest with your memories. We have to keep them clear with the accuracy of how things really were rather than warping reality with the hindrance of self-serving hindsight. When we do that, we affect our present and future because we engage in selective memory: only recalling the parts that help prove that the days of our past were far better than the ones we have now.

No one can afford regrets. Regrets are a total waste of time and energy. They simply bog you down and pull you into the pit of despair and darkness. Pass it by!

Every great pity party serves up plenty of hindsight. – Charmainism

Chapter Three:
The Darkness before Dawn

Unhappiness is relative to an individual's perception of it. Frustration, anxiety, disappointment, etc. are what we feel they are to us as well...but none of those emotions seem to have the impact as that of being "unhappy." It is much easier to get over those other seemingly more temporary and less impacting emotions rather than have the impending doom of "unhappiness" shadowing over us. So in a way, perhaps happy people keep unhappiness at bay by interpreting their negative emotions as the temporary ones that are the easiest to overcome. – Charmainism

By the time I was old enough to know what a bad mood was, my mother had become very negative about her life and had somewhat given up on anything ever being right in her world. She therefore was focusing only on what her religion had taught her, that the "New Order" of the world, the time after God would cleanse it with the second coming of Christ and the final battle of good vs. evil, would soon be here to save her. That's when everything would be perfect again (after Satan had his rule for a thousand years first). If one could pass the test of vying with Satan for a thousand years and remain a faithful servant to Jehovah God, then the reward would be everlasting life in a paradise here on earth for all God-fearing people to enjoy.

Even though I couldn't understand all of her issues at the time, what I did know was that being pessimistic was Mother's right, but the little girl that was me was a genuine clone of her highly optimistic, happy-go-lucky father – and nothing could ever dampen my zest for life or make me think there was anything I could not do! I wasn't waiting for the "New Order!" To me, as a young child with everything to look forward to, life was already in the right order. I was loved and I was happy!! That's all I knew.

Perhaps you tend to be more melancholy lately. More often than not, this tends to occur when one gets caught up in too many daydreams about better times. Soon, one is stuck living in the past with no reality called the present. When that happens, you can quickly destine yourself to have no future. The melancholia could be due to tremendous loss, heartache, disappointment, disenchantment, or from any of a hundred other reasons why people begin to feel at first sorrow and then watch it grow into self-pity. They forget that there always is, within their grasp, a healthy end to every dark period.

It happens far too often when some suddenly find themselves at the bottom and wonder how the hell they got there. Having fallen too far down into the depths of darkness, the person has hit rock bottom. It's very easy to become exhausted just thinking about what one might have to do in order to ever find a ray of hope. They know they must get busy and dig themselves out of this horrible and dark hole in which they've hidden their thoughts and feelings from others. The top seems unreachable from so far below.

That person could be any of us. And what would we do if we over-think such a scenario and find ourselves thinking ourselves right back into that deep, dark corner, and having no clue as how to crawl out and become ALIVE again. Would we not wonder if perhaps we'd ever again see the light of a really good day?

The light is here and always has been. We simply must learn to change our perspective on how we see where we are in life. We have to learn that we aren't alone and that darkness shrouds us all at some point in our lives. It's normal. It's human. And it's also reversible.

The thing is that most people who walk around each day with a lilt in their step don't have perfect lives. They too have problems, issues, concerns, and all the other normal imbalances of life tugging at their shirttail. They just don't wear it on their sleeve. They don't let it run or ruin their lives because they've never thought themselves singled out as a plaything by the only black cloud on the planet. They find a way to be happy. And so, then can you.

There's a growing trend to wear one's troubles on the sleeves. It's a trend that can't go out of fashion soon enough for me. Everyone has woes. It is what life includes along with the good times. How one handles the tough days is what gives strength, or a lack of, during the super rough times. When heat from the blazing sun of adversity hits, all that time wilting in what later will be recognized as shade, will not help. It's all relative. What is seen as an immense challenge today, in comparison to far worse situations of tomorrow or yesterday, is really just a blip on the emotional radar. Stay positive by keeping things in perspective! Know you can handle anything because the sheer joy of living gives you the power to do so. It's the WEAK end! – Charmainism

People who choose to be strong in the face of adversity are those who have learned to keep their emotional balance from teetering off into pits of darkness by keeping their thought processes rational. By doing so, they neutralize negative thoughts and turn them into positive empowerment! It's within you to bring your positive being to the surface and let it knock all negativity from your life force. It can be done and you can most certainly do it.

What about deep loss? Dealing with the stresses and grief of deep loss can also be handled in a manner that allows you to retain your sanity. We have to remember that death is as much a part of the human condition as birth. Being positive and realistic can help you through any of life's hurdles. There's nothing you can't handle. You simply have to make sense of it, and it's my intention to help you do just that.

For darkness to become light, we have to believe in the brightness of another day. – Charmainism

It's not that others haven't done things to you which have caused intense pain or grief; it's more that if you fall into the trap of thinking you deserve to fall apart because of it, then you'll fall very far. You may fall too far.

It's as if the more we love someone, when we lose them, we must solidify that great love by using the longevity of grief as a testament to our devotion. As if we grieve forever, we then adequately pay the person we loved with our tribute of sacrifice and give them their genuine due. But that simply isn't true!

We cannot honor those we've lost if __we__ lose our minds. – Charmainism

Certainly, everyone is entitled to mourn. But when mourning goes on for too long, it's no longer mourning about another, but a selfish mourning that is more akin to wallowing in self-pity. It's a thin line, but it's one that most who have endured great losses must learn to keep in balance. There's a time to come to grips with the fact that Alfred Lord Tennyson's words from his poem, "In Memoriam" (1850), ring oh, so true: "It is better to have loved and lost than never to have loved at all," is so very true. Even in the face of loss, we must be thankful for that which we had.

Our memories will ensure we'll always have what was lost even if we can't touch it one more time. Our gain will always live within us if only we can stop suffocating it with the deluge of tears and fears that have taken over what used to be a life in balance. We've come unglued and are sometimes not sure we really *want* to be put back together again into a life that will never be the same as it once was. We want things the way they used to be. That, of course, is simply not possible. So we have to adapt and choose to swim in the calming and peaceful waters of a life lived with joy; and we must do so quickly or drown in our sorrows.

To gain positive insight, one must

rid the mind of a negative outlook. – Charmainism

Everything is positive when it emanates from a truly positive being. Positive people have position dispositions. Some are seemingly born with it as it flows out of their pores and their lives exemplify their positive nature. However, for most, this positive nature has to be brought out and up to the surface; then kicked into high gear in order to be able to grasp that power. It's that power that allows us to attain the state of being known as inner peace.

Until you decide to stand up and face your fears, including accepting great loss as a part of this journey called life; then life will continue to waste away for you at great speed. Knowing that truth also causes you great distress as you awake each day wondering when you'll ever make the real changes you so desire and <u>need</u> to make! You've put off doing anything positive for your life for so long, you've forgotten you have a choice!

The menu of life has a plethora of entrees.

Choose from those that don't give you heartburn. – Charmainism

Consider what's likely to occur if you don't change the things you know you must. You've no doubt in your mind that your current problems will multiply and magnify if you continue to let procrastination lead the way. Left unchecked, neglect in any form will always take its toll. So the realistic answer will always come back around to the fact that you *must* make the changes necessary in order to gain control over your life again. But it's that *"must"* that gives you pause. You despise being pushed or forced to do anything.

So you fight with yourself about it. You flog yourself time and time again when you let the opportunities for change come and go without acting on them. Your anger is more about you than anyone else, yet you take out your frustrations on everyone around you. You don't have to hate yourself in order to better yourself. Motivation does <u>not</u> have to come from disgust! We can't produce positive change by using negativity as a resource.

So when terrible things happen that are out of your control, how do you deal with them with optimism and find the strength to forgive, forget, and move forward?

Imagine being fourteen and going steady with a high school varsity basketball player and have to go back to school the next day and explain you're no longer dating...but you didn't quite break up...it's waaaay beyond that. What you have to explain is that the boy you've been going steady with for eight months, the boy you're so infatuated with because he's so much like your father... well, turned out to be that very thing. VERY much like your father! In fact, far too much like your father because he's your father's son! Yes. He's your brother!

Dare I say, quite literally, an "Oh, brother!" moment?! Ugh! The *agony*.

I dealt with it by soon after becoming anorexic, though I didn't realize it at the time. I'd never even heard of the eating disorder or diagnosis. Before I knew it, I was running at least five miles a day and down to eating one hard-boiled egg and one carrot per day. That was it. My goal was to weigh 70 lbs. I was out of my mind, yes. But at the time, it made sense to me. Little did I realize that though I could not control what was happening in my life, I was asserting myself to take control of my own body. And I did...though it was out-of-control in an entirely different way. It never occurred to me that my behavior was not normal. I couldn't see the pounds melting away, not even when I'd lost over 30% of my body weight. To me, I looked the same as when I started. Yes, I was ill.

I never whined or complained about any of it. In fact, I was very matter-of-fact. To me, the anorexia had nothing to do with any of it. It was just me, I'd say. My parents were at their wit's end. They thought for sure I was trying to kill myself. I began to have physical ailments due to starvation. My kidneys weren't working properly and I'd severe headaches.

My mother said we were referred to another physician, a specialist, and that we'd an appointment to see him. I was like, "Fine." When we went to the Clinic, it was a medical center of many, many different doctors. The waiting room was huge. When my name was called, a woman came out and directed us through a hallway, around a corner, and to an office door. It had glass in the door but you couldn't see through it. There was a name on the door, but it flashed by so quickly I didn't read it. The whole thing was just so odd. Or so I thought.

We walked in and there was a man sitting behind a desk. He stood up and greeted us. As he extended his hand, there was no hand. Nope. It was a pincher or something. Prosthetic. I thought well, this guy's definitely not a surgeon!

He asked us to sit down after I rejected shaking his pincher. It just didn't feel right at all, and I knew that without even trying. That's when the small, gratuitous, bowl of peanuts came into view. Then the light bulb went off: there were a lot more nuts around here than those in the bowl! And as the Pincher Man began to speak...wait for it...uh huh...wait for it – he asked me, "How are you feeling?"

I just couldn't even believe any of this. This was truly surreal. However, I was very calm and respectful to him...but inside I felt like screaming to the mountaintops. Didn't anyone even think to ask me about anything before resorting to something like this? I mean, to not tell me...like I wouldn't figure out what was going on? Please!

Hold it together, Betty. This was no time to let my emotions surface...nope. There would be no Thorazine in my future any time soon. Keep calm. And I did.

And I then told the doctor that I was _feeling_ like a complete idiot.

Standing up, I calmly announced to Mother that we couldn't possibly afford any of this and that I'd do better and get better but this was all totally unnecessary. I then said I'd be waiting outside in the car, and turned around to tell the physician there should be no charge for this visit.

Mom came out about ten minutes later with her face still wet from tears of frustration and wasting the doctor's time. After all, she was a nurse – at that time, a nurse at her wit's end. Oh for heaven's sakes! Truly, I'd no idea until that time, the hell I was putting my parents through. It was easy to see that my mother truly knew not what to do. And it was also obvious to me that she would've done just about anything to save me.

You have to accept the fact that you really do want to change and you want to be happy. There's no failure in making those determinations. Decide you want to be happy. From this point on, a happier person will be making decisions with a clearer mind and a more positive outlook on life. Is there any doubt that "Happier" can think better?! "Happier" can certainly get the ball rolling! "Happier" has learned to accept the fact that happiness comes from within.

Learning to accept that which cannot be changed will free you from the bondage of bitterness and self-pity. Acceptance is a nutrient on which happiness thrives. Thrive on! – Charmainism

The key here to greatness comes with your acceptance of what you DO want. This is how you get over being overwhelmed at the very thought of initiating change. The change you've made is all positive, not negative. Your desire is there, no doubt about it, but your motivation has to be such that it brings happiness to you just knowing you're making moves in the right direction. Then "Happy" can get on with life in a much more positive light. That's when things immediately become better for you.

Therefore, decide right here and now that you're going to become the key to your own destiny. You're going to make every effort to help yourself by making amends with your past and facing your fears. In time, with all you'll learn here, you'll begin to see the beacon atop the lighthouse of your present and future. Your life is about to change as you understand more about yourself and the things you need to do to make positive change in your life.

Right now, you need to embrace a figurative action and Shake Hands with Yourself. You know you're more than ready to do so. Let the "Shwy" Philosophy shine through you!

Every morning, relish the opportunity of another glorious day to SHINE! – Charmainism

Chapter Four:
Shake Hands With Yourself

Shake hands with yourself. Forgive yourself and you can learn to love yourself and others in the manner that brings you the greatest fulfillment of all. With love, all things are truly possible. –
Charmainism

The Significance of Shaking Hands

Just about anyone will offer their hand to a total stranger as introductions are being exchanged. Shaking hands signifies, "all is fair." With a simple handshake, you give a person the benefit of the doubt as friendship is offered. With those who have wronged us, shaking hands symbolizes forgiveness and a fresh start. Whatever happened before is over and done with and both parties decide it's time to forgive, forget, move on and press on that handshake to seal the deal.

There's no doubt that sometimes we all take a handshake totally for granted. We forget what its meaning is about and find ourselves doing it more as a learned social action rather than a meaningful action.

Learning the benefit of shaking hands and forgiveness is the bridge that can turn an uncertain path into one of certainty. Following a bitter disagreement, when we shake hands with the opposing party, we're announcing that we're now good with that person. We've let go of any ill that was harbored and we're therefore no longer suffocating with the lingering thought processes filled with negativity.

The bridge of happiness has no breaks in it and therefore nothing to fear. There are no holes to fall through or asterisks above your head to come crashing down, causing you to lose your footing. It's solid! That's the type of solid foundation you need! It's a foundation that leads to the path of enjoyment throughout your life.

You'll never truly understand how much frustration has to do with a less than happy life until you overcome frustration in all forms. Many fail to see how refusal to forgive is perhaps the biggest frustration of all. This is a promise: when you begin to truly forgive, you'll be well on your way to attaining inner peace. It's a freedom easily understood and appreciated once it's put into practice and becomes a way of life. Walk on and over the bridge made up of your own two hands, shaking each other in harmony, to begin rebuilding your happy and peaceful life.

It is my belief that perhaps the biggest test you face as far as religious beliefs, is can you live up to being simultaneously tolerant and loving of your fellowman throughout whatever transpires. Those who continue to be stoically "holier than thou," need the reminder of the virtue of humility. Until all who profess to follow a higher power actually "LET GO and LET GOD," religious differences will continue to be used as an excuse to wreak havoc on this earth. It shall be man's own undoing. – Charmainism

Realize that it's in your own best interest to choose to forgive and be negative-free, and then the life that is positive and happy will find you. Most worries, concerns, and fears are made up more of that which you embellish to the point that your negativity makes them seem worthy of monopolizing your life, rather than them being actual roadblocks on your path to happiness. Negative thinking actually has you blocking yourself from what you desire.

This is why you must Shake Hands with Yourself! Shaking hands is a very simple gesture. See the big picture here? What you routinely do in the name of fairness and friendship, you hold back from offering to yourself. So many people never give themselves a fair shake. People tend to be their own worst enemy. They're forever picking at themselves.

After a while, with no letup, self-loathing and its nasty companion, self-pity, take over and darken all that used to be a life vibrant and fulfilling. Both of these soul-sapping vultures move in and won't leave one's side until they're evicted once and for all. Though a person can be helped along the way to do so, no one can remove those parasites for you. You have to do it yourself. This is why shaking hands with yourself is so important. It says: "I'm ready and committed to make this change." Yes! It means: Let's do this thing!

You need to gain adequate motivation to give you the courage to face your fears, overcome them, and proceed on to greatness. You must cease the habit of holding your breath when in turmoil by remembering that your brain needs all the oxygen possible in order to think clearly and make well thought-out decisions. Serious business! Remember to breathe! And breathe deeply. You may wonder if there's any real truth to that. Well, the next time you're in a situation that's a sphincter factor of more than six, check to see if you're breathing. We all hold our breath when we're awaiting some finality. And some of us do a lot of shallow breathing that's not really healthy at all.

Remember that a fresh breath of life follows every sigh of exasperation. Breathe in, breathe out, and ENJOY every moment. It is how everything begins and ends. – Charmainism

You need to be reminded what it's like to be joyful and full of gratitude for this wonderful life you've been given. Look, no one can begin anew while carrying the same baggage each and every day. So go ahead, tell yourself, "Shwy," "Shwy," "Shwy!!" Yes! Shake hands with yourself and agree to leave that baggage on the curb and get on with this newest leg of your journey called life. The only thing you'll be carrying from this point on is the smile of inner peace on your face. That's what you've to look forward to and soon it will be yours.

When our minds are negative we have an aura of negativity surrounding us. We aren't approachable, though we have no clue as to why everyone who looks our way seems to project surliness. Perhaps we need to look at each face that comes our way as a reflection of what we ourselves project. If nothing else, if we're not smiling, that thought surely will bring one to our face. A smile usually brings back a smile. – Charmainism

It's always wise to know the moves your opponents will most likely make and to be prepared to effectively defend against them. It's not a bloody battle, per se, but rather a competition much like chess in that it's a game of the mind. Your goal is to neutralize your affinity to be negative and to also keep your opponent (out-of-control emotions) under control. This is how you can acquire a more positive disposition. It takes time to cultivate . . . but it's so worth it!

Understanding how your emotions play against your progress towards happiness is how you can ultimately gain the upper hand by then learning to harness that negative energy and turning your victory into a positive force. We all are fully aware that it's completely counterproductive to allow our emotions to wreak havoc in our lives. This is where learning how to neutralize our fears by taking claim of a positive disposition will serve us very well.

Cultivating Your Positive Disposition

We are human and make mistakes. Understood. However, as we mature, there comes a time when we think to ourselves that by now we should have figured out how to keep our frustrations low on the radar in order to better control over-emotional, negative reactions – the ones where we tend to blurt out words faster than our brains can compute the futility of it. The ones that make us feel like a penny waiting on change at the checkout of progress. The ones that make us feel lower than low and sillier than stupid could ever be, and whatever other self-deprecating analogies we can throw at ourselves. We become, once again, our own worst critic. We simply can't seem to get out of our own way!

Happy people are those who learn that it is a high priority to utilize the most efficient and effective ways necessary for our minds to make sense of, neutralize, and put far behind us any situation that breeds negativity. – Charmainism

Attaining happiness is far easier than riding that ever-vicious cycle of self-loathing that people do day in and day out. Even when ingested in its smallest doses, self-loathing wears one out faster than anything. Exhausted with the fight to just maintain a good front for others, there's not enough energy left to work on improving the situation! We wake up and wonder why we have to struggle so much. Why can't we simply find peace and just be happy!

If only we could just keep the peace in our lives floating on the surface, ridding ourselves of the "what ifs" and "should haves" that continue to undermine our quest for inner peace and happiness. It seems we are never quite content. Not content with others or our selves. We're forever chasing the dream of fulfillment and contentment but don't have a plan to attain any of it.

Happiness is a conditioning of the mind and body so that happiness is totally within the way you perceive things and handle situations in life. You choose to be happy; happiness doesn't choose you. – Charmainism

This is why so many people are forever searching for something to fill a void that really isn't a void at all. You see, there's most often no hole that needs to be filled. Rather, what's missing is the ability to control one's emotions and keep frustration and the fear of failure at bay.

Sometimes it's as simple as not making a big deal out of a funky mood. We have to learn to not make things worse than they are! One need only have a method of dealing with such normal things in a likewise normal manner. This is how we'll learn not to be overly dramatic when it comes to simple situations. Funky mood? Then roll with it! Let's not over magnify its importance to our day-to-day living. I mean, *think* about it: It's your drama, so why not decide that this time it will be a light-hearted drama instead of overly dramatic! Come on, write your own script and enjoy your leading role of acting like a sane, well-balanced, "I-got-this" kind of individual!

So how does all that babble help you with a funky mood? I hear you…yes, I do! What I do is to put some music on! Whether I have to wear headphones or whatever it is I have to do in order to hear it, music soothes my soul as nothing else quite does. Music is the inside, the outside, the up and the down of life all wrapped up into notes of endurance. It doesn't matter whether it's instrumental or with voice, music is what my body craves.

Put on some music you really like and just enjoy the blessing of listening and breathing for awhile. Sometimes we don't need to shake these moods, as they do serve a purpose. And it's okay! When kept in perspective, that dark blue becomes a much lighter shade! Just work on lightening the shade for now by doing something just for you! – Charmainism

This is how you learn to control your emotions. You feel them getting out of hand or going the wrong direction, and you nip those suckers in the bud! Every person on the planet can become a better person by learning to better control their emotions. Even the most gentle of persons must work diligently on this most admirable characteristic. This means having the wherewithal to use restraint to keep situations from escalating into petty battles. Sometimes "restraint" is a mere diversion or something by which to change your mood to a better one. That's when you can think so much more clearly and get back on track to doing what's in your best interest to do: maintaining your inner peace.

When we become a person of peace and gratitude for the simplest of life's gifts, we become a person who exudes a positive disposition. Soon, that positive disposition enters a room before we physically do so. It brightens the aura of the room as the rays of the sun. Everyone is in a better mood because you are too!

When thirsting for zest, quench first

in the simple emollient of __being__. – Charmainism

A positive disposition isn't draining or wearing on your being. Negative energy is what weakens you. As you begin to put what you're learning into practice, you'll quickly notice how doing so transforms your outlook on life by changing you from being a person in turmoil to a person who personifies inner peace. It all depends on how quickly you embrace the concept of cultivating your positive disposition.

Understanding how you got down to the tumultuousness where you are now and changing your thought processes from those that are self-effacing, full of guilt, remorse, and self-pity into those that become enlightening revelations, will be a freedom you'll find easy to embrace. Gone will be the internal twin-headed monsters called Frustration and Fear that have held you back for so long. They'll no longer have a hold on you because you'll no longer allow it. No more 'what ifs' or 'if onlys.' Hindsight is a complete waste of time. No one can go back and make changes in one's history. It is what it is: history! Learn from it and move on.

A moment spent fretting about "What if?" is a moment lost for solving "What is." Positive thinking does not waste time or sap your energy. Rather, it empowers you! – Charmainism

Own up to the fact that changes have to be made and consider that an awakening, not a detriment! You won't be tired or downtrodden once you discover the positive energy within you. You're in the midst of embarking on a resurrection of that person inside you who used to be happy! And yes, it's about time. But trust in that everything happens in its own good time! This is no different. You had to get to where you are now in order to catch a glimpse of that faint beacon of light flickering in the distance. That is the light of great hope. That is the light of inner peace.

Each day, somewhere, someone is fighting for their life while others are wondering what they'll plan for dinner. Whoever crosses your path; remember that we know not what burdens are carried along with their gait. One simple gesture can convey that there is love and caring in this world, a SMILE. Life can be tough, yet a simple smile can truly brighten someone's day. Sending smiles to all of you to carry forward. And yes, I am loving you! – Charmainism

Gerald, my brother-who-used-to-be-my-boyfriend {like you'd actually forget?}, suffered a nervous breakdown shortly after losing his temper and slapping me in the face out of frustration. Truthfully, I asked for it.

It really was my fault. Gerald was upset because I started dating a good friend of his who was on the varsity basketball team with him. They were both three years my senior, and I wasn't taking kindly to being pushed around by anyone! So that "Little Dog Syndrome" of mine reared its yapping little head, and before I knew it the smartest little attitude I could muster up, the Freshman in me told Gerald it was none of his business as I wasn't his girlfriend! If that weren't enough, I started in on how he couldn't be my "big brother" *and* play the part of the jealous ex-boyfriend too! Well, that about had him blowing a gasket.

It's not like I was deliberately trying to stir the pot and upset him, it was just that I was as frustrated as he was about all this. I just had a way of dealing with it and putting it out of mind. Up until this point, I'd put up a good front about it all and was doing well. Deep down, my intent was to get on with my life, but when this mess kept resurfacing and impeding my progress, it began to get the better of me. I was tired of it, and unfortunately, I lost my cool.

In truth: I also was angry. I just wasn't going to face it. So I took it out on Gerry.

He then asked what all I'd done with this friend of his.

"What all I'd done?" Imagine that!! Now *I* was furious! How *dare* he!

In reply, I told him, "I'd done whatever it was I liked!"

Now Gerald knew he and I'd never had sex and never even came close to it after eight months of dating. He knew I was the type of girl who was going to be virtuous for my wedding night. However, a lot had changed since Gerald and I found out we were siblings. And perhaps he thought I'd be so angry, as he was, that I'd become wild and promiscuous because of it. And he knew how his friends talk about girls in the locker room!

When I said anything I want...well, that was it. Gerald was 6'3 and even at only seventeen, had very large hands and size 15 shoes. His hand almost completely covered my face. When he slapped me, he practically knocked me out of the room.

Immediately my face began to swell. I turned away from him as his cousin Butch grabbed him by the arm and pleaded with him to not hit me again. I told them both they'd better leave.

Gerald began to say how sorry he was and he really didn't mean to hit me that hard. He lost his temper and he was sorry. He kept saying that. I just told them to go.

Not ten minutes later, my little sister, who'd been in the room the whole time, had a look of horror on her face. I went to the mirror and saw that my face was disfigured with swelling and completely black and blue on the right side. Mom would be coming home shortly and I had to get out of the house before she got home. She only worked one block away from the house.

I went to the house of one of my two closest girlfriends; my sweet "Suzi Q." Suzi knew I always had her back, and of course I knew she always had mine. But this time, Suzi threw a fit about all this. It was hard for her not to, and had the shoe been on the other foot, I'm sure I would've reacted in the same manner. Then her Nana wanted to know what was going on and then her dad came home. Oh my…trouble, trouble, trouble! This was not good. When Mr. White saw my whole face…well, he was <u>livid</u>. They all were. Livid.

Mr. White demanded to take me home and meet with my parents. I knew Daddy would break Gerald's neck over something like this. How could I fix this and possibly not cause the Smith Family Furious to breathe fire all over Gerald and ruin any chances of him becoming a real member of our family? He didn't deserve any of this, he really didn't. I loved him so much.

When one can't let go of fear, those fears can alienate the very person with whom you wish to be. If you can't trust them at all, they'll have a hard time thinking that the relationship is worth the effort of constantly reassuring you. That gets old. You have to trust. Even if you're wrong in the long run, in the short run did you not find some happiness? Won't the experience of that relationship have some worth as far as helping you to narrow down the parameters of what it is that you're looking for in a companion? You have to let your life's experiences do its job for you! Push fear to the curb and live your life. What happens will happen and you'll survive and move on at that time. You have to OWN that positive philosophy or life's disappointments will own <u>you</u>!

Each one of us makes choices every day. Sometimes a choice of another has a disheartening effect on us. Remember, though, that it is up to us how much that effect erodes our hearts. We can stop that erosion by being fulfilled with whatever we had prior to the fall. No one cries over losing something they never had. Be happy for what you did have and relish in the memories of a better time. – Charmainism

When you consider that whether at work, at home, or wherever you are, if you're unhappy, it doesn't matter where you physically are. It can't be simply that all those different places make you unhappy. Even though your mind tells you it could be this or that, him or her – you know deep down that unhappiness isn't controlled by outside forces. Rather, it's residing and growing inside you.

One has to remember that controlling one's emotions plays a big part of the key to this puzzle of finding happiness. If you decide to be happy, there's nothing to stop you. Only you can control your emotions and how you determine to receive input from others. It's up to you to have on positive receptors. Even when others err and don't acknowledge it, what difference does that make to your happiness? None! Not if you don't allow what others do to affect your emotional state of mind.

In other words, it's not really what others actually <u>do</u> that gets beneath your skin, but rather, it's how *you* perceive and grasp what they do <u>as it pertains to you.</u> Somehow, what they're doing becomes all about you! But it isn't all about you at all. Honestly. Sometimes we make our own traps and then step into them with both feet. We have to keep a handle on quelling negative energy each and every time it surfaces. We don't have to entertain it by allowing it to feed off our friends and family. That's just not a good thing.

Just because something is perplexing to you, as far as a manner of someone's thought processes, doesn't mean you must understand just why the person thinks that way. You keep prodding and interrupting them until you get an answer. An answer you think is appropriate. Well, you know full well the person has been backed into a corner and doesn't know exactly how to respond. They don't <u>have</u> an answer as to why they think the way they do!

Treating people this way is called plain and simply, picking a fight. Oh, yes you did…and yes, I called you on it. Hey, we're all guilty of these things at some time or another, even if only to very small degrees…but no matter the magnitude, it's always an ugly outlet for venting frustration. We all have times when we definitely awoke on the wrong side of the bed, but we need to know that despite that, controlling our frustrations and emotions is what's best for us. So we shake hands and play nice! We can calm our turbulent waters (and bad hair days) and decide to choose a better path when dealing with those grumpy times. And yes, we all do have them!

Great relationships are consistently cultivated in order to grow with vibrant, optimal blossoms. They flourish when nurtured with sunny dispositions, quenched with caring and encouragement in all kinds of 'whether,' and adding a bit of fertilizer every now and again can work wonders (as long as no one has to wear hip boots as it's being applied). Being kind is one of the easiest things to do in life; yet being consistently kind to those closest to us is often the biggest challenge. Remember to embrace LOVE! – Charmainism

Do you get angry when somebody fails to put the cap back on the tube of toothpaste, or when they squeeze the tube from its middle? LOL Well, I'm trying not to laugh because, at times, I too turn into that type of controlling person! Yes, really. Human beings can do the silliest things and get so into a perfect way that things should be done … that it's carried to the point of ridiculousness. It's one thing if you're helping a youngster learn good habits or courtesies, but quite another when the person you're "helping" is a full-grown adult. No one wants to be barked at! No one.

When you think about it, few people actually try to listen to barking dogs.

Harping should be limited to musical instruments. – Charmainism

It is evident that it's easier to be positive with total strangers or acquaintances rather than those close to us. We must be careful about taking for granted those closest to us. They too do have choices also!

And especially when the nitpicking is over something as trivial as whether or not silverware should go up or down when placed in the dish rack right after washing.

Actually, it really doesn't make a difference. Serious business. Well, it does…to *me…sometimes*…but I'm working on not making a big deal of it. ;)

Hey now, LOL. Yes! Most certainly, I work on such things just as anyone else does. Depending on whether or not I'm hydrated properly right after awaking can make a huge difference in my tolerance level. Staying hydrated definitely helps me maintain my positive disposition. Of course, being dehydrated just invites negative energy to come and soak up all the remaining moisture I might have at the time! No thanks!!

What we have to remember with all these things is that people are individuals. We all have our quirks and silly little idiosyncrasies. And those get worse as we get older... believe me on that! The thing is that we either accept someone the way they are and take them, along with their ridiculousness, or we leave them behind and move on. They don't have to be the "bad guy," when we do...it's just a clean break, and everyone is fine thereafter—just apart. There's nothing wrong with that at all. If that's what you really want.

But if we do decide to accept them as they are, then we must do exactly that and make no more quibbles about it. We can't truly accept someone and then nitpick and nag them over the things they do. That's simply very unfair. In the big picture, what does any of it matter? Sure, you may have found the most efficient way to do something and expect others to take your lead; but to someone else, that efficiency may be neutralized for them by adding in not only the time it takes for them to remember to do it, but also the pain of trying to remember the many other things to do that don't come naturally to them. It all bogs them down because they don't have the same thought processes as you do. They don't think like you at all. And that's okay too.

And that's something of which I must remind myself a *lot!*

So the little things that people do that get on my nerves? Well, the small stuff has to be kept in the proper perspective too: LET IT GO! It's easy to remember it when your mind is consumed with enormous challenge; but the less time you spend on important issues and the more free time you have to bicker about things...the more you notice the things to bicker about! Keep it in perspective. There's no reason for bickering at all.

Born prematurely, I was a tiny little runt of a thing with no doubt some bits of "Little Dog Syndrome." Actually, it was probably more due to there being such a large gap in age between my two older siblings and myself. After a five-and-a-half year gap, I was born third in line and was being treated like a peer by my two older sisters as they'd desperately wanted a third sibling so we could play jump rope together! Yes: two to turn the rope or ropes and one to jump! My sister Cheyenne used to tell me how she and Sylvia would try to tie the jump rope around my wrist while I sat in my baby buggy. But it just wouldn't work. They just couldn't wait for me to grow up big enough to hold the rope by myself and embrace my duties as the third sister!

That gap in age was also probably why I was the only child in my household to ever have an imaginary playmate. My playmate's name was "Bossy!" Bossy was neither male nor female. "Bossy" was just a pretty cool companion, but had to be kept in line from time to time. Imagine that! Ha!

In 1987, while finishing up the season playing in a 4.5 Volvo tournament tennis league, my congenital spinal stenosis was diagnosed. I was thirty years old. This was my second year playing the USTA Volvo League, and the first year I'd been team captain. Both years I was named MVP for my teams. The second year my MVP included an engraved trophy stating "Undefeated." Team Captain Sue McCain presented it to me, and I thought to myself, that's pretty good "for an old gal." LOL I'd thoroughly enjoyed playing local and area tournament tennis for about ten years and spent many, many hours in preparation on the courts.

Being a totally self-taught player (Bill introduced me to tennis when we were dating.) I hadn't taken tennis seriously at all until around 1975, the year after my son was born. My sister Cheyenne and I'd get n the courts and soon she was loving it as much as I was. She was very athletic and fast on her feet. Growing up, I was probably the most athletic of the family, being a total Tom Boy and a natural born swimmer from day one; there was no sport I wouldn't try. I was very competitive in everything I did. That made for some great matches between my sister and I, as we were becoming more a part of the local tennis scene.

My tennis was a passion and I loved every minute of it. I loved the sounds and the smells at the courts. I loved all the people. It was a fabulous time with a full schedule of playing and practicing. My son Bj was literally raised on the courts of Washington Park. It was a routine thing for players to see him in his playpen in a shady corner courtside.

Throughout all my tennis tournament-playing years, I knew there was something wrong with my body. However, I always found a way to play through it. It got to a point, though, where there was no more playing through it. The pain was too severe and my hips felt as if they were going to break in half. The gnawing in my back and stomach was terrible. It got to where I could be on my feet for about five minutes and then my legs would stop working.

The escalation of my congenital spinal stenosis and its obvious deterioration hit me pretty hard. Even though my doctors were impressed that I was an accomplished tennis player despite it, they were saying my tennis days were over. In fact, they were saying I'd probably be sitting in a wheelchair far more than ever actually walking again. My body was done...as in "put-a-fork-in-it," DONE.

Long story short, chronic pain has been a huge part of my life for as long as I can remember. However, just to show you how everything is truly relative, the pain over the past thirty years has had its ups and downs that sometimes made a formerly unbearable pain later feel like that of a comforting massage! No kidding. It can be so brutal. You think you've felt all you can feel...and then something says, "Really?" And hits you with a grenade. Yow!

Too, thinking of someone else's pain could also make my pain take another serious downgrade. It was important to me to keep things in perspective. If you give into pain it will run your life and ruin your life. So I suck it up and deal with it. There aren't many choices, as far as I'm concerned. Life is pain. I have to not let it get to me and simply get going!! I'm going to hurt no matter what I'm doing, so I may as well at least be trying to do all that I can possibly do. DOING is always better than MOANING!

Fifteen years ago, sitting in a wheelchair where I'd been trapped the previous three months, when I was told I'd never walk again, that was just not an option for me to choose that as my new reality. Not if I'd any viable alternative. After begging and pleading with my physicians to please help me and just do a disco gram (I felt it would show I'd blown a spinal disc and if that alone were removed and fused, then I'd be able to walk again). They were hearing none of it because the spinal stenosis was so bad there were at least three other areas that could produce the same type of permanent problems at any time. Their view was that my time was up! Their argument was what's the point? The time had been coming since the day I was born when one day I'd no longer walk. To them, that time had arrived.

They wanted me to get over it.

Yeah. They did.

In hindsight, I can't blame them. My spine was and still is a mess. I get it. But I got this.

Anyway, I kept fighting and my orthopedic surgeon decided it might be worth it, but deep down I don't think he felt I'd a chance at all. However, it was my dime and my body. If this was it for me as far as playing tennis, walking, biking, and all that other wonderfully good athletic stuff...well, no one was going to convince me that the surgery wasn't worth the effort. I mean really! The surgery would be an anterior (incised through the abdomen) spinal fusion at L-5, S-1. Titanium cages would be filled with a bone graft (from my hip) and inserted for support. I highly doubt there was ever a more excited and eager patient than myself for this surgery. No fear whatsoever! Just a "Let's do this thing!" attitude all the way!

I never spent one minute in physical therapy (not because I wasn't supposed to, but because I knew I didn't need to). About two days later, I was on a flight to Scottsdale, Arizona. I've been running and jumping and biking and playing tennis ever since. I'm sure my surgeon wonders what ever happened to me. I never saw him again even though he deserves my deepest thanks and admiration for seeing something in me that was worth pushing the envelope. Thank you Dr. Timothy Van Fleet!! It's been a fabulous fifteen years out of that wheelchair and has done me a world of good...sailing all over the Caribbean, playing tennis, biking, loving large (can I get an "Amen"), and another favorite, shadow dancing topside on the deck of the boat in the moonlight!! I've loved every single minute of it. With pain, even! No problem.

Of course my spine has been fighting me every step of the way ever since, but hey, I expected that and proceed to whip it into submission on a daily basis. LOL It's like trying to live with a screaming spoiled little brat, determined to reach way up on their tippy-toes, but who still is just out of reach of the Oreos. Ha! Not a happy little camper at all. But hey, the alternative has four wheels...and I'm not yet there again. So I'm fine with every bit of pain that comes my way. It announces to me that I'm alive, up on my feet, and living life LOUD!

One day I won't be walking. Okay, I've no problem with that. One day, everyone who is currently on this planet also won't be walking anymore. It's all relative. I'm good with it. But until that time, I'm going to be doing all I can to stay on my feet and as physically active as possible. I've learned some lessons throughout my life...and a lot of lessons while writing this book. I'm finally making the efforts to take better care of myself.

When I start harping on others about this or that, being somewhat of a stickler for commonsense things; I remember sitting in that wheelchair pleading, "Please, please let me have one more chance to walk again." Nothing else was on my mind at the time. Really.

Help neutralize pain by feeling it as part of the joy of living! -
Charmainism

All I could think about was just getting out of that wheelchair and having one last chance to walk again. Even though the pain was excruciating, there just had to be a way. I was consumed with finding a way. And I did. That was fifteen years ago and I'm still on my feet.

During dark periods in your life, you'll find that when your quality of life is <u>really</u> on the line, the petty stuff takes a distant backseat. There's no *time* to think about toothpaste being squeezed from the middle! Not even a thought!! No time to moan and groan about wiping up crumbs that made it look like Hansel and Gretel just walked through the house. No time to wonder how coffee grounds got all over the kitchen countertops. Nope. None of that stuff matters at all.

Which means none of that stuff ever really matters.

We have to remember to give people the benefit of the doubt, especially when whatever it is we're questioning doesn't matter in the slightest. We don't walk in the shoes of other people. We've no clue as to what mountains they climb on a daily basis. Just because someone looks refreshed and good doesn't mean that their day isn't an enormous struggle. We tend to think only of what we're going through...and that's very selfish. Doing so gives us lots of sustenance for feeling even more sorry for ourselves.

The thing to do is to let the things go that really don't matter. If we keep things in the right perspective, we'll learn this lesson very quickly:

LIFE IS **NOT JUST** ALL ABOUT US.

LIFE IS **NOT JUST** HAPPENING TO US.

LIFE **WILL JUST** GO ON WHETHER OR NOT WE GO ALONG.

I decided long ago to remind myself *often* about letting go of the petty stuff. When I realized that here I was thinking I'm cool because of accepting the person with their silly quirks, it became so clear to me that my aversion to what I considered being *the molestation of a tube of toothpaste* had to rank right up there with how I felt about them not really caring one way or the other about it. I had the nerve to be irritated by their inconsideration and lack of respect for a tube of toothpaste! Have mercy!

Lawd, I can hardly type that! Whew! Okay, but I got myself in check! Yes, it came down to me realizing we're *even* and I didn't even know it at the time, but now I do! LOL Our quirks cancelled each other out…petty silliness! Hahahaaaaaaaaaa

Those who have a positive disposition do <u>not</u> sweat the small stuff. REALLY. That means even the small stuff created within your own mind, the stuff that really has so much more to do with you and how you're dealing with your personal world of aches, pains, physical ailments, and general turmoil. Don't waste your life moaning and groaning, whether at yourself or anyone else.

One person's ache is another person's blessing: for she who once could not feel a thing, now can feel again! So is it pain or the pleasure of knowing we are still alive? Let your mind be positive and your life will flourish because we are the masters of our own happiness. – Charmainism

It doesn't matter whether or not you have a *right* to do so, or even if you have a valid *reason* to do so...it's that your life will be so much more wonderful when you let all of that go. The time spent burning up a steam engine of negative energy could be instead a time having a fabulously positive, and quality experience building solid relationships with those you care about and love. Or just a good time alone with yourself, loving life and letting your gratitude be the appreciative smile on your face. Look, it's your life...but doesn't it make sense to ENJOY it?! Not just when things are going great, but all the time. ENJOY it.

Life is short. There's no time for pettiness or picking on yourself or others. Give yourself and everyone else a break and enjoy life! It's so much easier when your mind is no longer egged on by a hair trigger just waiting to go off. Only you can change that.

One reason for that hair trigger is that we've too much time on our hands (or we're so overwhelmed with obligations that we're spending more time conjuring up any ridiculous stuff to either get mad and frustrated about, or we just are angry anyway!). Bottom line: Get busy doing something constructive. Get busy and spend that time working on you! You're not angry with anyone but yourself. Whether it's because of pain, or worry, or illness, or bitterness, resentment, or whatever...making a big deal about petty stuff won't make you feel better. I promise it won't. So don't. And it's so unfair to those we love when we make our family become the Ogre-who-lives-in-their-house's whipping posts. Few things are worse than seeing little kids cringing in fear of what not to do when an adult who hates their job comes home.

Even if you don't recognize it, *if* you hate your job...everyone in your household knows it. But look at the bright side -- you HAVE a job! Be thankful for that blessing and let gratitude carry you to higher ground. You can soar far above the grit of office politics if you just keep your head from dragging among the coffee grounds and work on your positive disposition. You *can* do this!

When you come home in a bad mood, especially after a hard day's work, it's not realistic to think that anyone else is in a mood to hear about all the very things that have put you in a foul mood. Think about it: what you know actually put <u>you</u> in a foul mood, so why would anyone else want to hear it and feel as you do? If you're looking for sympathy, you might get some lip service about it, but it's not real sympathy. And I'm sure the listener is very tired of hearing about it and so wants you to stop ruining the nice evening you all could be having.

If it's to explain just why you're in a bad mood, that's just inconsiderate thinking! Hey, I've been there and done that, and it's a very self-serving way of seeing things…but that still doesn't make it any better for the captive audience. Your family lives with you. You come home and there's at least a one-hour rant about your messed up day when you come through the door. Change it.

No one *needs* to understand how you feel. Because you don't really need to <u>know</u> that others understand how you feel – you just *think* you do. You think it will make you feel better if others understand how you feel. Wrong!

But that's okay. Just suck it up and forget about it when you come home. Your home is your escape. It makes no sense for office politics to drive you crazy at least forty hours a week, and then you carry that at least an hour more after the workday is over. And weekends? You guessed it: full of moaning and groaning about what's going on at the office. I've had people I just met start telling me about the things going on in their work environment. They're so disgusted, disgruntled, and overwhelmed with their anguish about it, that they even forgot to even introduce themselves!

Don't let this be you.

Positive energy is a wonderful thing. It's your energy <u>not</u> working against you. The choice is yours. – Charmainism

Don't sabotage relationships with your family. Make for good; quality family time no matter what else is going on in your life. This will become your down time when your positive energy can really soar. Being with those you love, when kept positive, will recharge your internal batteries and keep you grounded on what really matters in life. When we make the mistake of focusing on the negative things (the things we can't change and therefore garners intense frustration within us), well, that's when we're standing squarely in our own way.

We need only to change our way of thinking and instead, focus on maintaining our positive disposition. Realizing what's really going on in our thoughts and the futility of it, then changing gears to focus on that which is more constructive and more positive will do the trick every time. Then we can enjoy spending time doing things we actually love to do and enjoying all others during the process. Why? Because we're not bogged down with the heaviness of futility…those silly reminders about pending issues that have absolutely no relevance at the time.

How you feel at the time affects how you receive and react to communication from others. You have to put on your objective eyes and ears in order to be consistently fair. – Charmainism

Good communication is imperative. Others, no matter how close they are to you, aren't mind readers. Don't ever expect anyone to be the one who "should know" what you want or need. Life just doesn't work that way. Speak up on all fronts and keep it positive! Relationships will reward you as they continue to feed off of and reflect your positive disposition back to you. And yes, this technique is effective in the work environment too!

Optimism is the filter for reducing the stresses of life.
Use it or lose it! – Charmainism

One person's inflection doesn't necessarily equate to that of another. This is how people get their feelings hurt needlessly time and time again. And this is how people get angry over something that someone else didn't even know they said! Perhaps that's because they really didn't say it, but you *heard* it anyway.

"It was his *tone*." Uh huh.

Perhaps the intentions of the individual weren't as sinister as if you'd said the same words to them. We all have differing scales of showing hostility. What's perfectly normal and benign to someone else may be abnormal and malignant to you. We can't compare our feelings to the feelings of others. When unsure, ASK. Communication is everything in all relationships. If something is bothering you, talk about it with the person if you feel their friendship is important to you.

The more important a friendship, the more important it becomes to gain clarity when faced with unclear reactions to situations. However, if it really isn't that important, let it go as if it never happened. Tell yourself you're making something out of nothing and be done with it. No anger, no resentment, and no need for revenge: all those things are negatives that our bodies and minds can't consume. Rather, they consume us! We can't afford the cost of upkeep for harboring negative energy.

It's not just what you say but how you say it that makes the difference whether something conveyed is received in a negative or positive fashion, hateful or loving. Tone really tells the tale. Make it a point to have a kind tone to whatever you say. Sometimes receptors are in a weakened state and tend to pick up negative vibrations far too easily. Kindness of tone is the solution to bringing back peaceful and constructive communication. It's so worth it! – Charmainism

Allowing emotions to get the better of us is counterproductive to our inner peace. Sometimes it's simply best to walk away. It's in one's best interest to do so. What could be a better motivator than remembering that simple fact?

Yes! It's often in our best interest to diffuse such situations by embracing a positive disposition and walking away. We have to realize that others don't necessarily think the same as we do.

So we let it go, we do so because it's good for us to do so. That doesn't mean we let others walk all over us. However, even if that occurs, it's our choice to decide whether or not we wish to continue a relationship that isn't worthy of our time.

We are in full control of our emotions, as how we react to any action by another is our own doing. When we own up to that fact, we are seldom hurt because we do not perceive a weakness by someone else as a hurt upon us. – Charmainism

We select the choice that's the closest to our own inner peace and happiness. Well, a positive disposition would most certainly be a boon towards that end! Yes! It really is that simple. Ponder not about how to respond to someone else, think more of how to maintain your total peace of mind and then your response will always be perfect. Being optimistic and bringing forth a positive demeanor goes a long way to keeping the peace.

When we spend too much time wondering what was meant as if we've missed a dig or barb thrown our way, we often are the very cause of the friction that ensues. We've done it to ourselves. We get caught looking for it! We must remember that actions of another aren't necessarily intended as if we'd done the same action to them. Having a positive disposition will allow us to give others the benefit of the doubt.

Good communication is vital to healthy relationships. What we hear is not always what is being said. Give the benefit of the doubt when unsure -- and truly listen. Assume nothing. People will tell us what's on their minds if we listen more and talk less. – Charmainism

Things began to get cooler with Gerald, as after the slapping incident, my entire family was furious with him. They told him not to come to the house until things got better. They blamed him but I didn't blame him at all. I felt totally sorry for him. It was right after that when Gerry had a breakdown at school. The hallways were crowded and full of students scrambling to their lockers between classes. Quite suddenly, Gerry walked directly over to a teacher and punched him in the chest with his fist for seemingly no reason at all. Gerald was completely out of control. My cousin Enyo happened to be right nearby when this all happened. He immediately reacted by wrestling Gerald down to the floor. Enyo was a champion wrestler, though he was a very slight build, and a fraction of Gerald's 6'3" frame. Enyo stepped in and took care of it.

But Gerald was never to be quite the same ever again. He was about to be introduced to the Psych Ward.

This was not a good turn at all and the home stretch to this nightmare was getting more bizarre all the time. My parents were realizing that Gerald and I had really been in love. UGH!! I spent quite a bit of time visiting Gerry, even though others thought it was best for me not to do so. When it got to where I felt that I was doing more facilitating Gerry's pity parties rather than helping him make sense of things…well, I stopped going up to see him.

I'm sure my parents thought I was next in line to be up there. They were very, very scared. It wasn't a thought of mine at the time, because when it came to having confidence, I had enough for the world. That was not going to happen to me. But my heart did ache because Gerry was going through all this and it was getting uglier by the minute. I could hardly stand all the drama. Drama was not my thing.

Learning to control emotions by rationalization and perspective is imperative to attaining inner peace and happiness, especially when doing so becomes peacefully instinctual rather than confrontationally reactionary. We must constantly remind ourselves that just because someone has said or done an action, doesn't mean that the intent is the same as if we'd done that same action. We have to learn to <u>first give the benefit of the doubt</u> <u>and not let our fears raise our defenses</u>.

We have to let go of that inherent need to fear. We don't need it anymore! We've become civil and social human beings who have learned the proper graces of general civilization and how to become disciplined enough to manifest our own destinies. It's only when we decide we've been singled out for unbearable trials and tribulations that we begin to think with our defenses heightened for battle.

Where compassion wanes, hate waxes. Keep your heart filled with compassion by judging less, forgiving often, and loving more. Though we cannot nurture the entire world, we make a difference when master gardeners of our own crops. – Charmainism

When that happens, we think that life is unfair to us. Unfortunately, there's the tendency at the time to also think that life seems to be fair to everyone else but us! That's the time we have to put ourselves in check and realize that the problem is more likely that we don't own up to the responsibilities our self-respect demands. Most times, the problem is ours alone. The good thing is that we can make the necessary adjustments to solve our own issues.

Helping you to understand yourself and who you are deep down inside, is very important in my quest to get you motivated enough to be able to see your own positive light and reach for it! So, if you haven't felt the need to *physically* shake hands with yourself, then please do so now.

Shake hands with yourself. Extend that simple gesture to yourself. Make the "Heart of Hope" with your own two hands. You'll be glad you did! It's an awakening you'll never regret. If anything, you might regret having taken so long to do it! But we don't need regrets, do we? Just enjoy it. ENJOY THE NOW.

No matter the weather on any given day, when filled with positivity there is no dampening of the beautiful day within you. Make all your days gloriously joyous by letting your thankful heart be the master of your forecast. – Charmainism

Now that you've turned a figurative gesture into a physical one, how does it feel? Seeing the heart being made with your hands as they clasped each other should make you feel as if you're truly on a journey of real self-discovery. It should, because you are. You're beginning to believe more in yourself and that you've not only room for improvement, but that this philosophy of making much easier work of the petty things in life can also work for you! You've taken really great steps towards your goal of finding happiness and inner peace.

It's a good thing to get to know yourself better. We all can benefit from doing so. When we do, we find out that we're not alone in our dilemmas and issues. We are simply human beings trying to become the best we can be. It's comforting to know there are others like us who have the same thought processes and the same problems owning up to our shortcomings. And we also know now that others too are often their own worst enemies.

We are imperfect; yet we still often expect so much more from ourselves than what's realistic. When we realize that imperfection isn't a curse but something we learn from and use to better ourselves, then we can relax more and enjoy life. No need to flog ourselves whether mentally or physically; and no need to take out our frustrations on others who really have nothing to do with our internal battles. Together, we're beginning to "get it."

The more you learn about yourself, the more you'll enjoy being who you are. You'll come to care about yourself so much more on all levels; as you acknowledge there's only one you in the entire Universe. Think about that: ONLY ONE YOU. It's quite amazing, you know…the miracle that is each and every one of us.

The light of day is the trumpet
announcing another miracle. – Charmainism

Chapter Five: Happiness as a Purpose

When we understand who we are, we will understand what we want. When we understand what we want, we will have a goal. When we have a goal, we have the motivation to LIVE and DO what is necessary as we strive to get what it is we desire. – Charmainism

Many believe there's some higher power that put us here for a purpose. And, for most who believe that way, their search for that purpose continues. It's very difficult to feel happy and fulfilled when believing one's purpose hasn't been met. Worse, most have no idea what their purpose *is*. But one can be happy regardless. That begins by understanding the meaning of a most wondrous seven-letter word: JOURNEY.

While looking for fulfilling one's sense of purpose, the journey of life itself is truly everything.

Whether or not we, as human beings on this earth, have a true and divine purpose will be debated until the end of time. For me, it's more reasonable to imagine that who we are, as individuals, and how we see ourselves is what drives our respective desires to excel at something. In other words, our ability to motivate ourselves can come from many sources. Wanting and fulfilling one's desire for PURPOSE is one of those sources.

Some may think that a life without leaving some mark behind to serve as a reminder to others that "We were here," is a life unfulfilled. Others think that their children are their legacy and they're quite content with that. As the decades go by, the addition of grandchildren and great-grandchildren solidify that notion for many.

However, there are others who are still not totally content with the choices they have made in their lives. As they get older, they question what they've done, if anything, to make the world a better place. Or they wonder whether or not they've done enough to please the Higher Power they worship.

This is when "purpose" comes to light again. It's something that everyone thinks about at certain junctures during their lifetime. I'm not sure how it became so natural to do so, but it's definitely happened to most.

Could be that it's because purpose is natural to our self-preservation. When making the transition from late teens to adulthood, having gone from the nest, there are choices to be made about which paths to follow. Some have solid ideals as to what they want to do with their lives, and others have no clue. So some wing it, as they "have time," to get it right eventually; while others go and chase after fulfilling their more guided "purpose" in life. And many do so in record time. It's as if they had a map directing them to right where they wanted to be at whatever exact time...and they do it!

Perhaps they've wanted to become a doctor ever since being a very young child; or knew they always wanted to follow the career path of a parent or other mentor. Whichever it may be how they knew what their choice would be, there was a dream that fulfilled their purpose and they were intent on making that dream a reality.

But for others, it's not that simple at all. So they wander around aimlessly wondering when the light bulb will go off...the one that tells them exactly what their purpose is.

Until that happens, if it does, they feel substandard and unworthy. They feel as if they haven't accomplished a thing and are no closer to doing so today than they were yesterday.

Let's face it. In the big picture, most don't get to do what they love to do and make a decent living at it. But there's no doubt in my mind that there are millions of people who have succeeded in finding a niche and settling into it. Could have been that luck had something to do with it (as in being at the right place at the right time); but most times, luck has very little to do with it, if at all. It's less luck than you think…because first, in order for something like this to happen to you, you must be in a receptive frame of mind in order to recognize the opportunity when it comes your way!

And to be receptive, you have to be flexible enough to know an opportunity when it arises! It may not be what you'd in mind…but will it do for now? And is it possibly something that might work out long-term? Could be!

If you're always ready…I promise you…
you will get lucky! – Charmainism

You see, if you're where you need to be at the right time, and the right person comes along to help you in your quest, then all that remains is that you're ready to snatch that chance before it continues down the street and out of your life. If you're indeed ready, then that's not totally luck, is it? No. That, my friend, is the benefit of being prepared! Such is the difference between luck and being up to the challenge to seize an opportunity when it presents itself. Even the luckiest person ever has to at least get up out of bed and be outside in order to make it possible for something to drop down from the sky and land in his lap!

Opportunities present themselves all the time, but if you're not in the right frame of mind, you won't even recognize it appeared! People who are up and ready, eager to seize the day and find their way to greatness, are the ones who usually need only one chance at an opportunity. It's immediately recognized and acted upon by them. They don't blink to think. Nor should any of us when a great opportunity comes along!

When Mom was in her fifties, she became the oldest person to ever qualify for a nursing school scholarship in our area. She earned her nursing degree and had a rewarding career in nursing. She even began driving! We never knew our Mom could drive! Her children finally got to meet the strong, intelligent and independent woman who was the same young girl that was Valedictorian of her high school class. We even learned she was on the basketball team...and played! She also ran track and played baseball! Wow! Who knew? Mom actually had a life! She was a real live person before she was our mom!

I was always very proud of my mother. She retired about fifteen years later. Some years after that, she began to develop signs of early Alzheimer's disease. It runs in her family, all her sisters succumbed to it as well. There's some humor, though, even in such a horrible illness. Yes. The beauty in this is that Mother completely forgot she despised my father! In her middle stages of the disease, Daddy became her Hero and she was very much in love with him again. I found that poetic, and still do...as just thinking of it now brings tears of joy to my eyes. It pleased my father. He finally got to feel like a King again, he got to feel like "The Kid," as was Mother's nickname for him when they first met when he was in the Navy, stationed at Newport News. Her love and affection was so very important to him.

I remember Daddy calling me on the phone and telling me that Mom was driving him crazy, that she was so full of energy he couldn't keep up with her. He then asked me how he could go about getting some Valium.

"Oh no Dad! You can't sedate Mom! You need to talk to her doctor because that might interfere with her Alzheimer's medications."

"I don't want to *sedate* her; I want to keep up with her!" he contested.

Long pause on my part.

"Uh…Dad?"

"Yes, darling."

"Dad?"

"Yes, Mainie, my love. What?"

"You don't mean Valium… Uh, you mean, maybe…Viagra?"

"Yes. Viagra. That's what I said. Wait. What *did* I say it was?"

Cute pause. I smiled, "You said Valium, Daddy."

"No, honey. No. No. I *meant* Viagra."

Lawd!! Did that make my head spin. Hahahaaaaaaaaaa!! Holy guacamole! I mean they *are* my parents! LOL I got the biggest chuckle out of that one, but I also loved it that Daddy felt he could come to me about it. We were like that. We talked about everything together. Most young girls would go to their mothers to find out the things they needed to know. Not me. I went to my Dad.

I always loved knowing that no matter how much my mother sobbed and cried her eyes out day in and day out throughout all of my childhood, deep down I knew she loved my father and my father loved her.

Knowing that my mother found her calling as a nurse, a most natural fit for her, was an incredible undertaking by my mother at such an age when many women are thinking about retiring and she decides to embark on a full-fledged career. I still display the photo I took while attending the ceremony for Mom to be awarded her nurse's cap.

If ever anything was earned, that was surely it. Mom worked hard and she and Dad fared much better financially as her yearly income was more than four times that of what father had ever made.

Daddy was proud of her too. *Really* proud.

We have to stay positive and ready to make a move when the opportunity presents itself. And if the opportunity isn't quite sitting on a platter waiting for our fork of approval, we have to take it to the next level on our own. For most people, one has to be "up" in spirit in order to even think in a motivationally positive fashion…and that's where we all can work on how we *think*. Even when a person is feeling down and low, with their energy as in the negative as the air around them, they've sucked all the positive karma out of the air for a long, long, way. But it doesn't have to remain that way. We can tell ourselves to knock it off and get with it! We don't have to chastise ourselves beyond that…just from that moment forward, decide enough is enough and become instantly positive!

Roll with the punches and want a positive disposition so much that you make it happen! No one is going to hand it to you. During the rough times, ROLL. Roll with those punches so that you hardly feel them and the blips disappear as quickly as they surfaced. Now you can get on with living life LOUD. Loud in the sense that you can feel your mind and body telling you, "Yeah Baby, I have arrived!"

And then get on your dancing shoes!

The wind feels wonderful, the sun is amazing, the sky is brilliant with the blue of life and you're so grateful and thankful to be alive that everything else is FINE. Not *wondering* time and again about *what your purpose is*; but knowing that IF there's such a purpose, you'll recognize yours when it's within striking distance. You <u>will</u> be ready, and you know it!

Happiness is infectious.
It's long overdue to go viral. – Charmainism

Now is the time to stop saying over and over again that you're 'trying' to be more positive and just simply do it. It's truly in your best interest to do so. Your present and future will become bright with the force of positive energy as you embrace it and get to know how it feels to be truly positive and optimistic. It's yours for the taking.

If you aren't happy with yourself, nothing else will ever make it happen for you. It's not something you can buy in the grocery store. It's not dependent on anyone else being in your life to give it to you. It is, however, yours for the taking once the concept of attaining it is completely understood.

Many people, once they have satisfied their physical "purpose" in life (i.e., materialistic successes), still feel as if they've not fulfilled their want for living up to their true purpose in life. For most, with all things said and done, it just comes down to being happy in its truest sense. Happiness isn't an accumulation of wealth or knowledge...happiness is a state of mind embraced by a person who understands its priceless value as the key to all splendor of life.

It's interesting when asked, "What do you want out of life?" how many people will respond with, "Just to be happy." It's a goal that most want to attain. Yet for most, all they really need to understand is that <u>to want it is to own it</u>. You can <u>own</u> being happy. It just takes knowing that happiness is a choice, an option just as anything else. But happiness is the ultimate option for a wonderful life. Because when you're happy, you are ready to tackle the day-to-day problems that come with life itself as something that's kept in perspective...so instead of "tackling" them as if drudgery, you readily accept the challenge! It's easy to choose something and embrace it once you genuinely understand that it's the answer to all your problems. Your choices can solve everything.

This is why choosing to be happy no matter what, is the key to attaining inner peace.

Whatever it is you think you're yearning for...look into a mirror and yearn no more. Don't wait for loss to help you appreciate all the gains you take for granted. Relish the now and enjoy every moment. Remember, everything done to this point has shaped who you are -- so no regrets, just more egrets. – Charmainism

What are you yearning for? What is it that you think will be the miracle that makes everything in your life suddenly perfect? There's no such miracle. Nothing is ever really perfect. With the right perspective, though, your life can be as near "perfect" as possible. Serious business! It's up to you to choose to see the lighter side of life as you continue to strive for being the best you can. You must have a genuine zest for life and unbridled love for all those in it with you. It really isn't difficult, that's the simple beauty of it all...we, as imperfect human beings, just have an incredibly destructive habit of over-thinking just about everything. We therefore have a tendency to make even the simplest of things extremely complex. We complicate tying our shoes sometimes and decide we have to switch to using Velcro. LOL

Recognizing our weaknesses and working hard on them by embracing the soul of a peacemaker, will turn your life around. If we truly want inner peace, all we have to do is *relax* to get it! It's already there within each and every one of us...we merely have to get out of our own way to let the peacemaker within come to the surface and take charge. And the first assignment is deciding to be happy each and every day. Happy. Yes.

And could it be, possibly, that since we humans tend to make everything so incredibly complicated that we've also done so with that elusive purpose we still search for? Perhaps the answer to the age-old question as to what our true purpose is as we rotate on this planet, is that we've been challenged with the task of learning <u>how to be content</u> <u>and happy!</u> Wouldn't it be something that if we can handle that task, all things are granted to us?!! All locked doors open up and the world is our playground!

But then again, the worrywart in you is wondering just how can anyone possibly be happy in a world that's full of mostly discontented, hateful, and unhappy people?

Here's my take on it.

Most of our evolution from whence we came to today's hyper-technological age has come with a price. Things are done in a simpler manner and on an enormous scale. We don't have to farm in order to have corn and beef on our dinner tables. We go to the market and buy it. It's all wrapped up and ready for us to choose and put into our carts. Multiply that ease of putting food on the table by all the other conveniences living in this modern age has to offer, and this, in turn, allows us more free time.

It's what we decide to do with that free time that has a lot of us spending more time wringing our hands in frustration rather than enjoying the free time afforded to us. And, heaven forbid, if while everything isn't perfect in our lives, we actually begin to enjoy having FUN! That's when the guilt trip meter sounds its alarm and puts a damper on the little enjoyment that could've done you so much good!

What's done with free time and how we feel about it after we've done it, is highly subjective. It totally depends on the person. We can use the time to sit around and complain about how things were so simple yesterday and now so complicated today, or we can decide that we're just another generation who's lost touch with the scope of progress and spends far too much time pining for the past.

You can thrive while relishing in the thought of another day, another night, and another chance to see this wonderful world and embrace all that it encompasses. Such are the choices. It's not about what has happened in the past. It is more about the choices we make when we are grateful for the opportunity to indeed have a choice! – Charmainism

Our culture has transitioned from a life that was very physical to one that's sedate in comparison. In today's norm, most people sit at a desk rather than engage in manual labor whether it used to be working one's own farm or someone else's. It's no wonder that so many of those who are in the routine of sitting at a desk forty hours a week, might find their minds wandering off as they dream of one day sailing off into the sunset on their way to big adventures by landing on one paradisiacal island after another. But will fulfilling that dream equate to a guarantee of attaining happiness and inner peace? Hmm.

Paradise is relative. The islanders want to get to the city, the city people want to get to the suburbs, the suburbanites want to move to the country, and the country folks are just wishing things would stay the same. The bottom line is paradise is within you, no matter where you may be. – Charmainism

In today's culture, we know just enough to drive ourselves mad with the vicious cycle of feeling as if we haven't measured up to being that which we thought we could be. Yet sitting around dwelling on it is the very thing that keeps us from any progress towards our goals. It's so much easier to *talk* about goals rather than to get up and do anything productive about attaining them.

And then there are those who seemingly have attained everything and *still* aren't happy. That's one thing that those who haven't reached their goals need to realize is a genuine fact. Human beings are very hard to satisfy. Every satisfaction seems temporary. Every satisfaction has an expiration date! The very thing that was once so highly desired, then obtained, is replaced by another want of something else. One quickly concludes that no matter on which end you sit – it mostly comes down to your perception of where you are in life. Your happiness is more dependent on whether or not you've reached realistic "goals" of personal growth, rather than the short-lived satisfactions brought on by "things" acquired. No tangible item or material gain will ever make a solid difference in your life unless you've worked hard to first earn self-respect. But with gratitude, everything becomes easier.

If we're not careful, we set ourselves up for failure. A genuinely happy person doesn't get up chanting, "I'm going to be happy all day no matter what." They just <u>do</u> it. There's no announcement, there's no pledge…it's just done! Their motivation to do so is the fact that it brings them great satisfaction to be happy and they've decided to attain it. Not for anyone else but for themselves. Besides, their gratitude for seeing the light of another day is quite enough for them to be wholly satisfied in all that transpires that given day. Nothing in this life is truly promised because we may not live to see it through. Such is life. No, such is the *gift* of life! Cherish it. Cherish every single moment.

The more we keep our promises close to our chests, the less we have to worry about backlash of failure from those to whom we've told our plans. It's not that sharing such things will sabotage our efforts; it's more that keeping things under wraps until all our ducks are in a row will free us from self-imposed pressures. We often use our friends and family in that capacity unknowingly. Don't put undue pressure on yourself or others. This is where silence can truly be golden – an adage, that when adhered to, speaks volumes in our lives by not uttering one word.

It's not up to anyone else but us to decide to embrace a philosophy and methodology that works for us as we strive to attain and maintain a level of contentment that works for us. We put it into practice without fanfare or celebration. We simply do it. There's nothing to fear when we embrace this concept. It's easy to do when filled with gratitude!

We all need this reminder, especially in times of uncertainty and heartache, the blessing of another day on this planet is always a LOVELY DAY. No matter what life throws into the mix, or what you're going through, you're never alone. Sometimes we have to make the extra effort to recognize that for which we should be grateful. – Charmainism

The Search for Happiness

Does there actually need to be a reason for us to be here on this earth? No. But somewhere along the way we've bought into that concept and put our own destruction up for grabs by fighting over who's right and who's wrong when it comes to telling the 'true' story of the origin of mankind. All the while, splitting hairs on the tiniest of details. It certainly makes sense to me that with an abundance of languages and cultures, there will always be differing versions of what equates to essentially the retelling of the same story. It's not a life or death issue as to whether any of us have it right or wrong. We all know that one thing remains the same, there's a common bond with all doctrine and spiritual belief: there's an ark somewhere in the picture! Noah, by any other name, would still be Noah if he indeed had an ark and an abundance of animals. LOL

I see it this way: whatever higher power there is, that power can no doubt understand each and every one of us for who we are. In our limited mental capacities, we'll never be able to understand all the ins and outs of our existence. It's not necessary for us to do so. There's nothing to be gained by that knowledge.

When you get exasperated and wonder from whence you came...look to where you're going: the hills and valleys of life. They're there for us all. We can either hold our breath as we rise and fall, or we can become determined to enjoy every moment of the ride...and wonder never again!

Loving life with all its hills and valleys. Riding and paying attention to the views all along the way...up and down, up and down...but still embracing the ride. – Charmainism

Which means that simple gratitude can take us through all of life's ups and downs and we can be satisfied with the acknowledgement of the blessing that it is to just have the hills and valleys to enjoy! We then give thanks and enjoy our lives to the fullest. We live with kindness and compassion in our hearts and allow life to fill all our wants and desires. Between birth and death, we enjoy all moments to the utmost capacity. Our cup runneth over. What happens after this earthly life should be of no concern or worry. Whatever it is, we'll know all too soon enough.

Life is what it is. Nothing is promised. We may not see the next minute. When you think of it that way, one minute of worry could be your last minute of hope! – Charmainism

Without a higher power to blame for whatever in life goes awry, we can happily be more proactive in making the changes necessary to have better lives. God is not sitting above on a throne in front of a chessboard just waiting to make your next move. The move is yours! You have the grace of the miracle of being born; it's all you get. The rest is up to you and on you. The Devil didn't make you do a thing and God isn't telling you what you need to do. One can't go through life thinking everything is scripted. For when it comes about that you do everything right and still bad things happen, there's nothing left on which to fall back for comfort. That's when one loses faith in record time. Setting ourselves up for such is just not necessary. Don't blame God, the Universe, or even Mother Nature for what *you* choose to do or not do with your miracles.

Perhaps the root of those who worry comes about more with the "unknown" part of that ultimate destination plan rather than anything else. It's not so much that one day we'll die, it's that what will happen between today and that time when we take our last gasp of air? Will we be okay with it at the time? Or worse, there are those that worry themselves sick over whether or not they'll go to Heaven or to Hell when they leave this earth. I still shake my head on that one. It's like; when that happens you won't be the same earthly human being that had this problem of over-thinking! Why not choose to find comfort in that and let it be?!

Really. We've no control whatsoever over many things in this life and learning that fact is one of the best lessons of all. If we weren't alive, we wouldn't have to deal with any of it. So why not "deal" with it in a positive manner so as not to suffocate any possibility of having a mind and body that's beautifully saturated with inner peace? It's your choice.

Every little thing happening in your life is yet another piece towards completing the puzzle of you. Handling life's roller coaster of peaks and valleys makes us who we are: an ounce of adversity can be met with a pound of strength! Embrace every moment whether cheer or challenge; as life is truly wonderful! – Charmainism

We can't worry about what will happen when we die because we haven't died yet. We're alive right here and now, yet wasting precious moments thinking about something that hasn't yet happened. Look at it this way -- whenever it does happen, you'll be a different person and not the person you are now. Therefore, you can't think today as if you are the person you'll be tomorrow. So let it go and enjoy the *now*!

This frees us to stop looking up to the heavens for every little thing and start looking within. God has made sure you have everything you need to be happy. It's simply up to you to get it. Happiness isn't a tangible like clothes, food, shelter, or any other thing that we can hold to make us more comfortable or to sustain life. Happiness is much, much more than any of those things. All those things needed for survival become easier to attain if we're happy while in the quest to acquire them. Once we have those things acquired, we can think about doing other things with our lives. This is essentially what life is. So why not be happy when doing it all?! Be happy with life itself!

Having received the greatest gift known to mankind should give you a feeling of immense gratitude. What we do with that gift is up to us. If you don't recognize yourself in this paragraph then you just might want to start back at the beginning of this book. You need to let it all soak in my friend. Now, if you totally get it to the nth degree and are eager to continue on in order to make the changes necessary to attain happiness and inner peace, then…well, *that's* what I'm talking about!! So please, my dear peacemaker-in-the-making, read on.

Freedom is the wind filling my sails to reach destinations beyond. What we do when the wind stops is what makes the difference in our lives. I've learned when there is no wind there still remains the planning and anticipation of my next adventure. Until the wind returns, sailing with the mind is satisfyingly fine. – Charmainism

Happiness Found In The Peacemaker!

To find peace, you must personify it. – Charmainism

The desire for inner peace is quenched when one decides to personify peace. Becoming a peaceful person in every way is what will bring harmony to your life. The frictions and frustrations lose their strength when up against a peaceful soul. This means that all offspring of friction and frustration are also gone: fear, impatience, anger, intolerance, and hate.

As you well know by now, this isn't about changing everyone else in your life or deleting a myriad of friends on social media. Rather, this is about you and your desire to become peaceful no matter what else happens among your family, friends, co-workers, etc. Because when you're at peace with yourself, your entire personal world follows in that peaceful path.

The more time spent appreciating individualities when interacting with co-workers, friends, and family, the less time spent dealing with frustration. It is our differences that make us unique. When that is understood first; our patience lengthens, our reasoning is more rational, and communication remains open to broaden. – Charmainism

We all need to find the right motivation to be eager to rise each day and do something productive with our lives. Productivity can be in the form of just knowing we are or were of help to someone who needed us. It doesn't have to be a plowed field or a sparkling clean house! Those are examples of the satisfaction one receives after working hard and seeing the end of a job well done. There are many ways to replicate that satisfaction: make it part of your purpose to find different ways of doing just that!

Since we are creatures of habit, sometimes getting out and finding new ways of doing things can be difficult – for some, almost stressful! We have to stop fearing change and get hold of that silliness right away! Such ridiculous fear of change reminds me of Nurse Ratched (the main antagonist of author Ken Kesey's novel, <u>One Flew Over the Cuckoo's Nest</u> (1962), played so incredibly well by Louise Fletcher in the 1975 movie that even to this day she can't watch her Academy Award winning performance!).

She was a cruel one! Nurse Mildred Ratched would spoil any chance at a patient's efforts to vary, in even the slightest way, any part of the daily routine of the group. She would defend her stickler stance by stating that any change could disrupt the fragile psyche of the inmates of the asylum. It soon became apparent to inmate "Mac" McMurphy (played by Jack Nicholson), that it wasn't *change* bothering the patients at all; rather, it was Nurse Ratched's being on a Power Trip and detesting any questioning of her laid out regime and authority! They were like oil and water, to say the least.

We all have a bit of Nurse Ratched in us, even if we don't realize it. And we also have a bit of McMurphy too. We *can* make different choices and we *can* enjoy the deviation from the norm! No guilt required! It certainly doesn't equate to being totally undisciplined. The McMurphy in us wants us to give ourselves a break from time to time. But the Nurse Ratched in us thinks that once McMurphy is unleashed, we may not be able to rein ourselves back in! That's the fear factor once again rearing its ugly head.

We aren't the new kids. There's no probie, no "*May*-o-nnaise," here who needs an iron hand of a Master Sergeant to get the job accomplished. We don't have to beat ourselves up in order to get in shape and do better. We can simply go about the business of doing it. One step at a time and one step in front of the other as we continue to climb to higher ground. So hush with the barking orders! (Can you hear Lou Gossett Jr.? I can!) Nothing is *that* big of a deal that we have to turn into drill sergeants and badger our family to get it done! LOL

Being temporarily overwhelmed is nothing when you realize permanently six feet under will be too late to know it. Enjoy each day, my darlings. Don't sweat the small stuff -- keep it in perspective. Every tear, whether brought on by joy or sorrow, begins a fresh shower of life's emotions: LIVE to the fullest. – Charmainism

Come on, enjoy a little variety and have fun with it! As long as you're happy and know you're doing a good thing, then don't flog yourself about what else you probably should be doing. There will be time for that later, and if not...then so be it. It's not life or death we're talking about here, it's just life. Because when the death part comes, it's over. Done. No more having to worry about choices or anything else when that finality comes your way. So why worry about any of it now? Make peace with being less rigid and let flexibility become a welcomed part of your new mantra. YES, you *can*! Just by exercising control over that which you can control...you become the positive, driving force at the helm of that ship of yours called life!

Having a sunny day is more dependent on the 'whether' than the 'weather'! Whether you will is entirely up to you. – Charmainism

Very early in life it was quite clear to me that being narrow-minded was not an option. It made no sense. The world was far too big for that! My mother felt that only *her* religion was the right religion and that all others were wasting their time and would not be saved come the doom of Armageddon. I couldn't help feeling that God couldn't possibly think that way. That's the way man thinks -- petty and narrow-minded. Dividing people into categories of the good ones, the super good ones, the good ones that were just goody good, and then pitting them all up against the not-so good, sometimes really bad, and the evil rotten evildoers!! If that doesn't sound more like a cartoon strip I don't know what does. It's like Rocky and Bullwinkle vs. Boris and Natasha on steroids.

What difference could it possibly make to God how a person chooses to worship Him and do right by Him? Using religions to divide brothers, sisters, and countries on this planet was something that mankind would do...but certainly not God. By the time I was ten years old, I felt strongly that we'd no right to dictate to others what was right or wrong when it came to their own *personal* choices that harmed no one else. And, if it were really about God and the Bible, as my Mother felt was the case, then it should be that much easier to "Let go and let God" [handle it]! I therefore learned many valuable lessons by being exposed to both positive and negative perspectives. If "Little Miss Sunshine," or so I was often called, could choose sunshine and blue skies rather than gloom and doom...well, that's a no-brainer for sure!

But my mother had other plans for the way I'd think. She pressured me a lot to stay on the straight and narrow with bible studies and work hard to succeed in the ministry. I'll never fault her for doing so, as those were her genuine beliefs and she wanted her family to be safe and in the good graces of God Almighty. And for a time, I embraced the ministry wholeheartedly.

Even so, I remained cognizant that it seemed the majority of so many problems people have is because they're too rigid in their ways and not flexible enough to see how compromise can expedite understanding. They would talk of being like Jesus Christ, but when it came to giving their fellowman an nth of the benefit of the doubt, they weren't Christ-like at all. It was their way or the highway, and that just doesn't work with most people. My approach to the ministry would go back and forth in a battle of minds, with my mother on one hand reminding me that the doctrine and organizational dogma was laid out long before I came along and it was therefore not my place to tweak it.

And I'd answer with something like, "Mom, being a weaker vessel doesn't mean weak minded. We can still think for ourselves."

My arguments with Mother often ended up with me just giving up as thinking of the condition of a weakened mind would more often than not, take my thoughts to Gerry up there on the Psych Ward. In and out, getting nowhere, really, but barely surviving sometimes. He had a terrible time taking care of himself and taking the medications needed to keep him balanced. He resented having to take medications at all.

I certainly understood that, but the alternative was not a good option either.

I'd try to help and tell him that he had to fight harder. He had to understand his condition and learn how to live with it. Others do and he could too. This was difficult for me because even though I could help everyone else with their internal battles, I couldn't help him. Gerry wouldn't hear me when I spoke. He just couldn't. I think it was far too painful for him to listen to me trying to be objective *and* his sister at the same time. It was a double blow of the black comedy of it all...smack dab in the middle of a life teetering off the scales of reality. He couldn't handle it. It was, truly, extremely hard for even me to handle it; and I was very skilled at neutralizing situations and making peace with things!

My family was afraid for me. They continued to hold their breath each time the phone rang, as any call could be the one that tells them *I've* had a nervous breakdown at school. When I think back on it, my family had every right to feel I'd soon be next in line, standing at a window of a Psych Floor pill dispensary, probably located in the same hospital where I was born fifteen years before that. Their impossible had happened too, when their skeletons were dug up and exposed for all to see, so why not expect more bad news?

Instead, a wonderful thing happened.

You'll get no argument from me that we can't change the entire world and correct all of its problems. However, what I know is that we can most certainly change our own personal world and effectively turn all our experiences and relationships into positive ones. It's all about changing our perspective when dealing with things and people so that instead of allowing any of those interactions to culminate into frustration and negative energy, we manage them in a manner that keeps us calm and peaceful.

Learning to view people and situations in a more positive light is highly ideal to achieving and maintaining inner peace, even when in the company of wolves in sheep's clothing. We can handle anything when we've the positive mindset to see us through it. When you keep putting forward the techniques of a peacemaker into practice, you'll continue to find them easier to employ each time -- until they become second nature to you. One person at a time is all it takes to make a difference in this world. Let it begin with you!

Happy are the Peacemakers, for they first shake their own hands! – Charmainism

Peacemakers are Affable

As we discussed at the beginning of this chapter, we have to be ready for when an opportunity arises. We have to be ready to seize it and run with it! That's just one reason why we have to be affable. Approachable.

The person who sits with their arms crossed, lips pursed, and totally unaware of others meandering by, will miss out on a plethora of opportunities that life has to offer. Few people will approach someone who seemingly wants to be closed off from others. Of course, the last person to realize they're perceived as unapproachable is you. Yet you sit there and ponder over why people aren't smiling like you remember. Why aren't they happier? Well, were *you* smiling as they walked along your way?

There's a growing trend to wear one's troubles on the sleeves. It's a trend that can't go out of fashion soon enough for me. Everyone has woes. It is what life includes along with the good times. How one handles the tough days is what gives strength, or a lack of, during the super rough times. When heat from the blazing sun of adversity hits, all that time wilting (in what later will be recognized as shade) will not help. It's all relative. What is seen as an immense challenge today, in comparison to far worse situations of tomorrow or yesterday, is really just a blip on the emotional radar. Stay positive by keeping things in perspective! Know you can handle anything because the sheer joy of living gives you the power to do so. It's the WEAK end! – Charmainism

We receive what we give. When we put out positive feelings and smiles, we get them back in return. When our outward disposition appears to be dour and sour…well, why should anyone let you put a damper on their day?! But a smile goes a long way. It's a wonderful thing!

Affable people are easily approached. A genuine smile is infectious and puts others at ease. When you're at peace with yourself you get there by letting go of all resentment, anger, bitterness, jealousy, envy, and all the other negative emotions that dehydrate your body of the quenching fluidity gained by the calm waters fostered by being positive and peaceful.

Become peaceful and you'll become a magnet for all others who are peaceful. – Charmainism

Instead of appearing unapproachable to others, you become just the opposite: you become a magnet for others who are also positive and peaceful—or those who want to be so! Those people are out there…you simply aren't currently in the frame of mind to notice. You must learn to become a peacemaker at heart and your heart will open the door to other peacemakers – and to those who have the affinity to become peacemakers.

A peacemaker has a knack for having just the right words at the appropriate time in order to neutralize situations that could've otherwise culminated in uncontrolled emotional outbursts by those overcome with frustration. Peacemakers see it long before it ever arrives. We pay attention to the weaknesses of others because it's in our best interest to do so. We're quite familiar with such weaknesses because we too are on constant guard against the same ever getting the better of us again.

A deep breath of thought before response is often all that is needed to cool hot air. Peace begins within each and every one of us. We can make it so! – Charmainism

Another knack of a peacemaker is the ability to put others at ease and allow them to communicate without feeling they're being judged. Sometimes it's very wise to comment with a question that provokes thought and downplays confrontation. Let them think it out on their own and soon they'll come to the optimal conclusion all on their own.

This doesn't mean that happy people are those who are totally carefree and just "consider the lilies of the field, how they grow" each day. No. They know they're not here on earth strictly for the amusement of a higher power. They may say 're, but deep down, I believe they know better. Some things are said due to habit rather than genuine rationale. Happy people have responsibilities just as anyone else; they just don't let those responsibilities become an all-consuming burden that destroys their sense of well-being and inner peace. They know it's up to them to make the best of any given situation. Instead of begrudging the thought, they embrace even the hint of a challenge!

Let's face it: no matter *what* happens, <u>it will happen whether you're happy or unhappy at the time</u>. You can only do the best you can with your choices. Most people make their best choices when they're not backed against a wall with no time left to breathe or think rationally. Everything doesn't have to be a life or death type decision. And in between those times of great struggle when decisions *have* to be made, you're happy!

You remain happy because during the in-between-struggles times, you aren't worrying about what else is *going* to happen. There's no need to keep pulling back the curtain on the window of the future to see what's coming down the road to blow you off your game. <u>Just play the game</u>. Enjoy the fact that you can still play. Don't worry about the what-iffers and if they're coming your way. Doing so will ruin any chance of learning to enjoy the *now*. So don't blame anyone or anything for your worries -- just stop worrying about what *could* or *might* happen.

Many people striving to become more positive unknowingly neutralize all their positive vibes when they dig into the negative rut of blaming others for their unhappiness. Happiness and a positive spirit are within your own hands. So shake hands with yourself to seal the deal of kicking resentment and blame to the curb! – Charmainism

For those who take the low road of placing blame on parental shortcomings; we need to learn very early in life that there comes a time when we have to make our own decisions; and until that time, we have to be thankful for the gift of life we've been given. It's too bad that many an adult has still not learned that valuable lesson. You see, we can blame our parents...but that doesn't make it the true place for accountability – not forever!

One must soon see that if they're old enough to place blame on the perceived failures of their parents, they're old enough to make some changes of their own. The first change is to take responsibility for making sure your life turns out as you see it should be. By seeing the negative forces that are out there, we can neutralize them by desiring and initiating positive change for ourselves.

And with that responsibility comes the wisdom to forgive ourselves for not measuring up to that which we felt we were capable of achieving long ago. Keep your head held high on this fantastic journey known as life. The same goes for thinking back to your roots. Perhaps your parents weren't the brightest intellectually, and perhaps you come from the Humble Road side of the tracks...but why should you be ashamed of gaining life and choice?! No one chooses who their parents will be.

No one. So be proud of your roots. You are who you are because of all you've experienced throughout your life to this point. There's no time for regret or shame. You must change your perspective and be grateful for all the nurturers who made sure you grew up to the age you are now. There's no time for any other way to think about it. If we don't, then we end up on the whiner's treadmill of life.

When we lose our sense of humor, our negative senses plant deeper roots. – Charmainism

People often find themselves at that juncture of holding endless pity parties. Sometimes the shame of doing so is the trigger that brings on another one. That's a cycle that has to be stopped in its tracks and fast! Otherwise it becomes a lifelong spiral to an existence that's truly wasted.

The sooner we learn the extraordinary benefits of shaking hands with ourselves and going about the task of finessing our lives into ones that can be positively magnificent; our personal worlds will be the better for it.

Stop fighting yourself. You have two hands. Use one hand to make amends with the other hand. Only you can do it: Shake hands with yourself! – Charmainism

I was fifteen years old with enormous eyes and, as my father would say, so thin I "could stand under a clothesline in the pouring rain and not get wet." Though I certainly wasn't aware of it at the time, I was turning many a young man's head and heart. When I saw myself dolled up for a school play, the sexy knockout standing in front of me was a bit surprising!

I'd just finished a talk at the Kingdom Hall and Mother had played the part of my householder. This was during one of the bible study nights where we honed our skills for talking to people when going door-to-door spreading the ministry. The talk went very well.

After the evening of services, my mother and I were preparing to leave as this man approached us.

"Hello, there sisters. I'd like to introduce myself. I'm Bill Ladd and new to the congregation. I've been studying with Art and Nancy."

Art and Nancy were two of my favorite people in the congregation. They were "with it" and smart enough to not waste time with others who weren't really serious about the ministry.

The guy with the cute smile before me was very nice and cute in a puppy dog sort of way. He was such a beanpole! Tall, and with lankiness about him that seemed to defy his age. He appeared to be about twenty-five or so (and, at the time, to me, that was getting up there! LOL). I probably thought he looked much older partly because of the mature suit he had on. It was a pretty green. Lighter than forest, but much darker than kelly; not flashy at all and very soothing, with light gold threads making patterns (though not a pinstriped suit). Very different, I thought, and it made his lovely blue eyes dance with just a tiny hint of a green tint. It was actually a very nice suit and a very nice selection for the man's physical characteristics.

His tie matched beautifully, and altogether, the whole ensemble played off the blondish highlights of his hair. He looked ready for anything. He was very professional looking. And his hands were clasped together in front of him. He looked very "together" to me. He continued by saying, "I wanted you to know how much I enjoyed your talk."

I thanked him and looked over at mother. Mom was not amused. Normally, my mother is quite charming, but this time…well, she just continued intently gathering up her things so we could leave and go home. In hindsight, I'm sure Mother knew full well that the man that stood before us was not too interested in speaking with *her*. Me? Well, I really was somewhat oblivious to that sort of thing at that time in my life.

"You know what…" Bill began to say. It was obvious it was more like the beginning of a thought coming out rather than being a question posed to me.

It was followed by this ever so cute and rather sly, but playful grin. Then…wait for it…uh huh. Wait for it… LOL This "I'm-Bill-new-to-the-congregation" continued his thought and said, "I think I'd like to marry you someday."

I laughed out loud. Well, not *loud* loud, just <u>out</u> loud. So let's just say I chuckled a bit and he heard me. It was funny and a cute thing to say. His eyes twinkled. He had big blue eyes with broomstick yellow lashes. His eyes appeared like they weren't quite all the way open, but definitely open. Oh yes! *Those* are what people call "bedroom eyes." The thought of it made me blush. Even so, I thought he was sorta cute in an odd kind of way. But I really didn't take him seriously.

But boy oh boy, my mother sure did!

She didn't say anything right then and there, but she was suddenly huffing and puffing to get her books together to get out of there. All the way home she was saying, "Can you believe that?"

And I was thinking, "Believe *what?*"

When we got home, Mother immediately walked up from the parking lot to the house and picked up the phone to call another sister from the congregation. I don't think there was ever a time I saw my mother walk so fast.

"Hello Karen, this is Essie. Sister Smith."

I couldn't hear Karen's side of the conversation, but I stood there and listened for Mom's as I got a drink of water.

"You know that guy that Art and Nancy are studying with?"

"Yes, that Bill Ladd guy. Well, he came right up to my baby Charmaine and told her he'd like to marry her someday. That's some nerve you know. I mean he's got to be like what, thirty-five or so? He's at least twenty years older than Charmaine!"

Then a long pause as mother listened to Karen.

Then…wait for it, uh huh. Here it comes:

"What! Nine*teen?*!! You've got to be wrong about that; this is a man. He's about thirty-five years old, Karen."

Then…silence. Mom was silent. Her lips were pursed and her jaws were tight. Then,

"Oh hell!" And Mom promptly slammed down the phone.

Hahahahahahaaaaaaaaaaaaaaa

Yup. Mr. Bill Ladd, looking so mature for his age that I thought he was about twenty-five and mother thought he was thirty-five, was just a mere baby himself at only nineteen. Sure, that's still four years my senior, but my mother knew that look in his eye was not "like" bedroom eyes, they <u>were</u> bedroom eyes! That young man was smitten by the love bug, and she was convinced his eyes had complete tunnel vision in the direction of her daughter.

Mind you, a daughter who already had her hands full with gut-wrenching realities in life. The last thing I'd need, or so my mother thought, was someone else to fall in love with or to have fallen in love with her. It could be just the additional trouble that none of us needed.

Even though my body was in trouble, I'd never lost my sense of humor. My mind was fine, but my body was a wreck. It was giving out because it wasn't being nourished and it was being pushed to the limit at the same time. Meeting Bill eventually changed all that. I spent the next few weeks saying "No" a lot...and that kept my mind off other pressing things, but during that time I'd talk with him and nibble on something. Food was beginning to be an option again. I'm sure that was the first thing my parents noticed.

But I wouldn't go out with him. I was adamant we'd not be dating.

Daddy took a group of us roller-skating every week, just as he'd done my whole life. When I was little, he was the guard at the skating rink. He was a master skater, a really fine ballroom skater. He was the guy who every female in the rink wanted to skate with, regardless of how young or old they were.

Anyway, Bill asked if he could ride with us to the skating rink. I said sure, there was no harm in that. We always took others with us. Besides, another brother from the congregation had started going along with us about a month ago. His name was Chuck.

Bill drove his little tealish-green Rambler to my house and was right on time for Daddy to drive us all to the Taylorville roller rink.

During that evening of skating, Bill and I talked a lot and had a really good time doing so. But then again, I had a great time with everyone no matter where I was. But this was especially nice because I really didn't know Bill at all. I was quite aware that he'd never met anyone quite like me; but I'm sure he had no idea that he also intrigued me a bit! That was a new thing for me! And there was another "new" thing for me that night: it became the first time I skated a moonlight skate with someone else besides my father.

Bill had asked me to skate a moonlight skate and I accepted. When I went over to tell my dad I'd be skating it with Bill, Daddy had "that look" on his face. LOL You know, one eyebrow raised and hearing the "Hmm" which follows. I immediately chastised him with, "Oh, Dad!"

Now, if you don't skate much or frequent roller rinks, the moonlight skates were the times where the lights were dimmed and the big glitter ball hanging from the center of the rink was illuminated. A slower, softer song was then played for couples to enjoy. It was very romantic and ballroom style, though ballroom skating was not a requirement. Everybody else who wasn't skating the moonlight skate, used the time to either go to the concessions counter and get refreshments, or watched…or a bit of both!

At the end of the night we went out to the parking lot and were loading up the station wagon. Dad got in the driver's seat, of course, and I always sat up front next to Daddy. Then Chuck went to get in the front seat, where he sat on the way to the rink.

Bill's hand went atop the front passenger door and I heard, "Uh, Chuck. How about you sit in the back?"

I turned my head to my left to look at Daddy and Dad was already looking at me. I grinned and Dad did too. We both thought it was funny.

The moonlight skate was nice, and Dad's eyebrow was right for Bill had made his move…and yes, I was impressed. I mean, my mind was a bit incredulous that this guy was not at all intimidated by my father *or* me! And if so, he sure didn't show it! That was new on *all* counts!! But even so, I still kept saying "No" when he asked me to go out on an official date with him. I just wouldn't go out with him.

It came down to Bill asking me out more and more and me continuing to say, "No," again and again. Finally, I decided to try something different and made this proposal to him: "Bill, *if* I go out with you this once, would you please stop asking me to go out with you?"

So that was the agreement. Little did I know how much I'd love being with him. Our first "official" date was at a pool hall. We shot pool for hours. Though naturally left-handed, Bill shot pool right-handed. I found that pretty cool since my father did the same thing. And he thought it was pretty cool to be beaten by a girl. LOL A girl who just whipped his butt by calling "three in the corner, off the six," and made it with that unmistakable sound of confidence and authority. When I learned to shoot pool, we called every single shot. There was no slop tolerated at any time. Even though I could feel his competitive streak surface throughout, this Bill Ladd took it like a man. I liked that very much!

When we got back to my house, standing on the porch saying goodnight, I told Bill that perhaps we might have to do this [shoot pool] again some time.

He said, "Uh no."

I knew that after all this time of him waiting for me to go out with him that I couldn't possibly be hearing correctly. Did he just say, "Uh, no?"

My neck and shoulders went backward. I said, "What was that?"

"You said that if you went out with me, I couldn't ask you out again."

"Correction," I said. "Yes, true. But I didn't say I couldn't ask *you* out!" We both laughed. There was something about him that was just meant to be. For me, for him, for us, for WE. The People of Tomorrow at a time when we could think about things such as that. Tomorrow. Promised to no one…but counted on nonetheless. For me, there was a chance that there would actually *be* a tomorrow…and I cared to be there. That was a huge improvement over where I'd been and what I'd gone through.

Mom and Dad were delighted and adored Bill Ladd. To the day my mother died, she called my husband by both his first and last name. She was so endeared to him. Now that I'm a mother and grandmother, I understand why my mother was so endeared to my husband: he saved her daughter's life. To her, that's exactly what happened. And that's why when he asked for my hand in marriage, I'm sure there was little hesitation because I was happy and getting healthy again. They weren't going to rock that boat because what was their alternative? Amazing how things happen. Any other scenario and there would be no possible way on this earth that my parents would've allowed me to marry so young.

But it was meant to be.

It used to crack me up so much over the years, when my father would talk about Bill Ladd's tenacious love for his daughter, he'd just say, "Uh, Chuck…how about you sit in the back."

Daddy always insisted that Bill never meant for Chuck to think he had a choice. "It was a statement," Dad would say, "not a question! Bill Ladd was not playing! So no question mark required!"

Hahahaaaaaaaaa Oh, how my father loved Bill.

It's even funnier when I look at my marriage certificate hanging on the wall and spot the names of our two witnesses: One was Chuck Elliot. Yes, the very same "get-in-the-back-Chuck." And we all remained good friends. The other witness was my mother!

We were supposed to have a nice wedding in November, scheduled on the date of my parent's wedding anniversary, but Mother began to fret and worry about every aspect of it to the point that I said, "Enough." We four went to the Court House in Decatur, IL, where Bill could get married without the permission of his parents. He was twenty years old. I was sixteen.

Peacemakers are Unselfish

Happy people freely give of themselves with their time and help. They also seem to have more time to do just that. Perhaps that's because they don't waste so much time sitting around in turmoil over being unfulfilled and unhappy. You know, it takes time to brood! It takes time to hold pity parties! It takes time to wallow in one's pit of darkness. Before one knows it, most of their time is spent struggling with how to lift their bodies up out of a deep, dark hole that's completely overshadowed any hope of a zestful and bright life.

When one is so very down, the best way to bounce back up is to find a way to give of yourself to others. Try it the next time you find yourself dragging around moaning and groaning about things you can't deal with. Go and help those who wish they could stand in *your* shoes! "Miserable," you know, is relative! We just have to be reminded of that fact from time to time.

There's much reward in unselfishness and the giving of one's heart and time. It gives us a purpose when we think we've no other. And the rewards are sweet. The rewards gained by giving of ourselves to help others are truly satisfying.

Sprouting a smile sows the seeds that cultivate and harvest happiness to and from others. – Charmainism

Every smile gained from another human being in gratitude for your efforts makes every moment assisting others well worth it. When you feel a bit down and out, often times the best thing you can do is get out and help someone. Go visit a sick relative or a friend who is feeling down; or pay a call over to the local hospice or nursing home and make someone's day really shine! There are places where smiles are scarce. You truly can help spread the joy!

What the expectations are of what should happen when we arise in the morning and all the way throughout our day is what can set us up for disaster and keep us from ever attaining happiness. We often find that we're standing in our way, blocking our path to happiness with unrealistic expectations. Why not be happy in the fact that we exist? It amazes me that so many take life for granted and have no clue they do so. If you aren't bringing in a new day with a big smile, then you've got to get your priorities straight. EACH MOMENT OF LIFE IS A MIRACLE.

You are the master and commander of your peace and happiness. Whether or not you are happy and at peace is not dependent upon anyone else but yourself. It really is that simple. – Charmainism

Whether or not you perceive yourself as "happy" is entirely up to you. The idea of being satisfied, content, or happy is entirely subjective: it depends on what those words mean to the person. Not so much what the person wants or needs, mind you, but how the person deals with life on a day-to-day basis; and how they think that compares with what their expectation of what happiness is. Their respective answers have a definite impact on whether or not they can be successful in attaining happiness.

Let the Master and Commander <u>in you</u> take hold of the "Shwy" philosophy. It will steer you where you need to go. Your happiness and inner peace are there for the taking.

Peacemakers Overcome Strife

When we think we will feel pain, we do just that. Depending on our level of fear and self-pity at the time, we can make this so unbearably true. – Charmainism

Life, with its entire splendor, is also full of strife, pain, struggle, and yes, even death. It is what it is. Yet we, as human beings, have taken these known characteristics of life and, after experiencing any one of these seemingly negative traits, use them as being reasons for not living fully. It just doesn't make sense to do so.

If you think you've a viable reason for feeling depressed, then the odds are that you'll most surely *be* depressed. Those who have been dealt a heavy blow are often told that perhaps they need the help of medication or grief counseling, and neither are necessarily a bad thing. However, the desire to remove the torturous nature of loss is so mind numbing that we may have an affinity for relying on those medications far too long.

During times of great grief, it's human nature to want to do just about anything to escape the torture of facing such a gut-wrenching reality. So we're often apt to either overuse prescribed medication or self-medicate to yet another extreme. Let me be clear about this: alcohol and drugs aren't your friends at times like these. They're probably your worst enemy. Let me repeat: *worst* enemy. *Not* the devil, mind you, as *you* will do a good job of becoming that for yourself if you succumb to self-medicating with alcohol or drugs.

Thinking of those I've known who have fallen down that path of what amounts to a slow and unrelenting spiral into total self-destruction, one chapter of this book was going to be titled, "Self-exorcism." Well, not really, but you do understand how we create the demons that manifest and make themselves at home in our lives. They're born from our own negativity and thrive on our bad moods and sour dispositions. They love the defeatist attitude in anyone! Don't keep inviting them back…change the venue and the menu! You can do it! Most definitely!

A lot of the torture comes from what we do to ourselves, which means we can therefore <u>undo</u> it. We can do amazing things when we don't feel sorry for ourselves and choose to face our fears instead. But when we lay the guilt at our feet, we then trip over it 24/7 and crave a way to neutralize it that will also allow us a period of relief: numbness. That never works. What does work is when we finally realize that life and death go hand in hand. We then can survive massive blows to our hearts and minds. We can live because life is worth living, or we can die because we feel so sorry for ourselves that we can't take it anymore. When we understand where our thinking has gone wrong, we can make the adjustments in our thought processes and wake up from the nightmare that was totally our own doing.

And we can realize that anything other than life or death can be dealt with in a much easier manner. And we're grateful for that. We merely have to remind ourselves of it time and time again, and keep things in the proper perspective. <u>The "Shwy" philosophy is you making amends with yourself and keeping your own self in check</u>. It's so worth it, just as any other preventative maintenance is.

My parents had seven children as a result of their union. But there were nine in total, counting my half-brothers. You know about Gerald, who makes eight; but long before Gerald, Daddy had been previously married and had a son during that union. The firstborn in that case is the ninth child for reference: his name was Robert Jr.

Robert Jr., or "Bobby," as we called him back in the day, was the spitting image of my father. He came to visit us every year, as he lived in Los Angeles with his mother (my father's first wife). When Bobby was seventeen, I was about six years old, I believe. At the time, we lived next door to The Starlight Tavern where Dad would go and shoot pool and drink with his buddies.

One night, Bobby was in The Starlight with Dad, shooting pool, and a fight broke out. The police were called and when Dad heard the sirens he told Bobby to go home, as Bobby was underage, and "home" was right next door. As Bobby went to leave, a police officer was on his way in. They simultaneously met at the threshold of the door. Bobby told the officer he was going home, next door, and that he wasn't involved in any of the going's on and knew nothing about it. The officer obviously misunderstood the situation, as Bobby was telling the truth when he stated he'd not been involved with any of the problems in the Tavern. But, for whatever reason, the officer raised his bully club and hit Bobby in the face. It cost Bobby his eye.

Dad helped Bobby sue the City and a settlement was won. This is where it gets very muddled. All I know is that after that happened; we didn't get to see Bobby. Dad wouldn't even talk about him. We knew he hadn't died, as we were told something bad had happened to him and it was about his eye or something, but then it was like our older brother had simply disappeared. Bobby never came back to visit us.

Every year we'd ask about Bobby. Why hasn't he come back to visit us again? There was always some reason or another, but each year there was more animosity in Daddy's answer. When I was much older and asked Daddy about Bobby, it turned out that there was some disagreement as to how the settlement money was to be disbursed. Apparently there were legal fees to pay, but it _was_ Bobby's eye and he left. That's all I was told at the time.

There were many times, through the years, that I tried to find and make contact with my brother Bobby. I was never successful. Little did I know that many of my other siblings did the very same thing.

My eldest sister, Sylvia had gone out to Los Angeles to see Bobby and the woman she thought was her mother, Bobby's mother Vivian.

I didn't find out about this until many, many years after the fact, but it was an honest mistake by La. Her birth certificate sure enough shows Bobby's mother Vivian listed as _her_ mother. However, the problem was that Daddy's benefits at the time covered his first wife, Vivian. For he and my mother, there would be big bills incurred if the Navy didn't cover the costs for La. Since his divorce from Vivian was not yet official, it left Dad in a bit of a pickle. He convinced Mother to say that she was Vivian.

I can't imagine the pain this caused for my mother, but I'm sure she was wholly distraught about it. First, she's connived by this charming and handsome man from the "City," and her father warns her about such men who come along in the countryside wooing down-home girls with big city promises. But noooo, Mother didn't listen. Turns out, Collossie Byrd hit the nail on the head!

None of this was made clear to me until I was grown and on my own. I only found out when my Aunt Juanita told me this story, and then my sister Cheyenne and I went and checked the birth certificates for ourselves: Cheyenne's birth certificate also listed Vivian as her mother too!

There's no question that Vivian isn't the mother of my older sisters. No question at all. However, it did make for some high drama when Bobby Jr.'s half-sister, who looked very much like La at the time, was convinced that La was in fact *her* twin and that their mother, Vivian, had betrayed them and had given up <u>her "twin."</u> Yeah, I know. But seriously, I kid you not.

Eventually, the whole thing probably served to mess up more than one life about all this uncertainty…I know for sure that it threw La for a big loop as what was she supposed to think?! But it also serves to illustrate that any skeletons dangling in the closet will one day eventually come out! All the bones will be rattling and Halloween will be smack dab in your living room as the witches and brooms unite for flight! Yup. Even if it's the Fourth of July. Yee-Haw!!! LOL

This also makes me understand why my mother wanted desperately to find redemption and salvation. She wanted to make sure that her daughters would never make the same mistake she did when being conned by a smooth talking man who promised her he was the one to turn the world into her oyster.

Forty years after the terrible night when Bobby lost his eye and was gone from our lives, he got in touch with Daddy. Daddy was delighted. When Bobby came to town after forty years of being away, I went to the train station to pick him up (he refused to fly, being fearful of airplanes). My husband, Bill, and my young grandson, Will, were with me at the time.

Not five minutes before, we'd sat down at the train station as the ticket person said the train would be arriving shortly. I got up to use the restroom and came back. There was a man sitting across from where my husband and grandson were sitting. He had on sunglasses so I couldn't see his eyes. But then I heard myself say, "Bobby?"

He got up and said, "Sis?"

I said, "Oh my goodness," as my arms stretched wide to greet him, "Bobby, it's me, your sister, Charmaine!"

He knew exactly who I was.

Oh! How we hugged and kissed and cried like you wouldn't believe. All those years apart completely disappeared. It was like he was still seventeen; that wonderful, big brother of mine who so coolly would effortlessly fall back into a lean on a car; simultaneously crossing his legs at the ankles. Just like James Dean.

It was an incredible reunion. A miracle of sorts, for sure! When Daddy saw him as he got out of our car, as we arrived back at Dad's house, it was nothing short of astonishing to everyone. Daddy and Bobby were dressed *identically*. Seriously. Same jeans, same blue jean jacket, same hat, same sunglasses, same checkered shirt, and same black tennis shoes. I promise you, I've pictures to prove it! This is the type of thing that you just can't make up because no one would believe it. LOL Everybody there just couldn't believe their eyes! It was like the Twilight Zone. AND they both sported grey Van Dyke style beards on their faces. They were TWINS!

There was a ton of crying that day. A ton!

We later had a celebration for my Aunt Juanita's birthday and for Daddy's…it was a big bash and to think that Bobby was there for it! It was a *miracle*! Aunt Juanita was so happy to see her favorite brother (my Dad) finally reunited with his firstborn son. I'll never forget it. There had to be over a hundred people there at the Lake Pavilion. It was a glorious celebration. A night I'll never forget. Mother had passed by then, but I'm sure she was smiling and happy for "The Kid."

When my sister Antoinette, was to be married, Daddy was bedridden, still recuperating from a bad fall. Bobby, or I should say, "Robert," as he then preferred to be called by then, stepped in for Dad and walked my little sis down the aisle during the ceremony in Los Angeles. As he escorted the bride down the aisle, brother Bobby looked exactly like a slightly younger version of Daddy. It was an absolutely riveting moment. It sealed his place in our family, and if he hadn't realized how much we loved him all these years, he knew it then. It was as if he'd never left. The forty-year gap had closed to being no gap at all. It was always that way for us, but for Bobby he didn't have the reassurance around him that we'd not forgotten him.

We were all so fortunate to have these great times with Bobby, as Daddy died shortly thereafter. Robert Jr. died two years after Daddy. He was diagnosed with esophageal cancer due to untreated Acid Reflux Disease. Bobby had no idea he had that either. From diagnosis to his passing was only about three months. It was a heavy blow to us all. We'd finally gotten him back after forty years only to lose him so quickly again. Though he'd lost his wife, Donis, whom he'd been married to since they were teenaged sweethearts, Bobby Jr. had found love again in a sweet lady named Anita. Bobby had told me how much he loved Anita and that she was actually the love of his life. Anita and I've corresponded and stayed in touch since Bobby's (she calls him Robert) death.

There are others who, over the years, have asked me how I felt when Robert Jr. abandoned us. Well, the truth is that I never felt abandoned by Bobby. Part of the reason for that may be that all I knew was that I loved him very, very much. I'm sure Dad and Mom made up a few stories to explain why he'd yet to return…then the stories went on year after year until we stopped asking.

None of that mattered to the little siblings that wondered what happened to their older brother. We knew in our hearts that wherever he was he was safe, and we also knew that we loved him very, very much. And we knew that he loved us too – and that was all we needed to know. Love conquers all.

Life is full of surprises, both joyful and heartbreaking, but we have to roll with the punches or get rolled over! With the laughter and joy also comes tears of grief and sadness…we can't have one without the other. It is what it is. And I love each and every minute, yes, even the hard times – otherwise I set myself up for shock and despair. We have to keep things in the proper perspective every step of the way. This is how we can enjoy our lives and live with the light of sincere thankfulness!

Even loss can offer up gain…
we need only to reflect with gratitude. – Charmainism

When you really think about it, mankind has been alive on this earth for as long as mankind has been dying. Why do we celebrate birth and treat death as if it were some monster that came like a thief in the night to rob us of those we love? Why do we let death keep eating at us until we ourselves wither away like a neglected arbor with grapes left hanging on the vine?

We don't have to let death devastate us to the point of causing our own life force to wane. But I'll readily admit it's something we have to learn to fight against. Losing those who are so close to us, especially at tender ages, will always be trying. Though it doesn't really matter if a person is 18 or 88 when it comes to facing the fact you'll never see them again. Fortunately, nowadays we're tending to accept death in a more natural fashion, with "Celebrations of Life," which permits a climate that's so much more conducive to embracing the joy of having known and loved the deceased.

The key to overcoming grief is to let it out when need be and then when it hits you as if you'll not last until the morning, you have to decide to curb and temper your grief or it will be the death of you. You have to find something to hold onto, a motivator so that you can get on with living. You're the one left behind and it hurts like hell. It hurts beyond hell. There are no words to explain it. Your entire being is an open wound with the salt of the oceans pouring into them. You're walking and functioning but only on autopilot. Every thing you do is just a reflex, a motion that has no meaning.

And that has to change. For then the crying comes again and it wails throughout your body with the force of the most threatening hurricane. Then you realize you might not make it through... you have to get hold of yourself.

We make things complicated but that doesn't mean things really are! Life is simple. We just got greedy. If we're not feeling the tingle of exuberance at every waking moment...then we must be dying. – Charmainism

That's when the desire to honor those lost comes to your rescue. You can't be selfish in this. You'll live for those who no longer can. We have to do it for them and to attest to the legacy of such great and powerful love we have for them – *we can and will see it through!* We must remove the power we've given death over us; that power of fearing impending doom. The breaking glass of death has shattered our once peaceful lives and we no longer feel immune to the worst that life can bestow upon us. The impossible has happened.

If we don't make amends by accepting that the impossible can and does happen, then we continue to torture ourselves with a myriad of questions that all come down to one: Why? Thinking and feeling this way will eventually rob us of our zest and gratitude for life as each time we plead with the forces of the universe for an answer.

Why?

We know why. We live; and therefore we die.

Does not our love for those we've lost mean more to us than anything else? Allowing a loss to render us defenseless against self-destruction is no tribute to those we love who have departed before us. We must pay great respect to that love by illustrating how love lives on! If we spent more time continuing to love them rather than feeling sorry for ourselves, we wouldn't be so melancholy.

That great love that has shown our sorrows the pit of hell will lead us out of that self-imposed darkness. We need merely to grasp that concept and allow our love to continue to flow. Just because our loved ones are no longer here on this earth shouldn't stop us from talking about them and to them. You have to refuse to lose them twice! The first time you could do nothing about, but the second loss is much greater because we do that one to ourselves. We tend to remove them and then it doesn't feel right. We say we do it so we can feel better if we put it all in the back of our mind; but you know that doesn't feel right. You can pack away the clothes and belongings and give things to Goodwill or the Salvation Army, or have a bonfire if you must...but you'll find out that deciding to forever include them in your life is a very good thing.

If you've put them out of your life so as not to bring up painful memories, you'll do so much better if you embrace the love instead of fueling the loss. Keeping them out of your life is a price you continue to pay and that toll is far too great a cost – too great for you and all those around you. Decide to put them back into your life and *keep* them in your life! This is how you can keep excessive mourning at bay. You have no regrets then. Your love for them is still there, front and center. There's nothing to get over anymore.

My only son has merely taken an extended trip, such is the life of a sailor; it just so happens that his destination, this trip, is unknown. I'm good with that. Sure, I know he's not coming back...not *ever*...but when thinking of him sailing, I can smile and really feel the *joy*. My only son continues to bring me great joy! If others are around when I sometimes speak of something he would like or laugh at, they're none the wiser that he's passed on. And for those who do know, they love being able to speak of him freely, without fear of saying the wrong thing or upsetting anyone. I get to enjoy each and every one of those moments.

If you truly could do it all over again, you wouldn't be the person you're today. Looking back with regret equates to not only a stiff neck...but also a stiff life. – Charmainism

The stark reality of possibly dying of a broken heart actually shook me out of excessive and unhealthy grieving. There's not a doubt in my mind it could've been the death of me. And what would that have helped, had I died of grief? It would've given my family and friends even more of a load of grief to withstand during that same tragic time. That would be a very horrible and totally selfish thing for me to do. Most all in my family got two calls that day, within minutes of each other . . . the first that my mother had died; the second that my son had died. No one was ready for a blow such as that.

At the time, I lived aboard my sailboat and was down in the Florida Keys. Bill and I had just come back into Boot Key Harbor after being out sailing for an entire week. It was glorious! Evening was quickly settling in, and we were hustling to get things back in shipshape before nightfall, at our slip at Sombrero Marina. Bill had come down below decks to make sure the central air was back online, when there was a familiar knock on the side of the boat. It was the knock of visitors.

I was in the middle of undressing to take a shower, so Bill peeked his head out of the companionway hatch.

"Yeah. Who's there? Hello?"

"Bill, it's Jack and Kathy."

Captain Jack and Kathy ("Munchkin"), two of our dearest friends. Captain Jack had gone on the first leg of the trip to St. Croix with Captain Dennis and our son Bj. There were some engine problems and other issues that caused too much of a delay for the rest of the crew who had obligations back here in the Keys, so they'd returned and Jack came back with them. First Mate Bj and Captain Dennis had finished the trip, having sailed from Rum Cay to St. Croix by themselves. That was three months ago.

Bj had been thriving ever since. He was working three jobs and loving the life of the professional beach bum. He was the hardest working "bum" that ever lived! The people of St. Croix embraced Bj with all arms. They adored him. You would've thought he had lived there all his life and was an Islander.

I heard Bill say, "I think it's Jack and Kathy," as he shut the companionway doors and stepped out into the cockpit to greet them.

I couldn't hear anything that was going on, but something wasn't quite right. Bill usually would be back by now with *something* to say, as more than five minutes had passed. I got my clothes back on and headed up the steps and through the companionway to the cockpit. The door shut behind me and I saw the legs of Bill, Kathy, and Jack all standing on the dock.

Peeking my head out from beneath the cockpit enclosure, "Hey Guys. What's going on?"

I wasn't alarmed, but I wasn't my usual zealously joyful self either.

Bill turned around and said, "Bj's dead."

There's no doubt in my mind he didn't mean to say it like that, so abruptly and so matter-of-fact. He was Bj's father. He was in shock.

"No. It's not him," I protested. "It's someone else. Someone has mistaken Bj for someone else. It's not him I tell you. It's not him." My voice began to escalate in volume with each and every word. Bill had come back into the cockpit and then Kathy and Captain Jack did too.

Bill was trying to talk to me, "Honey, Captain Dennis called Jack because we were out and he couldn't get hold of us when we were out of cell phone range as we came in. It's Bj. There is no doubt." Bill's face was deprived of all its color. He looked like a ghost.

And then I tried desperately to dive overboard. It was just a natural response for me. I've always loved the water and the ocean was a place of solace and comfort for me. It may have seemed to others that I'd lost my mind. . . but for me, I merely wanted to escape the deep pain in my chest and soothe it by swimming. To where? I don't know. Cuba, perhaps. Bill grabbed me and took me down below decks.

Peace was ripped to shreds as the tears began to fall.
My mind said, 'Swim fast, far away from it all!'
Struggling in panic, the strokes were nowhere around.
Had to then focus on simply how not to drown.

Captain Jack and Kathy came down with us. They were devastated and grieving too. We all were in shock. After about fifteen minutes of gut-wrenching chaos, I thought I had to call my father. Then I'd call my daughter, after I talked to my sister Cheyenne. Breighan's "Aunt Cheyenne" would make sure she was safe. There was so much to do. I made the call to my father and it was more like a "Who's on First?" skit...a very black comedy sketch this time.

Daddy thought I was calling about my mother. I didn't know my mother had just died.

When Daddy finally figured out that I was talking about the death of his grandson, I could feel the dagger of despair plunging deeper into his heart. My father had a heart as big as the universe. At that moment, his heart could've burst with the pangs of helplessness.

Daddy then said that Breighan was at the nursing home with Cheyenne. He said, "Mainie, your mother just died." When he told me, my legs buckled from beneath me and I fainted.

When I regained consciousness, Bill was hanging up the phone with Daddy saying he'd call Dad back in a little bit and that I'd fainted. Kathy and Captain Jack were tending to me. They all had only heard my end of the conversation. They thought I'd fainted from the stress of talking with my father about Bj. They weren't aware my mother had just died.

It was like a fog rolling inside my head…and it got thicker in my brain. I remembered hearing Daddy talking and being confused. My mother had died. My father's *wife* just died. Oh my…and…oh God no! Not my Bj. My poor baby. My poor son. How could this have happened? He was so happy and in his element there in St. Croix. He was meeting all sorts of people and everyone on the Island knew him. He was off and running with three jobs and many more prospects. Everyone who came in contact with him found his joy and love for life refreshingly infectious.

But this IS real and it IS happening. Captain Jack and Kathy are here. The impossible has happened. And now my father's grandson has died on the very same day as his wife…my mother. Everyone will be devastated. How can I possibly tell my daughter that her brother has died. This just can't be real. But it is. It is real. This is so bad, so very, very bad.

And now I have to tell Bill that my mother has just died. Oh for heaven sakes! Let me wake up from this nightmare!!

Life often throws us curve balls. We swing but often cannot seem to connect. Every day may not be a grand slam or even a home run…but it is most certainly a hit. Why? Because we're still in the game! – Charmainism

Being overwhelmed is a very common and normal event, but convincing yourself that it's the first step to doom is an embellishment none of us can afford to entertain for even a moment! It's our panic, when those types of feelings occur, that overwhelms us right over the cliff of sanity. So right here and right now, let's get one thing perfectly straight: being overwhelmed from time to time is a perfectly normal part of living! We simply have to recognize what it is and treat it as such by doing something about it and then summoning the courage to move on. You must change your outlook from dour and negative to one that's optimistic and positive!

When your inner sun is shining,

every day is a GORGEOUS day!! – Charmainism

Having a positive outlook will allow you to see hardships as they really are: simply another of life's challenges that can be tamed by the experience of a willingness to embrace all of the lessons of life. What began as a negative can be turned into a very positive experience. Each experience is yet another chapter in the book of you! As time goes on, you can rely on those learned lessons to help you in the future. As with any skill or art, you get better and better at it with practice!

When something is seen for what it is, and only that, one learns to go through the process of dealing with it – just as with any other occurrences in life's routine – and then move on. This goes for even the most horrible things that can happen in life. Yes, even death. We can survive and thrive through anything and become the better for it.

Peacemakers Personify Peace

Peacemakers are the ones that are happy regardless of what's happening in their lives. When you're truly happy, it doesn't matter where you are in life. You'll be so happy just to be here on this planet that nothing else really matters. This is a genuine zest for life that will serve to carry you through all that comes your way. Good, bad, the beauty and the beast, no matter…you'll smile all the while as you take on the challenge of whatever it is, and with gratitude at having the opportunity to do so.

May your day be filled with positive thoughts and cheerful reactions. No one can get you down unless you allow it. Stay UP! The air is so much more peaceful there. – Charmainism

There are some people on this earth who are happy no matter what life throws their way. They realize that life is simply a four-letter-word that we make mean what's best for us. There are no real measuring sticks as to who is happy and who isn't, as it's not about possessions because we all know full well by now that we can't take what we have with us when we depart for destinations unknown. We've come across some people who seem to get through each day with a smile on their face and a lilt in their gait, no matter what they have or don't have. They just seem to be happy no matter what. And they do not worry about tomorrow.

Keep life balanced by first having the heartfelt desire to attain (or maintain) inner peace. You know when inner peace has been attained because you'll recognize the crumbling of the foundation for self-doubt: frustration. With frustration kept at bay, life immediately becomes harmonious and balanced. Being at peace with yourself is the first step onto the path to genuine and lasting happiness. – Charmainism

Peacemakers personify peace. Fortunately, for some of us, it's a natural way of looking at things. We are the truly grateful and it oozes from our pores. We're at total peace with ourselves. We do not worry, fret, or fear that which may or may not happen tomorrow. Tomorrow is promised to no one. Why worry about a hypothetical outcome of a hypothetical event that hasn't yet transpired?

Embracing happiness as a purpose will get you to see yourself in a different light. This is a light that glows with the essence of who you are and what you can do for yourself. As you continue to discover how simple it is to attain peace within yourself, there's little you can't do. Inner peace is the real path to happiness. It's all within you and has always been there in the shadows waiting to be released into the light of day.

You may have forgotten that you're a peaceful dove on a journey to find your path to happiness. But I'm here to remind you!

Happiness is not dependent upon outside sources.

It lives within you! – Charmainism

No matter how hard it is for you to get the things you need for survival, when you don't blame others for your plot in life, you're on the road to happiness. You don't have time for the blame game, as you're simply so very grateful and happy to be alive. That's probably the most common denominator of all those on this earth who are inherently happy: they don't expect much, but whatever they do get – no matter how small – they're happy with it and make do with it. And they feel the same happiness when good things happen to other people as they do for themselves.

And here we are. We understand ourselves better and are honing more skills to become adept at making sense out of the nonsense that clogs our arteries of the good life. Still learning, still letting the good vibes soak way down deep. Ah…yes! You know, it just might be a good time for tea. Or coffee if you prefer! Sound good to you? Well, it certainly sounds pretty good to me.

I can make out a light that's perhaps not so very far away…is that a lighthouse beacon? Well yes *sirree*…I do believe it is.

Where there once was only darkness and despair

came forth light and hope. – Charmainism

145

Chapter Six:
Making Changes into the Light

Acceptance

Acceptance extinguishes the smoldering of frustration. There comes a time when one realizes there are things that cannot be changed. Acceptance, ultimately, is paramount to sanity. – Charmainism

Some put off making changes for so long that by the time they know they have no other choice; the task seems far too daunting to initiate. As the months and years fly by without action on their part, they fall deeper into the darkness of self-pity and shame. Many then choose to do nothing. They've given up and resigned themselves to a life unfulfilled and desperate. It's not difficult to see how self-imposed exiles keep others from ever enjoying a world that could've been far more productive and so much happier for them.

~ **I saw a man with holes in his soles.**
His eyes told me of a man whose soul was not whole. ~

The above is a little ditty I made up and used to say as a child. It was about "Old Man Washington," an elderly, kind soul of a man who used to regularly over imbibe and end up passed out drunk on the sidewalk in front of the tavern next to my house on Washington Street in my hometown. There was no fear of him by me, but other children in the neighborhood would cross the street instead of walking past him. If anyone else had empathy for him, other than myself, it was unknown to me. It was no matter; I'd enough sympathy for him to cover all those who didn't.

Those who are down and out are unfulfilled by way of broken promises, broken dreams, and broken hearts. They're broken links in the chain of mankind's progression on this earth. Do we not know something of fear, concern, and hardship? We can't change the word, so we must accept that which we can't change. However, we can change our own world. Acceptance allows us to carry on and do the latter.

If we're living in the realm of thinking happiness is merely being content to be alive in the first place, we find acceptance is our best friend when it comes to the things we cannot change. Sure, we may be a bit befuddled by things that occur, sometimes even hurt; but occupying one's time harboring resentment, anger, fear, and the like, is wasting time that would be much better spent on finding ways to change only that which we are capable of changing. - Charmainism

Bill, Captain Jack, and Kathy could not believe what it was that had made me faint. It was just something that couldn't be happening. Not for real. But it was. I told them that Daddy had just told me that my mother had just died.

Now I must get back on the phone and call my sister, Cheyenne, who is with my daughter, Breighan, and get her to Sophia's, her best and most trusted friend whose mother is like a second mother to her.

Here Bill and I are in the Florida Keys and Bj has died in the Virgin Islands. My mother has died in our home state of Illinois. The Land of Lincoln. That's where the majority of my immediate and extended family members are. That's where our daughter Breighan is.

She'll be safe there with them when she's told that her brother has died. Oh my, I thought, anguishing at the complexity of it all, this is so bad for Breighan. This is so, so bad for my precious little girl who's taken more blows than anyone her age should have to endure. There she is helping her Aunt with her grandmother and now she'll find out that her only sibling is dead. Her big brother, ten years her senior, who she adores with all her heart, is gone from this earth forever. This is so hard. I don't know if I can bear it. But I must. I must do this and think of my daughter and how to keep her emotionally and physically safe through this until we can get back and be with her.

When I called Cheyenne, I first asked her not to say my name aloud. Then I asked if Breighan was with her. She told me no, Breighan had just left. I told Cheyenne to call her and tell her to come back to the nursing home. I wasn't sure what else to do.

 "I don't think that's necessary because she's taking it pretty well, but she's very hurt. She loved Mom so much," Cheyenne said.

"Cheyenne, the impossible has happened. We've lost Bj too. Bj has died."

The screaming was horrific. I could hear my sweet Aunt Juanita, my father's little sister who was also a dear and close friend of my mother's, she began to scream, "What in God's name is happening?"

Cheyenne must have thrown her cell phone. Aunt Juanita picked it up.

"Who is this? What's happening?"

Cheyenne continued to wail with the cries of a thousand mothers who have lost their babies. Her pain was so deep that *I* couldn't breathe. We'd always been so very close. Her son was like my son; my son was like her son. Bj and Cheyenne's only child, Jon "Shooter," grew up like siblings rather than first cousins. Much like my siblings and Aunt Juanita's kids. Sister-cuzzes and brother-cuzzes – which means we are much, much closer than being first cousins might indicate.

When I told Aunt Juanita what had happened, she too was in disbelief, shock, and mourning at a magnitude few know. We were all crying horribly. For all of us, the IMPOSSIBLE had happened. All my sisters and brothers reacted the same way as Cheyenne. We all were that close. For my little brothers and youngest sister, Bj was much more like their little brother than their nephew. My heart was empty for each and every one of them. And then there was Bj's little son, at the time, my one and only grandchild. He too, at only seven years old, will have to make sense of losing his great-grandmother who he loves so much and his father.

Everyone in the family got two calls that horrible Memorial Day. Imagine that. MEMORIAL DAY. My dearest friends and even acquaintances were also distraught. How could this have happened? None of that mattered. LIFE happens and DEATH happens.

Breigh was in excellent hands being with Sophia and her mother Sheila. They were family to us. "Sophie" (as I call her, as well as "Sofa Soph"), had lost her father in a tragic traffic accident just six months prior. Jack was like a second father to Breighan. We were all still reeling from that tragedy when this happened. Our hearts had been so down for them over this horrific loss. The timing and gravity of all this for so many, was beyond comprehension...beyond imagination.

In my despair, I thought about my family and friends, especially my daughter and my son's children, and how my death could possibly affect the remainder of their lives. That, along with a crying jag where I thought my heart would literally burst through my chest unless it was immediately ceased -- well, it brought me back to my senses in record time. The deep, dark well of tears would no longer be filled by contributions from me! I wouldn't add further grief to a time of terrible heartache.

And I also thought about how this happens each and every day -- just not to us personally or even indirectly. We don't feel it because we're not aware of it. But it happens 24/7 around the planet and the Universe. People and things alive...ultimately die. It's so important to keep it all in the proper perspective. And yes, it is so much more difficult when things that happen are senseless and cost us so much, but the weight of it all kept my mind on those who'd have a very difficult time with this. They don't have the life experiences that we adults do…they need all of our attention to help them overcome such devastation. My daughter Breighan had just endured a tremendous blow with the death of Sophie's father.

And then there was my grandson, Bj's little son.

How very tragic this all is, a little boy has to deal with this. My cherished grandson is going to have his little heart broken today. And then there are my siblings who have had their hearts ripped today and will soon find it ripped out even further. My father…can he live through this most heavy blow? And then I realized that I had work to do. There was a ton of healing to be done! I had to get my act together.

This is how my refusal to die of a broken heart came to be. How could I dare dishonor the lives of my son and mother by such a selfish act? I needed to do just the opposite: I needed to honor them by allowing my deep love and gratitude for having had them in my life serve as a beacon of light for all to see the power of love and how it can help overcome the heartache of loss. Yes! Let everyone see that one can actually experience <u>Good</u> Grief and flourish thereafter.

It is a wonderful life when we don't box ourselves into narrow tunnels but expand our horizons by looking to the sky. There is light up there; and our hearts, even when heavy, can soar once again. – Charmainism

Changing my perspective kept me from succumbing to the beast of premature mortality. No doubt it's possible to cry yourself to death. You can indeed grieve beyond what the body can handle and never be able to recover. We have to remember that life is death. We can't have one without the other. Instead of grieving endlessly over death, I chose to rejoice in the celebration of the lives that have been shared with me on this earth. Doing so was a great testament to the power of being positive despite the odds against it. It was my way of honoring those lost. The losses didn't just happen to <u>me</u>. They happened to my family and friends as well as the entire world. All loss is this way. We all feel a ripple of those who have departed, we just don't always recognize the impact because we weren't close to them and weren't aware of their contributions to this earth.

Loss, heartache, hardship, or whatever it is that's weighing so heavily on you, will continue to do so as long as you let it. Often times these events, which play an enormous part of our life cycle, are intensified by our feelings of pain, guilt, blame, confusion, and a general overall unwillingness to accept that which has occurred. All these things are counterproductive to a healthy environment for our mind and bodies. We've made the mistake of thinking we'll never reach happiness until we have a satisfactory answer for every question the mind puts forth.

"Why is this happening to me?" you ask. You'll never get an answer that will satisfy your quandary and give you meaning enough to want to overcome it. It's not about "Why?"

It's not a requirement that we understand and make sense out of every bump encountered on the road of life. We just convince ourselves that finding a valid reason is a requirement for understanding and peace of mind. It isn't. Most times things probably have no reason at all, they just happen. No big meaning behind it, just that whatever it was it simply just happened.

Life, and all that transpires within it, happens to us all. –
Charmainism

It's a wonderful thought to believe that everything happens for a reason…until something happens that you can't understand or explain in the slightest degree. That leaves you scratching your head and trying desperately to make some semblance of sense out of it so you can move on. Look, moving on is an option that is always there no matter what your beliefs are. Cut your losses and move on! Give it no more thought and carry on with your happy disposition leading the way.

In the event there's someone you blame for that bump in the road, that's when it can be very troubling and difficult to overcome. It's then that you feel most helpless to make it right. You want revenge but perhaps can't have it. The one you feel is rightfully to blame can never replace what you've lost, even if you do succeed in exacting revenge. Such realization leaves you drowning in a sea of waves filled with even more intense helplessness and hopelessness.

Revenge doesn't help any more than anything else when it comes to making peace with situations. It's a negative energy that can burn a hole through your life! The only viable alternative is to accept how the situation played out and be done with it by making peace with it. Anything other than that is wishful and unproductive thinking. For most people, this only serves to begin a cycle that keeps them going around in circles, to no avail, serving only to keep one ensnared in the web of one's own pity. One thinks everything will be fine once revenge is had. But that's not so! Harboring hate puts a dagger in the heart of inner peace and happiness.

Once we put our happiness first, all the other issues either find their place or lack of space on the pathway of inner peace. It's nothing less than liberating to understand how ill will towards others simply poisons *you*! It's almost impossible to think badly of someone else and not leave the tale-tell signs of bitter thoughts around your mouth, hanging on to the skin like the crumbs of cynicism. We are drinking the very poison we put out for someone else. It certainly doesn't make much sense to do that to oneself.

Learning to accept that which cannot be changed will free you from the bondage of bitterness and self-pity. Acceptance is a nutrient on which happiness thrives. Thrive on! – Charmainism

Blame is a vicious cycle that refuses to release countless unfulfilled human beings who really want to stop their futile obsessing once and for all, because deep down they know their lives are being smothered by it. Being constantly smothered is not really living. Rather, it's akin to treading water to avoid drowning, yet all the while ignoring the notion that all one has to do is stand up and the treading can stop.

The waters of inner turmoil are only a foot deep and it's your foot! Just move it out of the water! Step out of the murky waters that have taken over your life as it clouds every opportunity of having a happy moment. Believe me, there are beautiful, crystal blue waters shore side, but you have to first say goodbye to the murky waters of negativity and open your eyes to the positive side of the shore! It is, once again, entirely your choice.

No matter the source of the turmoil you're going through, be it loss, or merely a fight within yourself for clarity and understanding; when you embrace the opportunity to enjoy the rays of the sun and the beauty of a moonlit night as if both were fine works of art, well, that's when real life begins!

All in life that transpires between the sunrise and sunset becomes manageable because your reward is waiting: another beautiful day in the life that is uniquely you! – Charmainism

When we let go of all negative energy and allow our minds to think in an optimal environment (i.e., free of self-inflicted bitterness and self-pity), we can thrive. This is how to change your life and drive in the positive lane once and for all.

Once you've experienced such positive, extraordinary change, and how it simplifies your life in such a manner that you're far more productive and accomplished than ever before, the thought of reverting back to the life that once was such a disheartening struggle will no longer be an option for you. Who'd choose to live any other way if they knew a better choice? No one.

In order to attain real peace, we have to make peace with ourselves first. Only after we decide we truly want to personify peace can we find peace. Despite the former confines of uncertainties that used to haunt our lives on a daily basis, we can make peace with anything and everything as long as we believe in our ability to do so. Things can no longer wreak havoc in our lives and gain control over our emotions and sensibilities unless we allow them to do so. You'll find happiness when you realize that it's only been yourself holding your own arms behind you and thus holding you back from attaining the life you want. Then it becomes so much easier to move out of your own way and proceed to make the changes within yourself in order to grab the peace of mind and happiness for which you yearn.

For the things you cannot change, accept! For the things you accept, no regret! The high road sits at the altitude of inner peace. RISE to reach it! – Charmainism

You're learning rationales that will begin to come to mind when you need them most. Understanding how it's in your best interest to let go of all that weighs you down is a revelation that will change your life and serve to effectively motivate you to retain my methods of empowerment. This is what's immediately going to improve your quality of life! It only gets easier as you reap the rewards of neutralizing negativity. Walking on a path that's wholly positive gives you an increasing lilt to your step and a song of joy in your heart.

Learning how to call upon positive thinking at the times when needed most is something you should be practicing right now. A positive disposition can be learned, practiced, and honed. Soak up every word and feel the power gained by way of a growingly positive disposition! The rewards for embracing the lifestyle of a Peacemaker are bountiful.

You have to know deep down in your innermost self that practicing these methods is indeed the ticket to admission to that happy place which has eluded you for so long. And that alone will become all the motivation you need to remember what it is you must do to preserve your peace of mind and happiness. You have a life-ring at all times because you're learning what will bring you back up to the surface at the first hint of going underwater. The surface is where you want to be from here on; it's up where you can enjoy and bask in the sunshine of happiness.

There's more to life than just hanging on -- your life ring should be your life's positive aura! Let it shine, and you'll float atop the rough times. – Charmainism

When one realizes just how counterproductive internal negative energy is to one's health and how it negates the ability to reason with any real success, we can once and for all rid our lives of negativity by not becoming a victim of frustration in the first place. Frustration is what feeds negativity. Starve it!

Without frustration and negativity, we then have more patience to think things out and determine whether or not we wish to pursue an alternative strategy, or perhaps enjoy the ability to engage an entirely new option: choosing to simply accept it, let it go, and move on without malice, resentment, frustration, or any negative feelings whatsoever. And you know something? It is liberating to do so! It's such a freedom to learn you have many choices when handling matters in your life. None of those choices should leave an imprint of negative connotations. It's all within you to make it so.

And the time for coming to terms with acceptance is now.

It is not the here and now that makes us unhappy, it is more so our unwillingness to accept the things we cannot change. Changing our perception of what we think "acceptance" is...is therefore the key. That single key unlocks a myriad of closed doors that keep us in the same unproductive place.

Use the key. Open the doors. ENJOY your life! – Charmainism

Embracing acceptance of the things you can't change will free you from the pangs of frustration. You can do this! You can make changes in your life that will improve your overall disposition and open the gate to happiness.

All one really needs is a real reason for change. Simple as it may seem, we all know that deep down inside, the first step is the most difficult. We have discussed fear of failure and you understand how that very thing can keep you at a standstill. Being at a standstill is no longer an option and you're well aware of that.

So why, then, is there the affinity for continuing to prolong the agony of making the same mistakes? Still putting off things that should have been tackled long ago for a better you? Perhaps for the same reason negativity has been a problem for so long: time kept passing us by while we were making excuses as to why we'd wait to "start change tomorrow." Tomorrow came and went, came and went, came and went, and we stayed right where we were yesterday -- and we're angry with ourselves for not doing what we know we should've been doing!

You're aware that procrastination isn't your friend. Nor is indecision. And you also know that the clock of father time is tick, tick, ticking away. You're well aware that you're running out of time and wasting valuable moments spinning your wheels. You want to get to where you want to be!

You're still here.

You've already made it...you just didn't know it! – Charmainism

And you're almost there!

Accepting that which you can't change is a vital step towards becoming a better you and enjoying a more positive life. It's also an integral part of the pathway that will lead you to the Lighthouse of Inner Peace.

Tomorrow may be the gift that never arrives.
Today is your present! – Charmainism

Change is internal more than it is external. When you're doing the right things for you, you tend to do the right things for others. It comes easier because you're content with yourself. This doesn't mean all things in your life are picture perfect. It just means that things don't have to be "picture perfect" in order for you to be happy!

No matter how long it takes for you to accept some of these truths, just know it's okay...because ultimately you will. However, when you *do* decide to accept all of the above, promise yourself you'll have no regrets about taking so long to do so.

Regret is a total waste of time and energy. Never regret a thing. Just forget about it and move on. We can't go back and change what has happened in the past, all we can do is improve upon our present and future. Not all people learn from their mistakes. We want to be one of those who do, yet also with the intelligence to know that dwelling on the past is a mistake. However, when one genuinely appreciates the lessons that come along with making mistakes, and what it does to brighten your future because of lessons learned, then there's no need for regret.

Retraining your mind to think in a different, more positive fashion is imperative to progressive change. You must only keep things in the proper perspective. Perspective allows us to rationalize the irrational so that we can more easily accept it as beyond our control and move on. This is how, no matter what occurs, your mind and body can make peace with it.

Had I decided to blame others and harbor anger and resentment or any other negative energy vampires during my times of great struggle at such a young age, I'd probably have never met my great love, Bill. I wouldn't have been open to loving anyone ever again had I let myself be so hurt and disillusioned by the things happening in my life that weren't under my control. That's what inner turmoil does – it destroys any chance at happiness and inner peace. This is why inner turmoil isn't an option. You must choose inner peace instead!

Never one to be bitter or resentful, my father instilled in me that life always presents options. Positive thinking options! I'm not sure whether or not my father truly knew at the time that I held no animosity or blame his way as far as Gerald was concerned, as I felt it was not my business. It seemed a very warped and ironic coincidence that Gerald and I met and became involved. Even though my body felt otherwise, internally, in my consciousness was where I immediately made peace with it all and knew there was no choice but to accept it and move on. Unfortunately for Gerald, his life was full of turmoil because his body broke down in an entirely different way. His mind let him down when he needed it most. No one can fault him for that. It truly was a most heavy blow.

So I have to be good with it. I've always been good with it because what's my alternative? Cry myself to death? Hate my father, as so many youngsters tend to do, by convincing myself that *he* did this to me? No, he didn't!! I didn't even <u>exist</u> when these things were being put into motion. And perhaps I wouldn't have existed at all if my father and mother hadn't separated and then reconciled. You see what wishing for changes would do and not do? There's no sense in trying to make sense of it. It simply IS. And that very <u>"IS"</u> is what makes me who I was back then and who I am today.

I <u>had</u> to make peace with it and help my siblings to also make peace with it. I didn't want them hating my father or our new "brother" for what they perceived as the responsible parties to my misery. Therefore I could not be miserable! So I made peace with myself and others…for their benefit and my own. I've made peace all my life with whatever comes my way. It simply is who I am because first and foremost, if I'm going to be here, I'm going to be happy doing whatever it is while I'm still here! Life is far too short for anything less. We owe it to ourselves and to all those around us who care for and love us.

Perspective

One afternoon, my husband was driving my father and me, and along the way we were passing through the downtown area of my hometown. Suddenly, my husband threw the car into park (in the middle of the street, mind you), jumped out, and proceeded to run over toward a man and woman on the sidewalk. The man was beating on the woman. He had one hand holding her by her coat and the other hand repeatedly slapping the screaming woman about the face and neck.

It happened so fast when my husband jumped out of the car. I'd not had the time to surmise what was happening or know what exactly he was doing. But when my father and I looked up and saw the ruckus on the street corner, we both immediately looked at each other and said aloud, "Oh no!" We both knew my naïve husband could very well get shot or stabbed for intervening in a situation of which he knew neither party.

My husband grew up in an entirely different world than myself. This was not a new sight for me at all. Having spent many, many years living next door to a tavern, there were few things I hadn't seen by the time I was ten years old. Add to that, my parents owned and operated a boarding house in the other side and upstairs of our large home on Washington Street. There were all kinds of misfits from all walks of life who lived there at one time or another. My friendly nature endeared me to many of them. I still have great fondness when I think back about many of them to this day.

And then there are those I'd like to forget, as young little girls will forever be easy prey to them. Few young girls have escaped some type of molestation, for most often we're too young to realize what's happening at the time. Some were visitors of our tenants, and others lived in the neighborhood. Some were much older and knew exactly what they were doing, and others were young and in an experimentation mode, albeit with a child much, much younger than themselves. It happens.

But we can survive and thrive despite it. We don't have to allow any of it to put a damper on our full enjoyment of life and love; or succeed in destroying our lives. Like all things, we must do our best to keep it in perspective, make peace with it, and move on.

Though my mother cringed at the thought of it, my being in a pool hall with Daddy, was, well, what other kids my age would enjoy about the community swimming pool. I loved shooting pool and shooting the breeze! A pool hall can be a great place to grow up, as it certainly teaches you about who is all talk and who actually walks the walk! My father was a crack shot, just as his father before him -- and by the time I was thirteen, this girl could hold her own or better with just about anyone!

So, at ten years of age, I probably knew the world a whole lot better than most. Tolerance and kindness was ingrained in me, but so also was a keen awareness of my surroundings. Even though I was somewhat fearless, it would be unwise to ever sit with one's back exposed. And one never, ever went looking for a fight.

It was an automatic thought to me that not many normally socially conscious people are fighting like that in broad daylight on a sunny afternoon. Well, especially not a grown man beating a grown woman like he's taking his daily exercise routine right out on a street corner. For them, it appeared as if it were all perfectly normal. And, mind you, the way she was hollering like she was being murdered, yet not trying all that hard to actually get away from her oppressor, was a good indication of what was really going down. It was in the middle of downtown and it was happening on a street corner. Do the math! How many people do you know who'd touch that?! At the time, I only knew one who did. Actually, I still only know one who ever did. Ha!

Next thing, both the man and the woman are cursing out Bill! Daddy and I sure knew it was coming, but Bill had no clue. As soon as the man saw my father sitting in the car, he grabbed the woman by the arm and proceeded to walk with her the other way away from Bill and the street.

My husband did what his conscience told him to do. He was quite naïve in those types of things. My husband had made assumptions that were based on a very limited amount of information and dismissed what should have been the glaring facts written on the wall of the nearby train station! From his perspective, he needed to intervene. From my perspective, some things are better left alone.

This is how some people unknowingly create and/or perpetuate drama. Their hearts and minds are in the right place, but somehow, drama seems to follow them wherever they go. Drama doesn't follow someone. The reality is that the person whose life is thick with drama is often the one creating it. My husband learned from his experience. The mistake he made that day was one he never repeated. He was not out to find drama or to create it; he thought he was helping out a damsel in distress. He simply forgot to size her up before he got involved. We're all guilty of jumping to erroneous conclusions from time to time.

More often than not, we perceive that which we see with a limited scope. Let's say we see a young man pull into his driveway and we then think, "What a nice looking guy." Then we think of how nice he probably is in everything he does. But then, as he gets out of his car, you watch him drop kick a child's toy across the yard. You're appalled! Now we've no clue as to why that happened, and the toy was probably in the young man's way, but his reaction certainly appeared to be totally inappropriate and quite immature to your way of thinking: that is, more specifically, to your perception of what you saw (or thought you saw).

Whether right or wrong in your assessment of what happened remains to be seen. However, until that time, little should be thought about what you saw, or thought you saw. This scenario illustrates how we can so easily tie our minds up in knots with the most meaningless things. In the meantime, if we don't let it go, we talk about it the rest of the day to whomever will lend a listening ear. The guy ticked you off and you don't even know him, or for that matter, you also might not really know what actually happened.

You have to make peace with your mind by remembering that the world needs less 'Alice Kravitzes' and more people who enjoy their lives enough to simply mind their own business. When one is happy with their own life, there's little time to be concerned about what anyone else is doing with theirs.

You can't save the entire world and all those in it. But you can have a wonderful life for you, your family, and those you love. That's well within your power to do. That is, as long as you don't drive yourself crazy thinking about why you shouldn't be able to achieve it. That's when excuses creep in and take the place of action! You have to work hard to keep the right perspective...that is, the one that allows you to maintain inner peace and happiness. Keep changing it until you get it right! The more you fall back on it, the more it will come to your rescue. Soon, it will be second nature to you. Not because you have remembered it, but because by then you'll have all the proof needed to know that your happiness <u>depends</u> on it.

Oh, by the way, the young man in the driveway wasn't trying to kick the child's toy at all. He was merely trying to remove gum from the bottom of his shoe. When he turned to the grass to slough the gum off his shoe, he hadn't noticed the toy in the path of his foot! Trying to miss it, he kicked way too hard.

Wisdom often comes with a price. Open your mind so your wisdom can grow. On the surface, it is difficult to understand that which is senseless. But when we understand that lessons learned define the paths to enlightenment, our hearts will beat with hope. – Charmainism

Look on the bright side of things by giving others the benefit of the doubt whenever it is easier for our peace of mind to do so. By honing your mastery of a more positive perspective, the little things that used to annoy you will cease to do so. Having the proper perspective allows you to tolerate more by being aggravated less.

Some people nearly cry at the sight of an invasive dandelion spoiling their otherwise impeccably green lawn. Yet a dandelion plucked by a sweet little child and presented as a gift can also bring tears, but of joy! ~ What a beautiful dandelion! ~ Perspective. Our happiness is all about perspective. – Charmainism

We have to learn from our experiences. Life is full of lessons that, if we're receptive to what we're being taught, will serve us well and keep us on guard from facilitating or perpetuating drama within our lives.

Even with the best of hearts and intentions, we can become caught up in something we know little about, but it's too late to hit the undo button! That's okay. Just know when to walk away and realize you've made a mistake. Apologize if need be. Don't forget to find the humor in things sometimes. When we crack ourselves up due to a "what-the-heck-was-I-thinking" moment…we leave all scars behind and get on with enjoying the day.

It's called immediate forgiveness. We forgive ourselves for our mistakes and we move on with a spring in our step and, sometimes, a chuckle beneath our breath!

We have to remember from whence we came. We were children who tried to live up to the expectations of our parents, just as our parents did for their parents. It's a life cycle that goes back a very long way, full of expectations from one generation to the next and more often each subsequent generation either being more lax about those expectations or more rigid.

It fluctuates back and forth from the extreme to a looser style as each generation continues in their chance at this journey called life. The truth is that it's a delicate balance and we often get it wrong; as all our children aren't the same, just as no two people are the same. Not all can be nurtured in exactly the same manner. Yet, if our expectations for them don't adapt to the individual, we may put the option of succumbing to failure in their minds.

In essence, it's what we do to ourselves as well. When we think we can't possibly live up to what we think our parents and elders want for us, we either do whatever it takes to show them and overachieve, or we give up and feel that we're a failure in life for the remainder of our days. Once we do that, we don't want our children to become a victim of the same cycle. It's then that we often expect far too much of our children and they, in turn, either begin to expect far too much of themselves or decide they'll never live up to your expectations and use that as an excuse to do nothing at all. They have rendered themselves a failure and will no doubt blame it all on you as their parent.

Just illustrating the HOW in all this can be very enlightening. When we understand how things happen and get so out of control, we become motivated to do something to counteract it. We can change our lives and the lives of those around us. We can make sense and peace of whatever happens in this life.

Not everyone has quite suddenly lost their only son and mother on the very same day and within the same hour, though nearly 1500 miles apart from one another, or five family members within five years for that matter, but somewhere some have surely lost *all* their family members on the same day. We have to keep things in perspective and be grateful for what could've been far worse. It's how I have to see things in order to keep my sanity and deal with life in its simplest of forms: life doesn't play favorites -- It's not personal and it's not a test: Life just IS.

It is my belief that it's no tribute to my beloved son if I harbor anger, resentment, or bitterness behind a wall of perpetual mourning and grief. No. He gave me, along with a myriad of others who knew and loved him; immense joy, and the world should know that. The blessing of having him in my life for thirty-one wonderful years instead of perhaps only a few hours is indeed worth every second of whatever happens during the course of that life – and life always, at some point, includes death. He could've died at birth, he didn't. For that I'm very, very grateful. I'm grateful for the thirty-one years we did have together. For that, I am immensely and intensely grateful.

Of course I'd love to have him back; and I often dream that I do. But upon waking up and realizing this daymare is real, I once again make peace with it. As long as there's a breath in me, he'll forever remain one of my greatest joys. And when I'm gone, others will live on and know that intense joy from what I've shared with them. Joy is a wonderful thing. Cherish it. It can soothe your deepest wounds.

Death will never negate the fact that I *have* a son. I'll <u>always</u> have a son. He may be gone from this earth, but he's not gone from my heart, nor is it accurate that he existed at a time and no more. And then we found out that with this most painful heartache, a miracle was on the horizon for us: Bj had a daughter we knew nothing about! We found out just a few days after his death. It was one of the greatest things to happen to my entire family. We all consider the blessing of our sweet granddaughter, Diana Jean, as well as her entire extended family that's embraced us all with open arms, to be a miracle! Our combined families continue to grow ever bigger and flourish with the enrichments of great love and genuine gratitude for the blessings that life brings our way.

There really are no words to express how dear Bj's daughter is to us. To think that our son was gone, forever, and then only a few days later find out that there's new life in our lives because of him. Out of death came life. His death brought forth the news and made us much easier to find. Our granddaughter's mother had been looking for us for nearly five years. As sailors, we weren't the easiest to track down if you'd no inside clues. The news of Bj's death hit his daughter's mother with the idea that perhaps he was still alive and decided to "disappear." She set out to prove that he was still alive.

In the meantime, the mother of our grandson, William III, was told by me to get over to the local social security office, where she could apply for benefits for her son. Bj was a hard worker throughout his adult life and would most certainly have benefits in place for Little Bj.

The paths of these two mothers crossed when they used the same social security office. One to prove that the father of their child was not deceased, and the other to apply for benefits. The story, of course, is much longer than this, but you get the idea. The rest is history…and a blessing! It's amazing how things happen.

My son's two children certainly attest to the fact that he still walks this earth. At the time, he simply walked in much smaller shoes. His children resemble him incredibly and their mannerisms and affinities are so eerily like their dad. They give me so much comfort and so much joy. Both Bj's children took part in the ceremony as Bj's artificial memorial reef was put into position off the coast of Ft. Lauderdale, Florida. It was as if they'd always been together. Diana has been a part of this family as if she's always been with us as well. In fact, even though only six years old at the time when we first came together, she said much the same thing when her great-grandmother remarked to her how nice it is to have even more grandparents. Diana replied, (pointing to Bill and me), "You mean them? I've <u>always</u> had them!"

My father called Diana, "Little Charmaine."

Life goes on my darlings. Life goes on.

I'll never forget the way my sister-cuzzes, Aunt Juanita's daughters, stepped in and took over everything to make sure things went as easily and smoothly as possible. My mother was like a second mother to them, just as their mother has always been to me. But what was organized by cousin Shannon as a "Celebration of Life" for Mother and Bj, was nothing short of amazing. Hundreds of people were there and it was just the type of gathering needed for healing. Family, by any name, is a wonderful thing. Friends who are like family make it even better. It was a "come as you are" gathering at my sweet sister-cuz Letitia and Bill's home. Letitia lost her husband, Bill, to cancer only three years later. He was a young and vibrant forty years old. Heartaches continue but all of our spirits rejoiced and celebrated the earthly life of Bill Anderson in April of 2008. He was a wonderful human being in every respect. He was so loved and is still so loved.

Life and death go on.

No life is without its share of heartache and loss. No life is without its share of ups and downs. But it is how we perceive such times of stress and strife that will ultimately determine whether or not our future is hopeful or hopeless; darkly clouded or full of sunshine. –
Charmainism

Changing our perception of how we see others and ourselves is at the heart of the art of finessing one's life. With the proper perspective in place, we can better rationalize that which used to give us pauses of grief and self-pity. As adults, we're smart enough to recognize that our manner of thinking dictates what we feel. Yes, I wrote "what" not "how." What we feel can be finessed into how we wish to feel. This is why perspective is so important to learn to master.

Great expectations can lead to great disappointments. For lasting success with finding happiness, expect less and strive more! –
Charmainism

In the book of life, we don't have to feel bad when the storyline is trying to indicate that we should feel bad. There's no absolute storyline for any of us. In the storybook of our life, we can change the sentences, the chapters, hey; we can even change the title if we wish. From "Great Expectations," we can rename it "No Expectations."

It's up to us to carve our path to happiness. When we're not on a path to anything we can be understandably confused and unfulfilled. Most of us just want a vision to live up to or a dream to ponder. We want to feel as if we're worthy of taking up space on this planet. If we can't be content with what we have and what we're doing, we feel as if we're failing. That's simply not the real state of affairs.

Rather, it's our way of thinking negatively that has us feeling the way we do! When perspective is tilted at an angle towards negativity, we're constantly exhausted at the very thought of being in the movie called "The Life of You." In fact, you may have already forgotten how to be yourself at all. You're the star of the picture!! What happened to the person who used to be you? Perhaps you're expecting too much from yourself and others. That kind of thinking is one of mankind's biggest pitfalls: Expecting too much and then being so disappointed when nothing manifests, that depression becomes your new best friend.

Mastering perspective is how we can change that defeatist's way of thinking. We've set ourselves up to fall far, far down!

Change the way you think and you will change the way you feel. –
Charmainism

When all is said and done, it will be your understanding of how it doesn't matter in the slightest why it took you so long to come to these realizations in order for you to have peace in your life. Did you really *waste* time actually waiting to do something positive for yourself? No. Once again, the proper perspective is key here. You have to get and keep the proper perspective on this matter just as importantly as anything else. Negativity is no longer an option. Positive thinking is the way onto the path of the Lighthouse of Inner Peace. Remember, your happiness depends on it.

Every second of every day that's transpired until this moment has made you who you are. Right now, you're the person who is willing to make the changes necessary to empower your life to drive on the road of inner peace and happiness. That's what I call progress! Real positive change of any degree is real progress. Be proud of being you and that you're still here reading this book and desiring real positive change!

Showering life with positivity will water your garden of optimism.
Flourish on! – Charmainism

Yes, they filled in all the blanks! It was their thinking that how could they possibly save face in front of the people present after being proved wrong by someone else?

Finesse your life by utilizing a positive perspective whenever possible. As long as your perspective is proper in that it assists you to remain calm and good-natured, then it's still considered positive. Doing so gets easier each and every time you employ it and reap the benefits. Using your mind as your best ally will change your life for the better. It's been your mind all along that's let you down, but now you know it can lift you up as well. You just have to remember to tap its strengths and starve its weaknesses.

And yes, you can most certainly do it. By now you know that anything is possible with the power of positive thinking and believing in yourself!

The most important lesson that will help you with all other lessons herein is that it's in your best interest to change. Yes, this has been repeated time and again and it's worth reading it over and over again. It's the foundation for the strongest motivator for change.

Not only to change, but to embrace your success immediately at the start of that revelation! This means immediate success! The decision to acknowledge the fact that one must change in order to become a happier person is the number one thing that will change your life for the better. Genuinely recognizing that there must be change, and then realizing that honing your new skills will produce a master gardener of your mind's atrium of inner peace, will keep you on the path to enlightenment.

As more changes take place, as to how things are viewed and put into a more positive perspective, you'll see that your mindset will change remarkably. Your perspective will progressively take huge leaps forward as you graduate to a life richer in every way.

Keeping things in the proper perspective reminds us that life is as much hardship as it is joyful. Treat each the same and you'll be forever happy. This type of positive mentality will help to make the changes so you can embrace every moment and make the best of each one. When you do so, nothing will keep you down. It can't, for your positive disposition is far too UP for anything or anyone to burst your bubble. You know you'll never come crashing down again. Those days are over. You're ready for final change and you're going to make your reality <u>the reality you want it to be</u>. You want to be happy and fulfilled, and so it shall be.

Here I am to remind you that there are a myriad of others who have gone through things far worse than most could ever imagine – and they too haven't lost their zest for life. Instead of digging holes for themselves and hiding, they're opening doors as others who know about their plight use their stories as inspiration. They serve to illustrate that there's a light at the end of all tunnels comprised of self-imposed darkness. Even though we may be inspired, some would love to have some sort of blueprint to help them find their way through to the light of a positive perspective.

We are all human and we all have our problems and issues. Some of us have merely learned to deal with life as it comes and have made peace with this earthly existence by embracing every moment of the challenges along the way. Challenges are just as positive as anything else if we choose not to see them as negative attacks on our peace of mind. It's not the challenge that does it as much as what we do to ourselves.

Do it for you because it is the key to you finding the path to inner peace and happiness.

A positive perspective is inherent to happiness because happiness begins within. Each day you have the choice to either roll with the punches or let the punches roll you over a cliff of emotional duress. Yesterday has come and gone. Forgive yourself, forgive others and embrace today! Life begins anew each and every day. – Charmainism

Neutralizing the Drama-rama

If we aren't unnecessarily hard on ourselves, we tend not to be hard on others. If we can forgive ourselves for making errors in judgment, we can forgive others for doing the same. When we make a mistake, we learn from it and we move on. When we're able to do that, it becomes second nature to extend others the same courtesy.

This is how we control the emotional tempo of our lives. No one has to be overwhelmed because of constant conflict. Conflict isn't really there as much as one might fathom. Remember, it takes two to butt heads. If one is forever wanting to be confrontational and the intended target is adept at keeping the matter in the proper perspective (i.e., This guy is always trying to get a rise out of people. How sad for him.), then it becomes easy to ignore the bait.

We cannot waste precious time trying to make sense with those who have made it clear they are addicted to nonsense. – Charmainism

Had you bit, what good would it do? So diffusing drama before it starts is an excellent choice in order to keep your peace of mind intact. No need to be upset about it, you proved you're mature enough to understand that some are at a handicap when it comes to the art of communication and curbing childhood hang-ups. You've grown past all that. Prove it each and every day by keeping the proper perspective when it comes to people who are addicted to drama.

For some, it's their lot in life. Or so they think. They're so used to having their emotional gauge on full blast 24/7. If things went smoothly, they wouldn't know what to do.

They too can learn there are viable options other than continuing life at the frenzied pace that constant mayhem fosters. The person who lives with drama as their life force has given up trying to change their life because they blame others as the cause for the drama.

But, as said before, usually, the one who has all the drama in their life is the common denominator sitting in the middle of a never-ending cycle of drama-rama. They're the star of the drama-rama show and don't even know it.

So their perspective must change! It's the perspective that their life is full of dysfunctional, confrontational people and therefore it will be automatically infused with drama day in and day out that has them blind to the real problem.

The real problem is that their belief that they have no other choice than to fight back against that which is dysfunctional has been allowing drama to continue in their life. They have become as dysfunctional as everyone else and are the last to know. They too are perpetuating the ridiculousness of dysfunction. It's the undoing of all involved.

Somewhere along the way, the truly fed up person decides their life would be far more rewarding and satisfying if they could figure out a way to deal with the dysfunctional people in their lives. Some are family members, some are co-workers, others are long-time friends of the family, etc. etc. It never matters who they are. How one deals with the issue isn't dependent on whom you're dealing with; it only has to do with how you become adept at changing the way you think!

This is how I coped with things early in my life. Big things like making myself understand just why my mother forced me to resign as Class President of my Freshman high school class. It was a bit disturbing, as she knew I was running for it. Daddy had helped me print up flyers for it, and she knew that too...but I think perhaps she thought I wouldn't win. But I did win. My acceptance speech was full of hopes and promises. The Class of '74 was off and running with ideas and the like. And then Mother's *other* shoe dropped. She demanded I resign.

Besides having meetings that would potentially interfere with my bible studies, she kept saying, "Our place is not to be a part of this world. This world will be replaced by the New Order." I lived in her house, Dad was no help because what could he say? Mom's religious convictions were very powerful. I'd no choice but to resign. I also thought that it was perhaps pressure from the Fellowship in the Congregation. She may have wanted to look the other way, but some members of the Congregation probably brought it to the attention of the Elders and they were then called to act.

That actually makes much more sense to me.

It was very disheartening for those who'd been counting on me. My friends understood, they were a very cool and "with it" group. They have remained my dear friends to this day. I felt the worst about my dear and precious high school counselor, Guy Anderson, who nearly worried himself sick over what would become of me. I'm sure there were many others like him who couldn't understand how a young girl with so much promise could suddenly do a total about face from everything she'd planned and seemingly dive off the deep end of a cliff down onto the rocks. Things were piling up and my life was beginning to spell disaster with a capital D.

This wasn't supposed to happen to me. Not the girl of so much confidence and hope, the girl with the disposition like the rays of the sun – the girl who could find her way through anything.

Guy and I've remained dear friends all these years. I try to get by and see him and his sweet wife, Maryann, whenever I'm back in "The Patch" (what locals call Springfield: "The Patch" is shortened from "Springpatch."). He understands now that what I had to do was the right thing for me at the time. That also included marrying so young. No doubt, very few would've given our marriage a spit of a chance. And I couldn't have blamed them if they did. But, just as I knew then, when I told my father that Bill is the man I'll be with for the rest of my life…these are the things that, in time, are proven to all.

I love Guy very much and always will. He will always have a special place in my heart. He means a lot to me to this very day.

This is looking at changing one's perspective to keep growing in a positive manner. The same goes for changing one's perspective in order to deal with the people and situations that are negative in nature. We adapt our way of thinking in order to protect ourselves from havoc. One need only to change their thought processes by being more creative with how they look at things: perspective.

We change for the better when we embrace the chance

to improve over our past. – Charmainism

Most grownups are still the little children they once were long ago. Not much changes about one's personality between those times. For most, you can still see behind the eyes, that kid of ten who now, at sixty, wears bigger and fancier shoes. Deep inside, he's still the little kid you knew so long ago.

When adults become frustrated, just as they did in their childhood, if they haven't learned by now how to handle their emotions, then they sometimes will revert to the temper tantrums of their youth. Many don't know what else to do.

By keeping that thought in mind, the temptation to fuel the fires of frustration wane quickly. There's no reason to give in to such temptation, because there will never be a productive result by doing so. Therefore, you find it in your best interest to take the high road and remain neutral to the disdain. There's no need to be defensively reactive. You aren't about to stoop back down to third grade for any of it. No need to express it, just let your actions lead by example.

Keeping things in the proper perspective
is imperative to a happier life. – Charmainism

This is how one's life can be rid of taking simple situations and constantly making them so complex that they become quagmires of frustration. You certainly know by now, frustration is the fuel that keeps the fires of being overwhelmed blazing in your life. Such are the fires that suffocate all the good air out of your life. It's what wreaks havoc in just about everything you do. You find yourself muttering, "Why does everything have to be so complicated?" time and time again. It doesn't have to be at all. You merely have to make peace with it as you put it in the proper perspective.

Most times it's because we feel we're entitled to be negative when things don't go our way. We don't do this as a conscious reaction, but the fact is that we've been raised on a diet of moodiness and that exercising our right to announce how we feel is God-given! This "right" gets magnified exponentially as the reasons for exercising the right increases. Such as when we've lost someone close to us due to death, or when we've endured some other major traumatic event that's changed our lives and dwindled our faith in all hopes that this world is a truly good place. We talk ourselves into acting the part of the downtrodden, and it's not pretty. We need to make peace with whatever it is and move on.

If we don't make peace with these types of events that occur, we become the dour and unhappy person we used to be. This is where a positive perspective helps us make peace with the things that aren't under our control. We can't change anything by being cynical. Being cynical poisons our desire to become a more positive human being. We can neutralize negativity by personifying positivity.

This is how we no longer become unapproachable as we used to be when we didn't feel like being around those who are jovial and in a good mood when we aren't. Before knowing the art of employing a positive perspective, we didn't want to rain on the parade of others. Our mind was drunk with sorrow and soaked to the core with it. We used to wear it on our sleeves.

In that state, you realized that a lot of people are pessimistic and negative. You even tried to tell them about your troubles and they turned the tables on you and began to start tearing into the myriad of black clouds covering their own lives. Thinking back on it, you thought to yourself, "Was I like that?"

If you find yourself surrounded by those who are miserable, take a good look in the mirror. We reap what we sow! – Charmainism

Things that happen in this world don't just happen to us, they happen to us all. We must keep things in the proper perspective. Before the urge to go crying to someone about all the downturns in your life, you'd better take a really good look at all that's been happening in the lives of others. Don't let your selfishness blind you to the woes of others.

We're all in the same boat — there are just those who rarely or never complain and there are those who constantly and loudly complain. Those who don't complain still have problems and issues, ones just like those who do complain. The difference is that those who don't complain or wear their woes on their sleeves know that their problems are no more important than anyone else's.

It may come to mind when reading all this that perhaps you've been a bit too judgmental when dealing with others. Perhaps you see that maybe people haven't gotten harder to get along with, but with all you've faced and are having difficulty coming to grips with, part of the negative change in your own world has been partially due to your negativity towards others.

You may have been too deep in your own pit to see that others around you have been carrying on despite the similar hardships in their lives. They're getting along just fine and you're still treading water, screaming at the top of your lungs for someone to save you. Now you realize they must have tuned you out a while ago. They have their own problems to deal with!

But that's okay! It happens to the best of us. We all can get a bit selfish and assume others have it better than we do. Life is dealing with life. Life encompasses everything that's alive, thriving, wonderful, and beautiful -- as well as all that which becomes death, stagnant, horrible, and ugly. It's all there each and every day. But how we choose to view what we see is our own perspective, and it's that perspective that's at the helm of our ship called life!

In my zest for life, I never forget that there are those going through troubling times. We all are, in one way or another. Our age of innocence long past, the reality that we're in a zone where we lose more than we gain is evident. We just have to appreciate the gains so much more and neutralize the losses with the joy that we are still here to absorb them. So many of our loved ones aren't. We live reaching for the fullest because they no longer can. Stay positive and strong! – Charmainism

Forgiveness

To err is human, but to readily admit it is angelic. – Charmainism

Learning to forgive is one of life's greatest and most empowering freedoms. When we no longer harbor disdain or ill will against another, we allow ourselves to be released from their negative hold on us. Yes! Holding grudges is actually holding yourself hostage to resentment and anger. It never really hurts the one who's wronged us...it only hurts ourselves by serving to hold us back from attaining a positive disposition.

Watched Betty White's "Off Their Rockers" last night. Funny stuff, for sure! Couldn't help but notice how much patience others display while being pranked. Spectators had smiles on their faces and their day brightened by the antics of these zany senior citizens. I keep thinking how much we can learn about human behavior from this show. With just a semblance of a sense of humor, a seemingly inappropriate action by another doesn't automatically produce a knee-jerk, negative reaction. It is our preconceived notions and assumptions that do that. It happens when we do not give others the benefit of the doubt. – Charmainism

Some of the things that occur on "Off Their Rockers," would cause great disdain and even violence if the offender wasn't a senior citizen. Since they're being viewed as relatively harmless and having earned the right to be a bit quirky in their advanced years, people don't take their antics as being wholly offensive.

There's a great lesson here in that we're often far too judgmental for our own good. We look at someone and quickly assess where we think they should line up on the scale of maturity and social adeptness. This is why we laugh when small children do the silliest of things but would be appalled if a young teen (whom we think should know better) did the same.

We have to keep the scales of how we perceive others in a better, more positive, balance. When we think we've the right to protest, even though the outcome would be no different (and never mind that we probably had no business intervening in the first place), we sometimes still feel we need to say something. It's as if we feel compelled to accept the challenge of putting someone "in their place." That means we first are making the assumption that we know best just what, exactly, "their place" is.

Perhaps it's wiser and better to learn to step back first and ask ourselves whether or not the effort to intervene has a meaningful purpose and will it have a lasting, favorable effect on all those involved. And yes, that includes you!

For those who feel their disdain for others has the backing of the Highest, please remember it is not our place to judge. Therefore, the saying and concept to "LET GO and LET GOD" is incredibly appropriate to neutralize so many of our differences...as it is more than sufficient for understanding the merit and virtue of 'letting go.

It is my belief that perhaps the biggest test we face, as far as religious beliefs, is can we live up to being simultaneously tolerant and loving of our fellowman throughout whatever transpires. Those who continue to be stoically "holier than thou," also need the reminder of the virtue of humility. Until all who profess to follow a higher power actually "LET GO and LET GOD," religious differences will continue to be used as an excuse to wreak havoc on this earth. It shall be our own undoing. – Charmainism

Learning the benefit of forgiveness is often the bridge that turns an uncertain path into one of certainty. Because when we let go of the ill will we harbor, it no longer suffocates our thought processes with negativity. It's done. Over. Fini. Now that the issue is finished, we can get on with the enjoyment of life! You'll never truly understand how much frustration has to do with a less than happy life until you overcome all forms of it. Many fail to see how refusal to forgive is one of the biggest frustrations of all. This is a promise: when you begin to truly forgive, you'll find inner peace. It's truly a freedom easily understood and appreciated once it's put into practice and becomes a way of life.

When one turns their life around in a positive fashion, there is often the tendency to replace former negative behaviors with disdain towards others who have not made similar changes. That is akin to taking one step forward and two steps back. Project your self-improvements by example and humility. Love others despite their faults and love will lead the way. Inner peace will keep you there. – Charmainism

When you realize it's in your own best interest to choose to forgive and be negative-free, then the life that is positive and happy will find you. Most suffocating worries, concerns, and fears are made up of that which we embellish to the point that our negative reactions make them seem worthy of monopolizing our lives and blocking the path to happiness.

We have the right to refrain from partaking in that which we have no desire to do (with the exception of death and taxes, of course!). Seriously, thinking of this reminds me how much some need the nudge to remember that the rights of others aren't something we have the right to impede; not when they are personal decisions that are of no detriment to rights of our own. – Charmainism

Seeing forgiveness as a forward move and going on about the business of our own happiness, despite what others may have done, is a great lesson for the person who's wronged us. They'll see they have no control over our happiness. And even if they don't see, it's of no concern to us because we're doing what's right for our own peace of mind. Makes them wonder how they can possibly be more like YOU!

We all teach lessons to others whether we realize it or not. Instead of thinking endlessly about how to 'get even,' do what's far better and more positive: show yourself that the person has absolutely no control over your life in any way, shape, or form. What they do or don't do has no affect on you. This renders all wannabe spoilsports totally powerless against you. They're no longer a factor regarding your level of happiness or your peace of mind.

And nor should you ever be a spoilsport towards others!

Know to learn to accept the things you can't change. There's no sense in getting upset or frustrated when doing so won't produce a better outcome. Therefore, a change in perspective will do us a world of good – OUR world of good!

And do not be afraid to correct your mistakes. You'll learn from your errors and grow from them if only you let them soak in and not create an embarrassment for you. You're entitled to make a mistake: you're human! Cut your losses and rack up the gains by correcting what you've done, make apologies if necessary, and then let it go. Forgive yourself, forgive others, and simply move on

No more looking back at past decisions that went wrong and using those mistakes as reason to stop trying! The enjoyment of your present and future are counting on you to make the changes necessary for you to live your life to the fullest!

Don't worry. With worry, we drag our feet hashing and rehashing hypothetical scenarios, wasting valuable time that would be better spent making the changes we know we must make.

Just DO what it is you know you must do, and needless worry shall be no more.

Worry is the fog that overshadows the sun of positive thinking. Waste not a moment on worry. – Charmainism

You must forgive yourself and clear the path for your progression to becoming a Peacemaker. Forgiveness starts with you! It's so much easier to extend the same courtesy of forgiveness to others when you're no longer harboring disappointment and resentment against yourself.

As painful as looking deep inside yourself may sometimes seem, it's important to face such truths because inner peace comes with having a better understanding of yourself. It's all within you and always has been. It's simply that the mind fears change and possible failure. Changing your perspective and the way you think is the most important way to defeat all that stands in your way.

How's your "whether?" Indecisiveness can drive even the most sane person crazy. Make a decision based on the best information available at the time and then just DO IT. If no decision is made, anguishing over the "whether" is not productive to good mental health. We all are just intelligent enough to drive ourselves nuts. Brighten up your "whether" by first deciding to be decisive and to not worry over that which we cannot control. Take a tip from Alfred E. Neuman: "What? Me, worry?" – Charmainism

When you forgive yourself you're saying you trust yourself to captain your ship of life. It is in no better hands than your own. It's your responsibility and you're up to the task at hand. It's a challenge for which you're ready. Challenge is what life is! When you begin to feel this way, that's when the world immediately becomes a much better place because your personal world has found the balance it was lacking. By forgiving yourself and letting go of the past, you can regain that trust in yourself and make solid decisions based on rational thinking rather than succumbing to erratic emotional reactions. When you make that peace with yourself, you'll find inner peace and be able to do anything positive your heart desires.

You can then get on with your happy life by dealing gracefully with the same situations that previously served to shred any dreams you ever had about having a life fabric made from the threads of happiness. You'll navigate your life with the deftness and skill of a world-class driver. No longer will you drive as a wreck-in-the-making -- eventually spiraling out-of-control over the cliff of despair. Our health is far more in our own hands than most of us realize. We just have to learn how to utilize all the bells and whistles of our life's vehicle. We can do more for ourselves with prevention than anything else! It's something I'm still learning: how to take better care of myself.

Forgiveness is the foundation for freedom from inner turmoil – inner peace is the bell tower. – Charmainism

The fog of futility is lifting! Soon you'll emerge into the light of living life to the fullest. Just surviving day-to-day is not living. Enjoying life is living. Living free of fears and frustrations is living. Feeling inner peace is living. You're learning a philosophy that will bring out the Peacemaker in you.

Loving peace and how your manner dissuades others who are negative without rendering them hostile is a beautiful thing! In fact, your new demeanor will serve to attract others who are also holders of positive and peaceful dispositions. This is how Peacemakers will gain strength in numbers – one Peacemaker at a time.

What is the difference between living and existing? When the ruts seem to be more routine than the hair-flying-in-the-wind-with-the-top-down times...then it's time to make some changes. You rearrange your furniture when it gets mundane, why not do the same with your routines! Change it up, mix it up, and pour yourself into a nice tall glass of fresher tasting LIFE! – Charmainism

Find forgiveness as you allow compassion to begin deep inside your heart and show yourself the ultimate in compassion and understanding: forgive yourself now, forgive all others, and let your light shine through.

It is never necessary to tear down someone in order to build up someone else. Instead, look to kindness and compassion: it's free, easy, and completely positive in nature. It also does a mind and body a whole lot of GOOD! The bright side of life really does exist, one need only to stay out of the shade of selfishness. – Charmainism

The beacon of hope is shining through!

Chapter Seven: Finessing Your Life with Positive Indifference

Positive Indifference – The Fine Art of Letting Go

When someone broadcasts to you from a Hard Rock Channel, choose to respond from Smooth Jazz 101. Use finesse in life to neutralize conflict and maintain happiness. – Charmainism

Drunkenness tears down the walls of inhibition and allows the mind and body to be set free. My father yearned for that kind of freedom and a good bottle of liquor could restore his faith in its existence. To the point that, when inebriated, my father's tendency to go off on a soliloquy was something out of the likes of Shakespeare's "Henry VI, Part 3." That play has the longest soliloquy of all Shakespeare's plays. My father could beat all those records, no doubt about it. LOL

But it wasn't just because of the liquor that my father would rant on and on about this or that, but it was his tendency to do so by nature. Honestly. The liquor just brought it to new heights of ridiculous babble. Sometimes the babble could get more sinister, depending on the mood of my father before he overindulged.

What I'm getting at is that my father had a tendency to rant about something even when completely sober. If there was something he'd told one of us kids to do and we forgot to do it, oh boy…if Mother was in a bad mood and had been harping on Daddy to get on us about what we forgot to do…then we were in for it. For the long haul!

Depending on how much Daddy wanted to erase all the harping Mother had put upon him, you could triple that and that's what we got. And I do mean harping! Actually, it was worse than harping. It was a whipping with words instead of the big black belt with the raised fake jewel stones in it. Daddy would whip you up and down with words. He would go on from breakfast throughout everything he was doing that day and be throwing words at us upside our heads and down our backsides. It was brutal.

"You know what happened to the kid who fixed his father a hamburger and put ketchup on it? Now, mind you, the father told his son at least thirteen times over the last five years, that he dislikes ketchup and to not put ketchup on his hamburger. He told his son to put mustard or mayonnaise on it, but never, ever put ketchup on it."

We knew this story because we'd heard it at last thirteen times ourselves.

Daddy continued telling the story as he went about his business doing chores around the house. When Daddy told a story, it was so melodramatic you could see every character...it was like listening to a radio show. Now the thing here is that no matter where you were in the house or on our block in the neighborhood...you could hear Dad bellowing out this barrage of punishment. To some, it probably sounded like he was frustrated about something and talking to himself. But noooo, he was talking to whomever it was who was perched upon the stool in the kitchen and couldn't move.

As Daddy walked out of the kitchen, you could still hear him as his voice would get farther away and you could get a moment of peace. But here comes his voice again, gaining strength and you knew he'd be in the kitchen at any moment with his voice at full volume and the story not missing a single word in the process: "And then that ungrateful little snot of a son of his fixed his father a hamburger. And what did he do? Did he listen to his father's instructions and obey them? No. He put ketchup on the hamburger. Not mustard, not mayonnaise, just ketchup."

Oh boy. Time to gulp.

"And the father calmly got up from the table and stabbed that little lazy ingrate of a bastard with a fork...right in the jugular. As his son lay on the kitchen floor, bleeding to death, the father stood over him and said, "Goodbye, son. Hello, no more ketchup!"

Now that's about the time when Mom would step in and tell Daddy that was enough already. It was a routine that went the same nearly each and every time; only the stories were different. They would all start as meaningful lessons of how one should do as their parents told them. Then, as the rant got louder, the lessons were embellished with much more violent endings until they got to the point where Mother would step in and make him stop. It was our warning that we could be strangled in our sleep if we caused too much trouble around the house. But we all knew he didn't really mean any of it.

It was the same with Mother sometimes. I recall being a very young child and running into the house after cutting my finger on something in the yard. It was bleeding. I'm sure it wasn't any big deal at all, but it was the first time in my recollection that I'd experienced blood coming from a wound.

When Mother told me to hush, that it was nothing, I said, "But it hurts."

Mom says to me, "Now, if your hand was cut off then your finger wouldn't be hurting, would it?"

I didn't complain anymore. I got the memo! LOL

The funny thing is that this is how we grew up. I was never afraid of their parenting methods, not really. I just would've preferred it if Daddy wouldn't have gotten so upset just because Mother was upset with we children. That, in turn, fueled his frustration as he felt like he was being punished too! Mother was making it seem that he wasn't doing his job parenting us properly. He wasn't a good disciplinarian, she was saying, because he wasn't around as much as he should be. It was always carried out this way and we all were used to it. Very little of it was really about the wrongdoings of we children at all, but more about how displeased my mother was with my father. It gives new meaning to the adage, "If Momma's not happy, ain't nobody happy!" In our household, that was the truth!

And so then he had to make it up to her. He had to prove that he was a good father and could get his children to behave and follow instructions. So he took the shortest path to get the job done. And it worked. None of we children were ever in trouble with the law or fell victim to alcohol or drug abuse.

When these tirades were going on, I learned to tune Daddy out – that is, unless I was the one who was supposed to be hearing it! When that was the case, the person being punished couldn't move from the spot on the stool or chair, which was the basic target of the verbal thrashing. Daddy would then "loud talk" as he walked around the target area as if you weren't even sitting there. Never was ever anything actually said about you personally, instead, everything was said in parables of sorts. Except these parables weren't biblical, they were more akin to something out of the likes of the <u>Creep Show</u> comic books. Even though he never had to look you in the eye as he loud talked, he made sure that you (and Mother, of course) could hear each and every word hurled your way like javelins of syllables.

Daddy couldn't let it go until Mother said it was okay to let it go. Even when she did say it was enough, Daddy couldn't just abruptly cut it off. Oh no. For by that time, he'd gotten himself so worked up about being forced to get this damn worked up!! Once he got started on his rantings, it was very difficult for Mom to get him to stop.

Mother would have to keep saying it, until she added another sentence at the end: "Smitty! I said that's enough already. *Why don't you go shoot some pool?*"

That would do it. Yup. Each and every single time.

Whew!

And then everybody could be happy again. Or pretend to be. It depends on whom you ask.

LOL

That was my father and I loved him, but wow…some of the things that went on in our house were something else. I'm sure to an outsider, they would be appalled. For we kids, it was Smith Family Usual. Ha!

To some extent, we all know people who are capable of ranting like this, albeit on a much less scale of dramatic flair. I'm thinking of the ones who tend to rant about things to keep them stirred up from settling on the bottom so they can be over and done with. They just keep on and on about it. They keep jabbing and nagging. They beat that dead horse until it resurrects itself and begs to please be put down permanently!

People such as that like drama. They relish conflict. They like confrontation. They revel in mayhem.

Becoming a peacemaker means you must be adept at utilizing methods to neutralize these types of people when they come into your life or come over to tea!

Throughout the book, there are a number of times where I alluded to a technique I've coined as (the art of unobtrusive), "Positive Indifference." You've been becoming familiar with it even if you weren't aware of it. So much so, that by now, you should have an excellent idea of just how this most useful concept can help keep you calm, levelheaded, sensible and grounded when dealing with people who are mongers of drama.

Positive Indifference is like always having cool waters at hand for dousing hot tempers. It's a neutralizer that everyone desiring a calmer life should practice and perfect. The reward is an inner peace that's attainable and maintainable! It's what's necessary to keep one's cool under the most stressful of circumstances. It's a different perspective along with a finesse that serves to keep all involved from feeding negative energy back and forth.

We use Positive Indifference to neutralize them when they're on a "rant" (er, mission) of wanting to stir the pot and make bubble, bubble, toil and trouble for all! Others in your circle of friends will learn by your lead. Positive Indifference works!

Pot-stirrers are the ones that forever remind you of what she said or he said or whomever-it-was-that-said that thing about you that was mean and ugly and cruel. - Charmainism

Pot stirrers, along with drama queens, magnets to mayhem, and gossipmongers will simply have to find something else to do when in your company. Positive Indifference is the way to handle all those who thrive on pitting those in their circle against each other. They love the attention they get from it and the resulting chaos it creates. Their need for purpose and importance by being a drama facilitator will be totally lost on you, and soon they'll know it!

Those forever stirring the pot are the ones that probably cause more nonsensical frustration than anyone else. It seems they're always biting at the bit for someone to misspeak about anything and then, with distortion and exaggeration, use that to expose glaring errors in the character of others. (Seems it's always the ones with the least character who want to bring others down to their place in the levy!) It's their self-appointed job in life to point out the inconsistencies and failures of others. And you've tired of their petty, trifling ways long ago.

Whether a family member or a person with whom you work, we all know people who are certified pot stirrers! They're the hosts of the Drama-Rama Shows.

We don't realize that we feed into their frenzy for fodder by allowing our reactions to butt heads with their actions. What comes from that is a collision of minds that will never see eye to eye on much of anything. Therefore, there really is no point in trying to make sense of the pot stirrer's nonsense.

Pot stirrers already know what they do! They know they're the masters of self-serving, gross exaggeration and innuendo. They don't, however, recognize the difference between an outright libelous untruth and slight embellishment to color a harmless but humorous story. Such is their usual modus operandi. They make you laugh with their outrageous stories. Before you know it, you're laughing at the others whom the pot stirrers talk about so disparagingly. The pot stirrers will be the first to let those 'others' know you were laughing at them!

And so it begins.

When you do find out what has happened, you're so angry you can hardly contain yourself. Even if you're well aware of the nonsensical ways of the pot stirrers, you still find yourself having to say something in response to what they have done. Putting the person in his or her place, you think, is important to clear the air on the issue.

The reality is that doing so probably won't do any real good at all. It certainly won't change the ways of the pot stirrer – and ultimately it won't make you feel any better about what happened; nor will it end the drama of the matter. Instead of getting the person's goat, your emotions will more than likely get the better of you. This is when it's best to accept a lesson learned and simply move on, albeit with one less pot stirrer in your life.

When our hearts truly embrace the blessings of giving; we aren't haunted by afterthoughts of whether we gave in or gave up. – Charmainism

Controlling our emotions, and thus taking control of our lives by doing the things we should be doing to make ourselves more contented individuals, is the only way we can ever really overcome the frustration we feel when dealing with those who are irritants. Knowing we have a manner in place by which to lessen the friction of irritation will ultimately give us power over the frustrations caused by it.

Positive Indifference, just like happiness, has to come from <u>within</u>.

Daddy was an outstanding billiards player. He taught me how to shoot pool with some of the best players in our town. "Your girl's got skills, Mr. Smitty," the guys would say. Oh, what fun we had! Those were super great times being out with my father. And you know what? I smoked my first joint with my father – or he thought it was my *first* joint. LOL "Skunion" was what he called it and it was nothing like what I'd ever had. It was the REAL DEAL. Daddy had been smoking marijuana ever since he was in C.C. Camp during his Navy days during WW II. That was the real stuff...the stuff that headaches and hangovers were made of! Well, that and those killer Rum and Cokes.

Daddy and I'd sometimes come rolling into the house in the wee hours of the morning looking for some leftover somethings..."Ooh," we'd say as we stood peering into the refrigerator, "there's collard greens and ham hocks," and then we'd hear Mom coming down the stairs. She had a good sniffer, my Mother.

Long inhale with her arms akimbo...then, "Hmm," she'd say, "so you been slummin' with your Daddy, huh?"

Mom would then follow up that comment with...wait for it...it's coming...wait for it...

"And *where's* Bill Ladd?"

LOL

Mother was <u>always</u> looking out for my husband.

I'd usually chuckle a bit and say, "He's at home in bed asleep. I'll tell him you asked about him."

Then Mom would say, "And that's where *you* should be, girl!"

It was always the same every time. She wasn't angry; as she knew by then that I was going to be a Daddy's girl forever and a day. I think even though she never really meant to let on to it, she actually liked it that I was much like my father. Perhaps she was just feeling sorry for my husband. Ha! Then I'd jovially tell her to lighten up and would embrace Mother with a great big hug.

Mom always loved my hugs, though she'd have to add something to say when they were "so cuddly"…(which was a signifying way of noticing I was once again gaining too much weight). Once the threat of anorexia was over, it was about five years after the birth of my son that the digs about my weight began. I thought to myself, I'm no longer starving myself to death, but I still can't win when it comes to Mom.

Look, if Daddy couldn't please her after all these years, I certainly was not going to join in that losing conquest.

My mother was forever stirring that pot! I used to say that she was forever "signifying" about something! LOL Mom wouldn't come right out and say exactly what was on her mind, she'd hint at it…or "signify." It was funny, though, most of the time, but I'll admit to sometimes thinking she would go out of her way quite a bit to get a rise out of Bill. I suppose that was his invitation to think he could put me in my place. I think Mom wanted to make sure I had someone strong enough to control me. But Daddy knew there was no such thing. And deep down, so did my Mother. And, more importantly, so did Bill. LOL

But what there _was_, I think both my parents quickly agreed on: when it came to me and that man Bill Ladd: it _was_ true love.

Both my parents knew that the love Bill and I had for one another would keep me safe.

But Mother, of course, *always* had to get in the last word anyway. Ha!

We can't allow others to hit our frustration button whenever they feel the need to get their "drama fix." We never want to be their "go to" person for such!

So we must learn to control our emotions and not allow frustration to drive our lives into the wrong lane. We want to enjoy the smooth road of inner peace and happiness instead of head-on into the lane of drama, confusion, frustration, and self-destruction. Positive Indifference is the way to mastering such control.

So do you think you understand the concept of Positive Indifference? No, it hasn't been fully explained to you just yet, but you should have a notion or two of what it is in theory and practice. Think about it a bit if you must.

Controlling Emotions with Positive Indifference

Positive Indifference is the game changer that will change how you interact with even the most ridiculous and nonsensical people. When you master this art, you'll have the finesse your peacemaking skills were lacking. Positive Indifference is the icing on the cake...the pièce de résistance of the "Shwy" Philosophy. It's what caps it all off and makes everything you've learned come into clarity with sharp vision focused on peace.

Young children have their little fits because they can't always verbalize their frustrations. Instead, they use actions to gain the attention so that others can attend to their needs. It goes without saying that adults can verbalize their frustrations, but their mental capacity is better utilized by learning to diffuse such behaviors. We can talk things out without allowing frustration to turn us into ranting, raving, out-of-control and unreasonable big babies.

Positive Indifference changes everything. It's the game changer you want to have! This means when someone asks, "You sure seem happier these days. What's changed?" The answer of your former self may have possibly been something like, "I just had to let that hate go. I can't stand my nosy mother-in-law, but I've decided I'm not going to let her make me unhappy and I'm not going to let her keep ruining my life."

See the problem in that response? Even though the person has decided to be happier, there remains the need for a scapegoat for the time previously wasted while going around and around with the person who'd become the nemesis. The declaration made is real proof of the harboring of anger and resentment against her mother-in-law. She's made changes for the wrong reasons. She's tired of the situation and has given up any hope of winning the ongoing battle. She therefore feels defeated rather than empowered. The reason for this is because she hasn't quite understood that the finesse of using Positive Indifference has to be based on the fact that doing so is in your own best interest. It's not about *anything* else! It's about ensuring *your* peace of mind.

Situations such as this can be finessed so they never reach the level of frustration this person has encountered with her mother-in-law. When executed properly, deciding to take the high road is an empowering choice.

Attempting to make amends is totally negated by doing it out loud. Yes, "out loud." Meaning we'll have better success when putting forth the olive branch in a discrete fashion. Such is a play of finesse! It's not necessary that anyone else in your circle know that you have chosen to finesse a situation. Doing so makes our lives simpler and easier in the process. Finesse, in itself, is a classy play. Classy doesn't need outside approval; classy knows the value of a stealth move! There are no smirks because smirks aren't classy -- smirks give you away by tapping the person on the shoulder and announcing, "I got you!"

In rainy 'whether,' classy chooses to play in the freedom of the sand instead of the bondage of the mud. – Charmainism

We can easily decide not to escalate a situation by simply refusing the bait offered up by another. We can opt to let it go and move on. The winners of duels of the mind aren't always the ones who got off the first shot or the last. On the contrary, they usually are the ones who found a way to diffuse the entire ordeal, whether the others involved realized it or not. Nothing matters except the situation is resolved in a manner that allows you to walk away without resentment or animosity.

So yes! It's an ultra classy play to take the high road! We choose not to waste precious time engaging in anything that erodes our self-respect and peace of mind. The more we handle situations in this most positive manner; the more it becomes second nature for us to do so. Our happiness is the proof that it's the right thing for us to do, and we become the happier, and better, for it!

We have to realize, once and for all, that in order to make necessary changes, we need not muster up anger, resentment, and bitterness as motivation to change. We need not ever feel fed up in order to find the strength for change. That's terribly self-defeating, as positive energy is never born from negativity.

Positive energy is always the easier choice. It comes with no regret. – Charmainism

Learning the art of using finesse and Positive Indifference for your own good is so valuable in many situations that can occur anywhere at any time: Let's say you and a friend are at a restaurant and the service is quite slow. The server is inattentive and not very sharp, but the beer is ice cold and the conversation is lively. So what to do? You could get vocal about the poor service and perhaps ruin the evening of your party and others in the establishment; or you could spend your evening complaining about the service to those at your table and listen to that turn into whining about other disappointments in life; or you can take a third choice: (unobtrusive) Positive Indifference.

You let it go as you realize you shouldn't be in that big of a hurry and eventually you'll get the food you've ordered. It's a Sports Bar! Deciding to be a "good sport" at a Sports Bar isn't a bad thing at all. Your blood pressure lowers and you relax. Now you're having a wonderful time again even though your food still hasn't been brought to the table. It's okay! In this scenario, it had to be realized that the server isn't slow on purpose. The server isn't singling anyone out to torment with mediocre or bad table service. They just need to be in a different profession (and we don't need to tell them that either). So we accept that and don't entertain silly thoughts of getting "even" or making it "right" in order to have a good time with the great company and conversation with our friends! We simply accept that it's a very busy night for all the servers and decide to have a good time despite the lack of better table service!

Indifference is something not commonly taught to children by most parents as an option because being indifferent is more often perceived as a negative. As if you don't care one way or another about something because you're callous towards it. Well, that's why I've coined this methodology as *"positive"* indifference. It's true that you're "indifferent," in the general sense of the word, but in the "positive" sense that when you say you don't really care either way, you mean it in a very "good" way – meaning it's the best thing for you to do at the time in order to keep the peace. And when it's decided upon, there are no lingering after effects of disappointment, resentment, bitterness, anger, or any other negative emotion as a reason for you to have made the decision.

Somewhere along the way, people got to thinking that they must be angry about something to "not care" whether someone makes this or that decision. It's like the saying "whatever." When it began, it wasn't really meant to be a negative comment. "Whatever" meant more of "Okay...whatever you say." Because most of the time when it's used, the person has run out of something else to say but wants the conversation to end.

To me, it's much better to say nothing more. Not a "Whatever," not a nothing. Just let it go. "Whatever," actually, is a pot-stirring word! So stop saying it.

Positive Indifference is used because it keeps you at your optimal level of inner peace. It ends things beautifully and calmly. There's no one angry or bitter after everything has been said and done. "Whatever" doesn't do that for you! LOL

Utilizing Positive Indifference is something you do for yourself and if affects those around you in a very positive light...and it works! Looking at what used to be simple "indifference" in this most <u>positive</u> manner will change the way you handle people and prevent people from affecting you negatively. You keep it positive by finessing the situation and others aren't even necessarily aware of it. In fact, that's the finesse of it all: they won't even know how you neutralized the climate from well-on-its-way-to-be-heated down to cool and calm.

Then there are situations where someone just won't let up until you satisfy their curiosity on whatever opinion about something it is that they want to hear. We all have our moods and sometimes we aren't on the same page as someone else as far as what type of conversation we enjoy at the time.

How do we let someone know that we aren't interested in discussing something at this time – or perhaps never with them!

How about just saying it. Well, not in the manner above, but more like, "Joe, having that conversation right now would be an exercise in futility. Now…how about them Cubbies?!" (Or whatever sports team or topic of interest you wish to use to obviously and purposefully distract their attention.)

So let's see how that worked. If said as it was depicted above, many times that won't work as well as if handled just a wee bit differently. Have you figured out what the problem was in the response yet? Give it some thought if the answer hasn't come to you crystal clear.

If you thought that the reason that response wouldn't work was because it was prefaced with something negative so as to have the final word…then you'd be right! The person began by saying, "Joe, having that conversation right now would be an exercise in futility". That wasn't necessary at all and only sparks the flame of return banter. And you put an exclamation point on it as you stomped your foot on the person's chances to reply by throwing in, "How about them Cubbies?" at the very end.

So instead, a simple "How about them Cubbies?!" works perfectly fine on its own. Add a light chuckle and you show you hold no animosity about the conversation. It's just time to mutually agree to disagree and move on. Most times, the other person will laugh about it too. It ends amicably.

Then it's so very easy to move on.

The other, and most optimal use of Positive Indifference is when someone has decided they aren't going to let up and try to engage you by being argumentative. They want a rise out of you. And you can handle that with ease too.

While out on handyman jobs, Daddy taught me to rely on my instincts for troubleshooting problems. He taught me so many things about plumbing and electrical work that served me very well during my time on the sea. With one's own boat, when you're out in the middle of nowhere, you can't just yell out, "Hey! Culligan Man!"

You had to tend to maintenance and repairs yourself. Some things your life depended on you finding a solution and fast! Those skills taught to me by my father will be invaluable to me the remainder of my days.

Those lessons carried over to many things throughout my formative years. Daddy also taught me from a very young age to question things if they didn't make perfect sense to me, no matter who was relaying the information. He would tell me that just because someone wrote something certainly didn't make it necessarily true, but Mother, on the other hand, would say, "Why would anyone print that if it were *not* true?"

At such times, Daddy would look over at me with that look of, "Don't ever think that way," without actually say it aloud. It was funny, when it would happen, 'cause he and I would've already turned our heads so that our eyes met at exactly the same time. As if our heads were on their way in response to what was said.

And Daddy would ask me, "Mainie, what do we know of the integrity of the writer?" The bottom line was that it was up to the reader to research such things and compare the opinions of many before making up their mind on any particular claim, issue, or debate. My father instilled in me that finding out what was truth was *my* responsibility. As he would tell me, "It is difficult to make a fool of a scholar."

There are those who do more than stir the pot…they are the pot! They walk around bubbling, bubbling, looking for ways to get a rise out of people who otherwise are happy and going about minding their own business. There are some who can't stand anyone who is happy and will do just about anything to ruin their day or, at the very least, get a rise out of them. Positive Indifference allows you to walk away from people like that without harboring resentment. You see, they win if you don't…because harboring resentment towards them is the equivalent of getting a rise out of you! It's what they wanted to do and you just gifted them their reward.

When dealing with people such as this, remember that even though they've chosen to act like a fool, that fact doesn't automatically make you one too.

It's their problem not yours. Walk away with a smile or a, "Well, I've got to run. Have a great afternoon." There's not much someone can do with that. It's hard to work that into some huge ridiculousness as to how you acted the last time you both were together. It gives the drama-rama majorettes nowhere to twirl their batons of negative banter. And as for the cauldron carriers? They just have to take their bubbling pot somewhere else!

It's always up to you to refuse to fuel any fires of debate if the end result isn't worthy of the friction it could create. Hypothetically, even though your opinion was asked, it's your decision whether to express it, change the subject, or make light humor from it. Humor works well in a lot of these circumstances. You can laugh it off and let the person know you're not even thinking about going there! LOL

Everyone, deep down, appreciates an honest response; even if it's not quite the response they'd expected. A lot depends on the personality of the person with whom you're speaking. Some people have a relatively good sense of humor, and others will use whatever response as an excuse to argue. Use good judgment in direct relationship with the person involved.

Now let's say you're the one who disagrees with someone. You think their choice isn't a good one, but they refuse to see things your way. At some point someone has to decide the matter has been fully explored, or at least for the time being, and just say, "Okay, how about we think more about it and talk about it later." That should be said with no hint of animosity or frustration in your tone.

Mind you, some will have to add a little dig, especially as they're walking away: "Well, if that's your choice…." Said in a manner that has the connotation of, "Well, if that's your stupid, dumb, ignorant choice…." You get my point, I'm sure. It's best to stay objective and give them the benefit of the doubt -- that the disparaging adjectives weren't included in their connotation. Remember, they said it; you might be hearing it somewhat subjectively and taking it a bit too personally.

Utilize the art of Positive Indifference and let the matter go. Doing so will have no lasting effects on you and not one additional ion of negative energy is added to the planet!

Once you've given your opinion on something and someone doesn't want to take it that's just fine. It has nothing to do with your friendship or relationship. It is, after all, just an opinion. Many times this type of scenario ends with, "Well, if you weren't going to use my opinion why did you ask for it!"

This is why the use of Positive Indifference is perfect for such scenarios. If you were right, and they didn't take your advice, then they'll learn from their mistakes – or not! No need to remind them of that later. There's no need to ever be the initiator of negative energy.

Life isn't a game where one has to be constantly declared the winner or loser. We all make choices and sometimes we err in judgment. Or sometimes we're mistaken and are wrong. And it's okay! When discussing matters with others, there's never a need for disagreements to come to a boil – not when one realizes there's always the option to agree to disagree; and in a most polite and civil manner! There's no harboring of ill will with that declaration because there's no frustration to fuel it.

You're impatient for your life to start lifting you up and making you happier. You have that backwards: if you want a happier life, you have to make it happen. It's not called your life for nothing! – Charmainism

Everyone is entitled to his or her opinion. The fact that the person can't agree with you doesn't lessen what you think about yourself. So it therefore shouldn't bother you in the slightest that you couldn't get them to see things exactly as you do. After all, the other person isn't you, and you aren't them!

By using the art of Positive Indifference, you finesse situations and they're diffused without the smoldering of disdain to be fanned into a blazing fire again later. Ultimately, when using Positive Indifference, there remains no baggage when the conversation concludes.

Learning to deal with situations from a mature perspective is true emotional stability. We all have the capacity to be emotionally stable. For many, it's a lesson that's long overdue.

We have to realize that we're often far more judgmental than we might think. The disdain our faces show when looking at someone else and wondering why they don't clean up their act or do things in the manner you'd do if you were them. We have to know when minding our own business is the best thing. Better for us because we don't get our pantyhose tied up in knots over that which should be no concern of our own.

You see, we're not that person! Never forget that we've no clue what other people go through in their daily lives. We can think we're filling in the gaps and have full knowledge of what would be best for them, but the real truth is glaring at us in our faces when we take off our hats of pompous righteousness and understand once and for all that their life isn't our life. Their decisions aren't our decisions to make. Never forget that.

The world could be a much better place, or I should say, the people in the world could help to make the world a much better place if those who think their choices in life are the best choices would refrain from thinking they have the right to be overbearing and demanding in that everyone else makes those same choices.

We have to stop judging other people and what they choose to do with their lives. To make peace with such things, we must remind ourselves to use Positive Indifference when tempted to convey our opinions on matters regarding others that have no bearing on our own lives.

Let people live their lives and you simply enjoy living yours. There's no reason to look down upon others and use them as scapegoats for all of your own personal problems. No one is that naïve to believe such to be true. If you're bitter and full of resentment, so much so that you must point fingers and hold others you don't even know responsible for your own disappointments – well, I couldn't be happier that you have found this book.

When we're not judgmental or full of disdain, we can see the lighter side of people. Lighten up on others and we lighten our own load. A match made in heaven! – Charmainism

There are many levels of need, but those who have buried their heads in the sand by blaming all their ills and all the ills of the world on certain people need to see that as oversimplifying by way of total selfishness. What you don't want to see you merely change in your mind's eye. No problem with that as long as the change in perspective does not harbor anger, resentment, ill will, or blame. To do otherwise is self-serving and delusional. Nothing good will come of adding negative energy to the planet.

There are talk shows on every day that convince viewers their problems aren't their fault. It's always someone or something else that's the culprit. Someone has done something to you that made you this way. Made you unable to deal with the simplest of situations. Instead, you throw a fit or yell and scream, or exhibit violent physical behaviors. Frustrations are at the top of the fool chain and are exhibited as if the ridiculous outbursts are normal.

Many times when someone says something negative, most people will respond with another negative barb. Such is how the feud begins and continues to be perpetuated. We do it to ourselves then wonder why there's always so much drama in our lives. It's there because we haven't diffused it by being totally, and positively, indifferent to it.

To learn how to use Positive Indifference, tell yourself that's what you'll use when you don't want to perpetuate negativity and aren't sure of exactly what to say at the time. Remembering the adage, "If you can't say something nice, say nothing," comes to mind. However, in this day and age, "nothing" is usually frowned upon as being more rude than anything and can lead to perpetuating the friction rather than amicably ending it.

That's why finding something humorous to say or something off topic but important (i.e. "Hey, what time did Renae say we were supposed to pick her up?"). You know, something completely benign but of some importance to mention. When you think about it, you can finesse it with something of little importance but that seems to be important! Such as, "Ooh, remember that recipe you had for buttercake? Do you still have it? I'd love to make that this weekend."

Then the person is off the original conversation yet still feeling of importance while getting you that recipe! It's a very positive way to diffuse sticky situations. And if you were waiting for a way to leave…you can yell out, "Hey, gotta run! I'll get that recipe later on. Thanks!" Everything ends quite peacefully and positively.

We choose to live life to the fullest
because it is in our best interest to do so. – Charmainism

Positive Indifference is the filler for those gray areas that used to drive you nuts. Positive Indifference will save your sanity, keep the peace, and remove all friction that used to wear away at your inner peace.

Freedom from Drama Using Positive Indifference

It's nearly impossible for someone to argue alone. Sure, there are those who will go on a rant and continue on and on as long as someone is listening. Don't be one of the listeners. Let them rant. Say nothing. Harbor no ill feelings towards them about the words they say when in this emotionally juvenile state. Because that's all it is: an adult who doesn't have a clue as to how to deal with his or her emotions.

This is perfect for dealing with others who tend to nitpick and are difficult to please. Don't feel angry that you can't please them. Be *positively* indifferent to the fact that you can't please them. You don't have to tell them, "You're impossible to please." Just go on about your business and enjoy the day!

When you really have moved on, it's over and you're no longer talking about it! It's put to rest and you've made peace with it. The value in this is because when you revert back to reliving it, you show you've not actually let it go at all. You're still rehashing it and potentially stirring the pot readying for Round Two! When you do that, you're making the drama!

When you let something go, that's all that need be done. You don't even have to announce it to the person that you're letting it go and are done with it. When it's done it is just that: D-O-N-E. And no patting yourself on the back or reporting your good deed to others either. This is how drama perpetuates itself within your life.

Those who find drama around them all the time have to realize that the common denominator is them! They continue to wonder why there's so much drama in their lives yet they're right smack in the middle of it each and every single time. We truly reap what we sow...many don't realize they're farmers of fodder!

They don't know when to walk away and just let things go. By not doing so, and always thinking they just have to have the last word; they continue to fuel the flames of the gossip grapevine, yet dare take the stance that they never struck a match! They don't get it. But they should. All they have to do is look into a mirror! If you're always somehow in the middle of the mix of drama, then you're more than an innocent bystander. Trust me!

And to remove all drama from one's life, all anyone really needs to learn is how to finesse situations so they can walk away from such confrontations with absolutely no resentment, anger, or bitterness within them. It actually is a very easy thing to do! It ends with you because you ended it peacefully and with no aftertaste or afterthought. This means it's over. No talking about it with your friends or anyone else. It's like it never happened. The grapevine of gossip about it has been cut. Service is discontinued. You're the operator! You can do that!

For when drama really does <u>end with you</u>, it's difficult for it to make headway into your life again. But that also means not entertaining those who love drama by sitting there and listening to their gossip and ridiculousness. Otherwise, (even though you might beg to differ at this point), you *were* doing half the talking... even though your mind says you were only "listening." "Listening" is keeping the pot stirred...you're the audience! I know all those tricks people convince themselves of in order to protect their role as "one who doesn't gossip or like drama!" If you're hearing it all the time, then you're in the middle of it all the time.

Read this again: If you're hearing it all the time, then you're in the middle of it all the time. It's true! If you're always in the middle of drama, you better believe there's a reason for it…and the reason is you. Just take a quick look at the common denominator. Uh huh. You recognize that person? LOL

So change it! If you don't want drama, you don't have to have drama. I promise you! But you do have to learn that there's a bit of finessing to do to in order to squash drama from your life. Many think they're ridding themselves of drama and create *more* drama simply trying to do just that!

Let's take a look at those we know who live and breathe drama…and get to understand them better. If we can understand them better, then we'll know what to do about handling them appropriately and not create more friction and drama in the process.

Those who love drama will sit and talk about all kinds of things waiting for you to affirm their stance. "Yeah, girl, you right!" Or that's what they hope to hear. Some would think a response of, "Girl, I don't get involved in those messes. Me Be a Drama-free Mama Bee." Then laugh it off and go do something else. That works sometimes, but other times it too will set off a spark of indignation. You just dissed someone, in their eyes. Since you referred to yourself as not getting involved in such matters and that you're drama free, what are you calling them? You see the problem? An even better response would be something like, "Girl, I gotta run. Don't let such things bother you. I don't." It's the way things are said sometimes and the words that are chosen as well…but when you want to snuff the raging fires of the gossip pyromaniacs, then you need to be sure you've done a good job of putting an end to others thinking you entertain gossip.

When you do, you won't be bothered with drama from that person again because you're no fun! Yup. You're not an ever-stretched ear hanging onto every gossipy word. Granted, they might come back a time or two with something they think ranks in the "highest of jucihood" categories just to test your resolve; but when they finally realize this isn't some phase for you but a new way of life and that you're seriously not interested, they'll give it up. It's easy for them to find someone else who will listen to their idle gossip rantings.

Now you might think that's what you were doing in the past, and you certainly will argue that you didn't agree with her delusions. Yeah, but the problem came about when you cracked that little smile of support! I'm sure you didn't think it was "support," but Miss Thang counts that half-smile as an "Affirmative, tell me more!"

And then there was that little snort you do sometimes when you get caught off-guard. I heard it all the way over here. Uh huh. I know what she said was funny. Just remember that your snort was all the encouragement needed for the gossip to continue onto "Floor Two: Undergarments." What you don't realize is that you think you're just hearing what's being said...wrong. What you don't know is that Miss Thang has dragged you right into the middle of the gossip grapevine again. Oh yes she did!

You see, to Miss Thang, after you've sat and listened to her gossip, whenever she thinks of you from then on, her assessment will be embellished to the point where you were agreeing with everything she said. And when she repeats the story of you both talking about it (even though it was grossly one-sided), they'll be sure to say you were right there agreeing with everything said in that too. It went from her talking about something to both of you having a conversation. You pulled yourself into it by being there listening to it; or, okay...half-listening to it. Don't give such people a forum to air their ridiculousness. Trust me, they'll find another more willing subject if they don't have you.

Don't entertain those who love drama by listening to it. It's not necessary to say anything about it, just walk away and start doing something else. Or, "Girl, I have to go." Then make yourself somewhat unavailable to that person. They'll get the message. Remember, though, when you say you have to run, make it a good thing. Positive, you know, with a lilt in your voice! You're the one conveying the fabulous feeling when you know that life awaits you and it's all wonderful. Personify peace and it will become you.

You'll probably become their next target, mind you. And that's okay too. It's a small price to pay when clearing your life of drama. Besides, everyone else knows the source and they've been there too. They won't believe a word of what that busybody says about you. If they do, then you're pretty lucky to be rid of them as well. Believe me, we all know the drama queens out there. It's just that usually no one wants to say anything to that person because they're unstable and somewhat delusional in the stories they believe and what they say to others.

By the way, did you know Miss Thang was your best friend? If you're entertaining her gossip (or doing just enough so that's what she thinks!), then she's got you marked down as FRIEND NUMERO UNO. People like Miss Thang thrive on drama and creating it everywhere they go. Without it, they'd have no interaction with others, or so they think. Maybe you might want to gift them a copy of this book!! If there are any redeeming qualities inside the Miss Thangs of the world, then this book and its philosophy will bring it out to the surface. They have only to read it and want to change.

It's okay. You're the sane one! What have you got to lose except a person who is negative, difficult to be around, and stirs up drama 24/7? That's no loss at all.

How, exactly, is that done? It all comes down to action and reaction. Just because we hear something and interpret it negatively, doesn't mean it *should* hurt us. Nor does it mean that it was necessarily the intention of someone to hurt us by something they said or did. For the most part, we hurt ourselves more than others actually intend to hurt us.

If not for us, then for whom? If not for the future, then for when? Our example will pave a path for others to follow -- especially our young people. Truly, it is my belief we can have a better world. Let it begin now, within each and every one of us. – Charmainism

What difference does it really make to your well-being when in the company of someone who is high drama? Their drama means nothing if no one is watching the show. They'll soon get the idea that they can no longer use their emotional outbursts to manipulate those around them. Or, at the very least, they won't be manipulating YOU! Others will notice how you handle the situation. That you don't let it bother you in the slightest!

People may do silly and petty things, but they rarely continue on that course when those actions don't produce what they wanted as a result. In other words, we often are facilitators of these needy people and don't even realize it. Once you learn the art of Positive Indifference and how good it feels when you reach the level where a clash means little or nothing to you, you'll see how simple this all is. It's not that you don't care…it's that you choose to care less about things that are futile to care about.

If we wear our emotions on our sleeves and take just about everything as a personal indictment of our shortcomings, we'll interpret a myriad of actions by others as personal insults. We're asking for it without knowing it. It's called paranoia.

We must realize that what we find upsetting is our own doing. We can be upset, yet not allow that choice to overly upset our lives. Becoming 'upset' is relative. Keep it relative to what works best for your own well-being as well as those around you. That means finessing the art of Positive Indifference! – Charmainism

"Is she trying to get over on me?" "What did he really mean by that?" Well, really, do you actually care? It's not a negative "I don't care," it's just that it's a choice you make to let the small stuff go and be done with it. You move on in the relationship as if it never happened.

Understanding the role that emotions play in our lives is highly important. Emotions are totally within our own control. Without emotional control, it's easy to see how the highs and lows of life can have us seesawing between soaring to the heavens in the middle of our best dream ever; or fighting for our lives during our worst nightmare. We have to understand that the power we give our emotions is entirely up to each of us. Again, it's about the choices we make.

The drama queens (and kings) are at the high end of those we want to rid our lives of, but sometimes that means cutting ties with family members. It doesn't fare well with the rest of the family to completely cut someone out of your life. It causes frictions and it also causes others to feel that choosing a side is necessary. It isn't. Why not? Well, because your goal, as a peacemaker, is to learn to deal with such persons instead of creating drama by drawing attention to the fact that you dislike being around them. The days of announcing to everybody in the family (and friends too) each time you decide to cut this person or that person out of your life and then top it off with a declaration of silliness like, "Don't invite *me* if you're going to invite *them*,"… is OVER! Yup. It's time to grow *up* and get over such foolishness my child.

Most of the troublemakers in families learn to manipulate the emotions of others from a very early age. They produce an action that gets a result that their emotional wants thrive upon. It's juvenile and immature, to say the least. But if you're the adult and mature with your own emotions, you shouldn't be bothered at all by the sophomoric antics of the adults in your life who are hell bent on being petty and small-minded. And that's okay too! Be glad you aren't them, but love them anyway and treat them with kindness.

It's much easier when dealing with acquaintances, as we can choose whom we wish to keep in our company. But when it's family members, the complications can and do begin! The way to neutralize the pot-stirring family members isn't to expose them outright among other family members (as they feel they have to take sides), but to kill the dirty dragon with kindness! One doesn't fare well in the light of the sun when someone is being kind to them and they're being hurtful in return. This is how you can disarm the pot-stirrers. You can't be stirred!

Be positive, considerate, loving, and kind. Because it is the only way to live one's life to the fullest! No matter what anyone else does, we have to live with ourselves and be content with everything we do. – Charmainism

It's human nature to lash back out when someone is barking at us. Right or wrong doesn't matter, it's that the person has invaded your space. Suddenly we see them attempting to drive a wedge between us and other family members or close friends. The pot-stirrers love to count those who are on this side or that side, and they keep track!

We don't have to expose them for what they are, as they do an excellent job of that all by themselves. So don't worry about it. Just let it go. That means really let it go. One never needs to use someone else to better their own light in the eyes of others. Doing so actually does just the opposite: instead of gaining the approval of others, it exposes your weaknesses.

You have the approval of yourself. That's quite enough for we who know true inner peace! – Charmainism

Peacemakers Finesse the Art of Positive Indifference

You'll soon master the art of Positive Indifference. You'll soon become a Peacemaker. But first you must learn patience for yourself and for all those around you. There's no hurry in life except that which we put on ourselves. It's our choice to choose to be productive in a manner that doesn't wear heavily upon us. We must remember to enjoy the journey, as our destination will soon be reached.

Patience and kindness aren't uncommon traits. It's just that in this fast life of the hustle and bustle; the displays of impatience and rudeness seem to leave the deepest and more lasting impression. We can change that. Look for the virtues shown by others and take not for granted that which is so admirable. It's out there! – Charmainism

We must learn to get along with others. If they won't meet us halfway, then we do what we must do in order to gain inner peace for ourselves. Why? By now you know the answer to that question: Because it's in your own best interest to do so!

Together, we can do anything. Divided, we shall never embrace PEACE and HARMONY. It definitely is within our grasp. But if we cannot get along with each other over our differences, how shall we ever make this world a better place. This is not a question but a fact. – Charmainism

One can't attain true inner peace without shaking one's own hand. Becoming one's best friend is so simple. You have to LIKE yourself! If you don't like yourself, then figure out the things you dislike and make a change. The moment you decide you're making changes for the better, the more you like yourself. We just have to make the first move and get the process of change started. Time flies by...use that speed of flight to change your life!

Until you shake hands with yourself and with all those you have blamed as being the cornerstones of what has held you back, then you can't move on. As you do come to grips with what's important in this life, you can and will find inner peace and total happiness. It's not an elusive dream. It's readily attainable by anyone who really and truly wants it.

Free yourself. Shake hands with yourself and forgive yourself once and for all! Only then can you move on to greatness! – Charmainism

Just remember, when you get close, there will be a tendency to become frustrated in the realization that you didn't make these changes sooner! Hey, it's human nature. I can help you understand the way the mind works and how we're forever getting in our own way... but I can't make you perfect. As humans, we're all imperfect. It's learning to deal with our imperfections and the imperfections of others that allow us to finally "get it" and get on with living the happy and contented lives we all can attain.

It's up to you to practice the art of Positive Indifference and be perfectly at peace with the remarkable change that being indifferent, in this most positive light, can do for you. It won't only change your life for the better, but you'll notice a wonderful change in how others interact with you. You'll finally command the respect from others that you always felt was missing.

Yes! The pot stirrers will find another muse! You're done with simmering! Frustration is no longer an option! If your pot never simmers in the first place, it will never come to a boil.

Instead of allowing others to put you through changes...make a change for yourself! Baggage exists only if you choose to carry it. Clean out your closet and let your life be cloaked in only that which you truly desire to wear. – Charmainism

Chapter Eight:
Love and Understanding

Maintaining Compassion in a User-Mentality World

When we are open to the fact that reality is often different than what our feelings may indicate, we don't get hurt much. We simply realize that we were caught doing a bit of our own dreaming and take ownership of that...and move on. Everyone cannot be as we wish them to be. But that's okay too. We either accept them for who they are, at the level we wish to have a relationship with them, or we lessen the expectations of the relationship and keep a friend. Or, we keep the intensity (or lack of intensity) of the relationship more on their terms than our own...or not. Whichever is entirely up to us.

— Charmainism

The term "Unconditional love" is everywhere, but few know what it is or how to give it. That may be due to the fact that it's a concept that's nearly impossible to live up to. Love shouldn't have "terms" or "conditions," and we can love someone despite the negative or self-destructive things that they do. However, that doesn't mean we should keep coming back to the trough for another helping of their slop – if that's what they're dishing out time and time again.

Daddy would get so involved in his pool shooting that he'd completely forget the time as day went into night and night went into day. Usually, these longer departures from his work routine would start with playing cards and drinking. Then the pool shooting would begin. And then there often seemed to be "that new guy in town visiting from New York City." Well, all the people at the local taverns say Daddy can take him.

It was during one of those similar times when Daddy came home just long enough to plop down two big Castors grocery store brown paper bags on the table and yell to Mother there was a "coon" in there he'd just bought over at the tavern. He then told Mom to cook it because as soon as he got done beating this high falutin out-of-towner, he was going to bring over Pasquale and Chico to treat them to a delicious raccoon dinner.

Mother was listening to him talk as he was heading back out the door. She noticed, as I did, that Daddy have put on more shaving lotion. Or that's what it smelled like to me. Most of the time, when Daddy was over at the pool hall or tavern, he dressed very nicely and smelled really nice too!

About three hours later, here comes Daddy with Pasquale and Chico. Mind you, those guys' names weren't really Pasquale and Chico; those were just the nicknames that Daddy called them. Daddy was always figuring out a nickname for somebody, especially new acquaintances. "Pasquale and Chico" meant there'd be two new guys we hadn't met yet coming over for dinner. Next time, if they were invited again, they'd be some other names that meant they'd been at our house before. LOL It was just his nature. I got the same propensity for doing so from him. It's been a part of me for as long as I can remember. I've always been one for nicknames.

Anyway, so Pasquale and Chico come in along with Daddy and they're all ridiculously drunk. Ha! Not so much that Daddy couldn't navigate walking home from next door, but they were all in a great mood and LOUD as all get out! Hahahaaaaaaa Ooooh, Mother could not stand this type of overt drunkenness at all.

In direct contrast to my father, when my mother was miffed, she would become quieter. More silent. So, she didn't say a word as the Three Amigos sat down at the dinner table.

Our dinner table at our house on Washington Street was fabulous! Daddy had made it out of a huge old wooden door. It was the thickest wood I'd ever seen and was solid mahogany. It was gorgeous and, obviously, one-of-a-kind. I'm sure whatever all that door had experienced in its lifetime of many homes; it's never been inside a home like ours and had never been used to display a huge platter of raccoon being served up for dinner.

As Mother put the accompanying side dishes on the table, Daddy began to carve the raccoon. "Umm, Johnnie! This smells and looks delicious!"

"Johnnie" was Daddy's pet name for Mother.

Mom was standing in the kitchen in the passageway between the breakfast counter and the cooking area with her arms akimbo. She nonchalantly remarked, "Well, it didn't smell much like 'coon when it was cooking."

Daddy paid her no mind as he was laughing and eagerly cutting portions for his friends. Daddy knew how to be a wonderful host to his guests and Pasquale and Chico were loving every moment of it.

They all began to eat and were deeply into the moment between salivation and satisfaction when Dad said, "You know Johnnie, I think this is the biggest coon I've ever seen. This thing is really huge."

Mom says, "Where'd you get it?"

Dad says, "A guy came by the tavern and said he was selling raccoons. He said he had one left and wanted to give somebody a deal so he could get back home. I'd seen him in there a time or two but don't know him very well, but others said he always had really good coon. So, since it was so late and I was starving like a Marvin, I thought I'd snatch the last one he had."

Mom had this odd look on her face...odd in the sense that perhaps she knew something that no one else did. Smug. Yes, that's it: Mom looked smug.

"Well, you know, if you think that's big," Mom continued, "I gotta tell you...the other half of it's in the oven."

"What?!" my Dad was incredulous upon hearing that.

"Essie, coons don't get this big!"

You know Daddy was starting to think something was up when he switched from sweet-talking Mom by calling her "Johnnie" to now being back to "Essie."

Mother answered in her beautifully calm voice, "Well, they do get that big when they don't come with their feet still on, Ro-bert-o!"

Wait for it...uh huh. Wait for it. It's coming. You know it is....

Said every so methodically, and slowly, Mom added...Personally, I think it might have been a dog."

Hahahaaaaaaaaaaaaaaaaaaa

Now that's funny. Though I was bit too young to understand what it all meant, because in my mind there was no way that my father and his new acquaintances had just snarfed down half a dog in record time...but it was hysterical looking at their faces after hearing what Mother said. Of course, Pasquale and Chico knew what Dad knew: you never, ever buy wild game if the feet aren't left intact. Otherwise, you won't know exactly what you're buying!

Daddy had never looked inside the bags.

And it if that wasn't bad enough, Mother had been cutting up celery and had the butcher knife in her hand, swinging it away with every syllable of "Ro-bert-o!" I think Dad's dinner guests thought their host's wife was some beautiful Native American woman who had a temper and probably killed the dog herself and cooked it up just to get even with him. It was really very funny. Like some skit on television or something.

"Ro-bert-o!" My Dad had a lot of names too. But "Roberto" was used a lot. Daddy was often called "Roberto" by friends and family members. He was "Roberto, the Commanchero." We kids shortened it to "The Common." "The Common" was just another one of Daddy's alter egos who'd come out when Daddy was drinking. Though even when sober, sometimes "The Common" would peek out his head and let everyone know that he was going to behave on this particular occasion.

"The Common" would still sometimes get into philosophizing, but he was more restrained. We used to think of him as Daddy's Cherokee side (my paternal grandmother, "Nana," was the granddaughter of a Cherokee Medicine Man) coming out and exploring the natural world in all its beauty while flying high but never leaving his chair. "The Common" would take us with him as he talked of the beauty of the earth and the waters that ran throughout it. We loved "The Common." He was a nice alter ego. If "The Common" came out, we knew that Mr. Hyde wouldn't be!

I loved my "Ma and Pa Kettle" parents. Their interactions were much like that old show, and I thought it was hysterical. I loved every minute of it.

Mother could be patient but to a point. Once the point arrived, you were definitely going to be made aware of it. Even if it meant possibly cooking up a dog and serving it up as dinner. Now, the truth be known, years later Mother said that it wasn't a dog. But then she didn't know the story of Daddy running in to that same guy years later. The guy was bragging to another guy that he used to sell lots of raccoons. When he ran out, he'd sell small dogs but leave the feet off and make some excuse as to why they were removed.

I thought Dad was going to beat that man half to death. Daddy loved dogs and now he had eaten one. And he wasn't very happy about that at all.

As a lover of all humanity, my propensity towards compassion and forgiveness of my fellowman is inherent. But no one wants to be anyone's fool. So how do we balance compassion and caring without becoming someone who is gullible and easily preyed upon? Unless we have "street smarts," how else are we to know when our kindness is being mistaken for weakness? Or worse, when our kindness actually IS weakness?!

Humankind. Yes, that describes us. But which __kind__ as far as temperament? Patient? Understanding? May your kind of humankind prove to be that which showers heartfelt kindness at every opportunity. That is the kind of human we all should strive to be. Humankind: May it aptly describe us in more ways than one. It is our choice. – Charmainism

We can love others and care about them regardless of what they do. But we can't be fools about it either. This is why there's "tough love" as well. Tough love doesn't mean you love someone less, it just means that they're worth saving and keeping in your life. Tough love is the kind that helps to save someone from their own self-destructive habits. Such habits can be anything from borrowing money and never repaying, to stealing money to feed a drug habit. Something in their life has to change or they're going down a road that will lead to a premature death or a life less fulfilled due to incarceration.

When you begin to feel like a facilitator rather than a friend, something has to change.

It happens when a relationship has to change a bit to become more on your terms because that's what's necessary for you to be able to keep your own balance of inner peace and happiness. This doesn't mean you dictate what the other person does; rather it means that there are certain self-destructive behaviors that you'll not be a party to entertaining.

It doesn't mean your life's mission should be to evoke change in others by issuing ultimatums; it is rather by being honest and letting them know that you're concerned about their welfare. You can lend an ear and help offer advice if you feel you're up to the task, but never admonish someone time and again and think you'll make a positive difference in their life.

Others are well aware of their own inner turmoil and unhappiness. If you feel you must say or do something to better your relationship with them, then by all means have a workable suggestion that can be of help to at least get the idea of change started. With no viable suggestions in hand, it's wise to simply let it go until you've something of a plan of action or a meaningful suggestion in place. If not, then the tendency to shoot from the hip can begin the same old harping, griping, nagging, and any other constantly negative feedback that's entirely counterproductive and falls upon deaf ears every time.

Giving Without Expectations

When we love someone, we should really love them…the *person*, not what they have or what they can possibly do for us…but them. True love is beyond all those things. True love is what remains after everything else is gone. It's there as you both stand stunned, stark naked, after being ripped apart by the pillage of hardship and injustice. True love is what allows you to stick by those we believe in, and it serves to carry us over every pothole in the road of life – even the potholes that are more like craters! We can because we know <u>love</u>.

When you talk the talk, you gotta walk the walk. If you profess to be loving and caring, do so without expecting reciprocation. Keep in mind that while busy counting brownie points, you're likely to miss what comes back to you. LOVE conquers all! – Charmainism

Sometimes it's very difficult for people to really give of their hearts because they fear being hurt; and sometimes they fear that their love won't be reciprocated in an equal manner. But we can't let the idea of counting those Brownie Points bother us and keep us from what probably is the ultimate in happiness: true love.

Love, like life in general, doesn't have to be fair in order for that love to be real or true! Nothing in life has to be "fair." That also means that not everything in a relationship is going to be "fair," not cut right smack down the middle and equitable in every way. When we fully understand that, we won't waste time getting our feelings hurt when someone doesn't reciprocate their showing of love to us <u>in the manner we think is most appropriate from our perspective</u>. You see, it's not our call to do so.

Their show of love isn't ours to dictate. When it comes to relationships and the showing of love and affection, the earlier in life one learns that great expectations = great disappointments, the better for all.

A heart filled with love is so beautifully flexible. - Charmainism

Life itself isn't fair, as there are people with agendas who are hell bent on stepping on the backs of anyone to get ahead in this life. Ordinary people are often caught in the crossfire and are thought of by callous, uncaring individuals as collateral damage. Such people give such things no more thought as they carry on to the next level of what person they can next destroy for a new feather in their cap of achievements. It's a sad state of affairs, but it's the only one we currently have.

Without a positive foundation at your core, interactions with ruthless people can cause good, but unprepared people, to crumble under the pressure. And then their lives are destroyed. Their marriage dissolves and their children are uprooted as the entire family falls apart under the weight of such turmoil. A once happy family becomes fragments of people who are destroyed and very angry and bitter about it. It doesn't have to be this way.

We must always hold fast to keeping our heads above the muck of the constant mayhem of this existence we call life on earth. For now, it's all we have. We must make the best of it at all times.

When one finally realizes that happiness is a state of mind rather than a tangible, the healing of wounds perpetuated by self-pity can finally come to an end and the flourishing of inner peace and happiness can begin. When one is happy with self, it opens an entirely new world: one of hope, confidence, and contentment. Happiness: It is within the reach of everyone. – Charmainism

Making the best of things also comes to play in everyday life at home with our significant other or spouse. The household is a breeding ground for resentment and loathing. I know, even when you have love in your heart...this is just a fact of life. Blame it on our imperfections...or blame it on the Boogey...but the bottom-line is that it's <u>true</u>!

This all means that even though you love your spouse, some days you'd love to twinkle your nose like Samantha of "Bewitched," and give your Darrin a bit of an adjustment. Or so you think. But then that would make him more of who you want him to be rather than whom he really is.

Oh...but you say in the way he shows affection. I hear you. But you can do many things in that regard to improve that situation, and none of those includes magical powers at all.

We can't expect to "change" someone and the way they're when it comes to showing affection, unless the individual has shown a *desire* to change. That's different. But if the only real change that seems to be in the works is *you* changing <u>them</u>...well, forget about it. It just doesn't work out well in the end. Honestly. So as much as you think that guy over there is the finest thing walking, if he's a Neanderthal inside, it will forever be coming out at the worst time. I'm sorry, that's just the way it is. He'll find a great woman for him who doesn't mind the fact that he's the most handsome total slob she's ever known.

Let love be love. Not an orchestrated conquest, but a match of mutual admiration, respect, genuine affection, and a glow that engulfs you when you both are together. *That* can be love! Remember that there are no rules when it comes to the love people have for one another. If it's mutual love and affection, then make it truly mutual!! Bring out some ideas, explore some new territories...make it really mutual and fun! Anything can get stale if it's just lying around looking same ole, same ole...you know! Get the things you want in life by initiating them yourself. Don't wait for an invitation. You know deep down exactly what to do! So just do it. Have fun with it. It's a challenge and you're up to the task at hand. Uh huh. *Yessirree!*

Why is it that we expect a person known to be absent-minded to be any less than that if we become involved with them? Instead, their manner is taken personally as we see them as being more thoughtless and inconsiderate. What was it about "absent-mindedness" we didn't understand? – Charmainism

Feeling love from others, or even a lack thereof, is a matter of personal and heartfelt perspective. When one understands that a person who loves you does so within their own capacity, and even though that capacity may not equate to the kind of love you feel you give them, then you must either learn to accept the love that person does give, or let the person know you need more than what they're offering. Or, of course, you could choose to give up and reject the love the person wishes to offer back and therefore pack your heartstrings in your bag and move on. Few things work as well as choice number one, especially if your love for the person is incredibly high. Time tells the tale when there exists devotion of an unselfish love. Many times that type of love begins more on one side than the other. But most times devotion wins out and both sides are the better for it.

It's when our expectations of love from another are such that we determine the love they're giving us isn't only inadequate, but probably equates to the person not loving us at all, that most often is the ruin of any chance for the relationship to succeed. Not loving "enough" does not equate to being "unloved." If you can rationalize things in this manner throughout your life, where you're intent on being objective, then life will hold very few disappointments for you.

We all have an affinity for setting ourselves up to be disappointed. We have to realize that each person on this planet is an individual who owes us nothing. Anything we get from them is then seen as something quite extraordinary and wonderful. – Charmainism

It's not possible that I'm the *only* person who sees things in this highly objective manner, but from my earliest memories it's how I saw things. I loved people very much and that fact was out there front and center. I don't think I could hold back my love and affection from those I care about if I wanted to…that's just not who I am. Perhaps it's due to my fearlessness when it comes to being hurt or rejected; it's just not something I think about at all. Therefore, I've no fear when it comes to expressing my caring and love for someone in the manner that suits me best. If they don't return my affection in a similarly enthusiastic manner, well, perhaps I never noticed that either because I wasn't expecting a certain response.

If you were to ask some of my siblings, with regard to our childhood, they'd no doubt tell some of the same stories I have from a very different perspective. The details of the stories would be the same, but how what happened made them feel at the time, would probably be quite different than how I felt.

For a very long time, the younger kids in the family really didn't feel secure and that took somewhat of a toll on them. The perceived lack for security from their parents, equated to some of them feeling unloved.

I remember many times defending my father in front of the other children, as to them; Daddy was the source of all the turmoil in the household. To me, things weren't quite that simple. However, I did agree that our father could make things easier on Mom if he'd just do the things he said he would do and then Mom would have peace of mind that her children were being taken care of.

That's understandable. But I felt that Mom often overreacted about things that to me weren't a big deal. So in between the crying wolf and the real crying, there were many different impacts of those emotional swings that had a negative impact on the smaller children.

I did my best, as a peacemaker, to make the kids feel better about everything, including themselves. We'd have fun doing all sorts of things that my creative little mind could think up and carry out for their enjoyment.

My bedroom was a classroom. Yes. I'd a large desk and even file cabinets as my hub. My room had my bed, of course, and then it was filled with eight smaller desks and chairs for students. I held classes every summer, all summer long for the neighborhood kids who needed help with their studies (as well as my smaller sisters and brothers who wanted to be there just to participate in what they saw as "Fun with Mainie!") It was a wonderful time. All my life, I'd wanted to teach others easier ways to find the solutions that eluded them.

All my siblings would agree on their feelings about my classroom antics…they loved them!

But as far as other things, it was a bit of a dance to try to keep the smaller two kids (later four) feeling content and safe. But I always did my best to make sure they were emotionally doing just fine.

The good thing is that after many, many years, some who felt unloved by our parents have changed their tune about it. And I'm very happy for them about that because I surely loved them!! (Of course they tell me they weren't talking about me!)

For other siblings, it took many decades for them to come to a peaceful place when reliving some of the happenings from their childhood. Especially when it came to our father and whether or not he did an adequate job of taking care of the needs of our family. Indeed, some truly did feel unloved or inadequately cared for, and interestingly enough, each for an entirely different reason than the others. Why is that?

It makes sense, when you think about it, because we're all different individuals with different needs. Just because we all grew up in the same house doesn't make us all the same. Their childhood and that of the other members of the family could not possibly be the same because even though we're siblings, as completely different people, we experienced a different dynamic throughout our respective years within the household. But even so, it still has a lot to do with perspective and expectation.

It also comes down to the ability of each particular child to interpret what's happening at the time. For many children, their interpretation is flawed because they're, in fact, immature and innocent children. There's a limited amount of information they can process correctly. They don't have the experience that adults do in order to fill in the gray areas. That means it's left up to their imaginations to create a full scenario as they mature. As each year goes by and the event is revisited, what was real and what was filled in with the mesh of imagination.

Remember, no matter what, we have to treat relationships, especially loving and lasting ones, as great friendships. Friendships we cherish, honor, and wish to keep! With friendships, we don't keep score as to who-has-done-what for-whom-and-whose-turn-is- it-next!! We can't be motivated to do things for others by expecting something in return. That's for business deals rather than acts of friendship or love. Do it for them because you love them.

In the game of relationships, those who refrain from keeping score are the ones who win their matches. – Charmainism

Therefore we must learn to be happy with whatever response the other person conveys to us. That should be good enough. They may have their insecurities and want to take things slower than you do. That's perfectly fine. This is what unconditional love is all about. We can't expect to have a lasting relationship with anyone if we're keeping scorecards under the table. What you feel or do isn't supposed to be reciprocated play-for-play by them. That's not a relationship, that's either a bartering partnership or it's a game. Life is too short to waste time with such nonsense.

Many ask me about true love and whether or not it exists. We all know true friendship exists, yet most doubt true love. True friendship has no hidden agenda. We do not try to stifle or change the individuality of our true friend; we love them for who they are. Through thick and thin, true friendship stands the test of time. In the simplest of terms, true love is very much akin to true friendship. If you have experienced true friendship, then you can experience true love. As one who has both, I wish them also for everyone. – Charmainism

Do what feels right to you. When it's genuine, others will notice it. If they don't, then they probably have been hurt or burned before by someone for which they cared and are cautious. No need to get into the past. Show them by example how it works. They'll soon find you're a person comfortable in your own skin and one who doesn't expect reciprocal action on their part. They owe you nothing because you're confident and caring. You care, love, and give without regard as to whether or not it's being appreciated, reciprocated, or misunderstood. What could be more fearless and peaceful than that?

When you really believe in your heart that life is good and that choosing to LIVE fully instead of DYING slowly is YOUR CHOICE -- you're then content and happy with the reality of what life is. – Charmainism

You love because you DO. Why is it so difficult for people to understand that a great relationship is no different than a great friendship? When others ask me, "How is it that your husband of over four decades is as wonderful for you to be with as ever after all those years?"

Imagine someone asking you the same question about a lifelong best friend? It doesn't happen, does it? No. (Well, my husband is my best friend too, but you know what I mean.) Finding the right person for you is as easy as just being yourself. That person will come along when you least expect it. Because when you're simply being yourself, you are as affable as you'll ever be. You don't have to spend a moment looking for love. Love, my darling, will find you!

Just remember that you can't keep score. You can't put parameters on your friendships and relationships. That's not the way to happiness at all. If you don't have any real close relationships then that's your first indication that your expectations just might be unrealistic. Most of the time a person will find they have an unrealistic laundry list of what they want or think they want in a mate. Finding a mate isn't like trying to figure out which coffee is your favorite brand. There's no need for a list. Why write down something that is YOU? Can't you remember who you are and what you like? Well, of course you can. You have simply complicated that which should be very simple. Don't over-think.

You have to do what's right for you. And you always think before you leap. However, being the imperfect human beings that we are, we often tend to grossly over-think before doing some of the simplest things. Especially when it comes to relationships, or even what to wear to a garden luncheon.

For most people there comes a time when they just aren't sure of where they stand in a relationship or what exactly is expected of them in a given situation. They want to be a great friend, but they also don't want to be abused by that friendship. They've been hurt and used as a doormat and are quite tired of it.

How does one be a great friend and yet still understand when it's necessary to simply say "no?" Once again, you have to learn how to use finesse to carry you peacefully over the humps of what could otherwise become a very unpleasant situation. We all have weaknesses and we're fully aware of those. But protection against exploitation of those weaknesses is an entirely different matter. It also can be done!

Protecting Your Weaknesses

No one can walk on you if you just stand up! – Charmainism

Just like anyone who reads vampire chronicles of any kind, the first lesson you know about vampires is they can't enter your home unless you invite them in. So sleep well at night because you shut the door in their face! They aren't coming in (and the garlic around your neck will help just in case you may have invited one in by mistake). The same with negative energy – don't let it in! Be it in the way of television, the Internet, newspapers, magazine articles, radio, or any other media source...do <u>not</u> invite negative energy into your home and into your mind. It works on you far more than you know.

As you can choose how to handle your life and keep things in a positive perspective, you also have to cultivate that newfound positivity by refraining from sources that you feel have a negative impact on your well-being and that of your household.

Negativity is the cornerstone of frustration. Frustration is the smoke of the fire to anger. We can choose to be positive, let confrontation roll off our backs, and take the high road. When we take the high road we know we have done the right thing for us. It's not like we allowed someone to get over on us or get away with something. Rather, we did it for ourselves. It's for our own peace of mind that we must refuse to allow negativity the power to poison us.

Yes! It's up to us whether or not we'll allow someone or some thing that kind of power over us. Who is to say that another person's opinion or comment should hurt us? The despair of getting our feelings hurt is something ingrained within us from a very early age. But we're adults now and can make sense of it. This should carry over to anything and everything that seems to have a negative affect on us. We don't have to let the actions of others annoy us to the point of distraction from what could be a very peaceful and happy life!

But this also means we have to watch out for our *own* annoying and counterproductive actions as well. We can be our own worst distraction! This means keeping the futility of stress and worry out of our lives and in the proper perspective:

Worry is a killer. Respect worry in that manner and you will find this murderous villain is much easier to kick to the curb than you ever thought possible. – Charmainism

When petty things constantly distract a person by worrying over them, it's a wake-up call that, simply, one has too much time to think. You have to get busy doing something else that takes your mind off of wandering around into pits of self-drawn quicksand. When we're sitting

around worrying, things around us become increasingly irritating. We're on edge and that edge is quickly eroding. We'll eventually slide off the cliff of sanity if such negative and self-destructive behaviors aren't put in check. We have to get hold of our mind and use it to get things in the proper perspective.

Stresses in life are more often caused by how we perceive a situation rather than the situation actually being stressful to the extent we have made it to be. Otherwise everyone would find the same scenarios equally stressful. But we do not. Not everyone sits around worrying their heads into a lather of total and futile frustration.

Much has to do with what we "feel" is happening. In truth, there's no real "feeling" that has bearing on any of it, but more of our way of "thinking" that has everything to do with how we handle any given situation. We convince ourselves we can't handle it, or we convince ourselves we can. If it's the former, than we worry about it even though it hasn't been proven that we can't overcome it.

It's our manner of thinking that is key to making peace with our dilemmas. If we think we'll be afraid, we so shall be. If we think we can excel, we so shall do. If we think we should worry because we aren't sure of what to do: then we'll let worry consume every possible positive option and allow negativity to convince us we indeed have something about which to demand intense worry!

This is a lot like feeling the need to place blame on something or someone for our shortcomings.

When we stop having the need to place blame on someone or something else for life's valleys, then we'll begin to see the distant outline of the path to inner peace up on the hill. It's there! We simply have to take responsibility for making the changes necessary to impact our lives in a positive manner.

People happy in their own skin rarely have issues with much of anything. When happy, there is little time to sit and ponder over that which is a waste of time and energy. When things aren't what one expected, that is when the self-serving convenience to find fault with most anything and anybody tends to surface. Scapegoats can take the most intriguing forms. As the adage states, 'necessity is the mother of invention.' Need someone or something to blame for your problems? Go find one. It's all the rage, you know. But it is definitely not in your best interest to do so! – Charmainism

When one is at peace with self, the world is a fantastic place. All those in it aren't feared but endeared. We embrace others we used to cringe at the thought of having to spend more than five minutes in their presence. How does this change come about? It comes about with the realization that we'd rather have that person living this life and thus retain the possibility of another encounter, rather than attending their funeral and never seeing them again. We have to keep things in the proper perspective.

We have to keep it real like that. Such is the reality of life! We moan and groan over that which should make absolutely no difference to us. Sure, there may be a sibling or other relative who is a loon, but would you rather have them gone from this life in order to make you happier? I think not.

Nothing and no one can make you happier as what you can do for yourself with a positive way of looking at things. We are the driving force that determines whether or not we'll be happy and at peace. It makes no difference what mood anyone else is in at the family reunion or Thanksgiving dinner, because <u>you're in a good mood</u> each and every day, regardless of the moods of others.

That's what keeps happy and peaceful people that way no matter what happens around them. They're happy and at peace down to their very soul. Down to the bone and beyond. It's who they are because it's who they choose to be!

If you've too much time on your hands and find that you're sitting around worrying about things, it may mean that you're uncertain about your own sense of purpose. Could be that you're doing a job that gives you satisfaction to some extent, but you think the going's on in the world are overshadowing any attempts you make to do your part to make the world a better place. You feel like things are spiraling out of control and the sense of helplessness is getting to be quite overwhelming.

Worry is the fog that blinds the pathway
to clear thinking and solutions. – Charmainism

You want the world to be a better place. You want others to show more love, caring, and compassion for one another. You feel the world has become spiteful, hateful, and bitter. You've told yourself time and again that you'll never be one of those types of people. So instead, you sit and worry not only about where the world is headed, but also about the questionable choices being made by those you care about and love. And then you worry about them too!

And you also have noticed that these days you usually find someone or something to blame the ills of the world on! You seem to see things very much in black and white anymore. Not many gray areas.

Well, let's be clear here about "gray." The world is full of gray areas. If you're seeing things in black and white and see them clearly enough to think you know who is to blame for every bad thing that happens in this world...then you're harboring resentment against some things. Because it is never, ever that easy!

It also means that you must be careful, because this is a very vulnerable time for you. It might be very easy for a vampire to walk across the threshold and into your home. And he might have brought luggage!

Well, not really a vampire. But in a sense, yes!

It's a lot easier to use people who don't know what they want out of life or what their path is to make the changes they wish to make. They're fledglings in a world full of grown up vultures who are more than ready to eat them for lunch and then wipe the corners of their mouths with what's left of the shirt that was on your back! They'll take everything and leave you with nothing.

People who abuse themselves by degradation and mental flogging are also very vulnerable to being abused by others. They allow it to happen because they subliminally think they don't deserve better. Or they're so lonely for companionship that their home has always been somewhat of a revolving door for any assortment of guests whether they walk in on two legs or four. Before they know it, once again they have a house full of responsibilities that actually don't belong to them yet are taxing their very being beyond their financial, physical, and mental abilities. They have had enough but can't seem to clear their home and their life of the never-ending stream of temporary guests who are always somewhat permanent.

It also happens when kind-hearted and generous people don't see the asterisk at the end of the definition of what "unconditional love" actually is. We can love our family and dear friends unconditionally by accepting them for who they are, but the mental asterisk should kick in that everything has its limitations. Some abusers use that "unconditional" cloak by which to hide behind and push you into a corner. These are the users. They were here before the term "unconditional love" ever crossed anyone's lips and they'll continue to be on this earth long after the buzz word is dead and buried.

The term has brought users to rationalize that using that "unconditional love" is a great way to seek out free housing, food, clothing, and miscellaneous assistance not only from we as taxpayers, but again when they want us to put them up in our own homes until they get on their feet. The problem is that they have never made any real attempt to actually get on their feet! If you turn them down, you're a number of different nasty names as they go through all your family and friends with their tale of how selfish you are!

If this doesn't happen to you, then consider yourself in far better shape than many others. Seriously, this happens far more often than you might imagine. Often times, the ones who try to help those who seem to need a helping hand are the very ones who already have the most problems prior to the addition of bringing in yet another responsibility. It's happens easily to households where something is already missing and the discontent is high. The household seems to function better when there are chaotic distractions away from that which was dull and boring...a rather mundane and routine existence before the visitors came. But what this situation lacks in boredom it makes up in increasingly more negative ways: drama, financial hardship, and hassles. Yet those whose homes have a revolving door, get in these types of situations time and time again with usually the same negative outcome.

And then the cycle repeats itself again. The faces of the visitors have changed, but the dance remains the same.

Don't be a victim. If you act like a victim, you're an easy target for those who can see the bull's eye on your back. It's sitting right beneath that long yellow streak running parallel with your fear of confrontation. You must stand up for yourself. However, this doesn't mean you have to be ready for an unpleasant showdown or a fight...no! In fact, it's quite the opposite. Smile! Be confident! When a person exudes confidence, others take notice. This happens quite naturally once a person finds inner peace.

Every breath brings joy when your heart is truly grateful for the opportunity to live. Forgetting that fact makes things far more difficult than they really are. Worry is an expense your mind and body cannot afford because it overshadows clear and constructive thinking. Bottom line: be happy throughout this journey called life. The peaks and valleys will smooth out much faster if you're whistling between them. – Charmainism

People who take advantage of others know exactly where they stand because your mood and body language tells them. They know the very moment when you realize you've been had and are having a problem getting them out of our house or your life! You avoid them, but when you do see them you ask if they have eaten. You see where I'm going with this? Your guilt and depression against yourself is rewarding them with the sweet life of sponging off of you! They don't see you changing anytime soon...so they plan on milking this cow for as long as they possibly can. This is why in such situations you have to stand up and stand up immediately. You don't have to waste one minute on being angry or frustrated. Just do it and rid your home of unwanted guests who are taking advantage of your hospitality. It's over.

Why don't most people stand up for themselves and/or others? I truly believe there are a lot of people who have a deep displeasure for confrontation – any kind of confrontation. This is something that has to change. Not every confrontation is a negative thing.

In this life, there's no way you'll ever agree with each and every person you encounter. Often, you have to agree to disagree! There's no harm in that at all. It's just two people on different wavelengths allowing mutual respect by deciding to feel just fine ending a conversation by meeting in the middle. Then it's done and you both can move on either together in a relationship, or apart and free from one another. Not everyone is compatible with each other. And when you don't meet in the middle...you meet where it's most comfortable to you. Then it's up to the other person to either accept you for the way you are or kick your friendship to the curb. And that's okay too. You can't possibly please everyone.

It's just the way life is. And it's fine. There are plenty of other people for that person to call "friend." If you're not comfortable with someone, there usually is a reason. Feel confident in that, and don't take it that there must be something wrong with you simply because you get a bad feeling when you're around a certain individual. No worries.

Instincts are there to assist self-preservation.
Learn to feel them. - Charmainism

One of the best things you can do for yourself is decide to never make a snap decision when it comes to an unusual request from someone who is more like an acquaintance than a near and dear friend. Especially when the request is to borrow money. Most of the time, the very first thing that should come into your mind is why doesn't this person have closer friends and family members to solicit? You're merely an acquaintance. Most times, it's because they have either burned their bridges with those closest to them due to never making good on the loans, or because those closest to them have cut them off so as not to be a facilitator of the person's bad choices.

One way of handling the money issue is to allow the person to borrow a very small amount of money for a very short period of time. Depending on the person, of course, you'll know whether or not they're important enough in your life to put forth this little test: when they don't repay as per the agreement, then *you* have paid very little for a lesson well learned. It ends the idea of using you as a lender because they already have an outstanding debt with you. Positive Indifference with finesse...to the max!

Learning how to protect your weaknesses is what will make you ultimately strong. The more you know about yourself, the more you can guard against the things that can occur when you just let things happen. There are others who watch you do that, and they're waiting in the wings for the time they can take advantage of you. It's up to you to not allow it. You don't have to fear it; you just have to have the confidence that you'll make the right decisions when the time comes. You've learned your lessons and understand how to empower yourself.

And you don't have to be angry about it. You know you can handle it.

When you truly love yourself, you can spread that love everywhere you go. And you can spread that love without the fear that someone will be right there to exploit it! You'll realize that when you're comfortable showing your love to others, that love doesn't have to expose your vulnerabilities and become a liability. The thought processes of a secure individual are pretty much the same as an insecure one when it comes to trying to be helpful and thoughtful to an individual in need. Only the outcome is very different!

It's a tough lesson to learn being harder on people than you'd like to be. But that's the way life is. We all have to do it from time to time in order to save our own peace of mind and keep our own families and dear friends in balance. When we say, "yes" to something we really don't want, we give out all the wrong signals. We make ourselves a target for the users of this world.

It's up to us to stop the cycle of allowing others to abuse us. It can't happen unless we allow it.

Let's say a person you haven't seen in decades shows up at your door. You all used to be good friends at one time but then this person had a string of bad luck, much of which was his or her own doing. They come to your door and bring a gift of cheap wine. Mind you, nothing wrong with cheap wine if that's all one can afford, but once inside the warmth of your home, they immediately ask for a cold beer. They didn't bring beer.

"Got any nuts or chips?"

"This is a nice place. How many bedrooms?"

While you're getting the nuts and chips, they're scoping out the sleeping situation... checking out the number of bedrooms and where they are. And all the while, you're talking from the kitchen as you think, "How nice it is they stopped by to see you after all these years."

You get my point.

The other shoe is about to drop. And you aren't even ready for it because you never heard or saw the first shoe come off.

A good-hearted person doesn't have to be a fool. There's no reason to let others use you as a doormat. They'll use you until you have no choice but to ask them to go out on an errand and change the locks while they're gone. Imagine that. The sad thing is that this scenario happens somewhere every day! It doesn't have to be this way.

Don't be afraid to use finesse to take care of such situations. For those who are shy when it comes to confrontations, finesse is your best friend!!

At the very first hint that this person wants more than what they brought along with them, you should put your guard up a bit. That simply means that your ears are pricked and your eyes are wide open.

When they began to ask about your house and number of bedrooms, after stating the number, it would be non-confrontational to say something like, "We've always got family coming in from out-of-town." That's when the person is backed against the wall if they were thinking of using you as a homeless shelter. They'll probably immediately ask when you're expecting company again.

You just say "Tomorrow."

It's as simple as that. You make it obviously inconvenient to be available to assist them. People have a way of telling their true colors during conversation as they prod and probe to find out how flexible you are when it comes to being manipulated. Kindly be inflexible!

Finesse is what shows them they can't pull the wool over your eyes, yet they don't even realize it — therefore, there are no hard feelings from them of which you might fear retaliation. It's a win-win for you because you're confident that you can finesse your way through the situation and smile all the while. This person has tuned you into just why they'll never make it past the front porch next time.

"Well, it was great seeing you. Thanks for the wine. I've got a few obligations of which to attend now. Sorry I don't have more time. You take care. Bye!"

And that's that.

Now the next time someone comes to your door, you know you have options! You don't have to hide behind a curtain and wait from someone to leave. They don't have to be invited into the house at all. Vampires are best left on the porch right in front of the garlic on your door!

When the hairs on the back of your neck stand up, so should you! - Charmainism

You can hit these issues head on and feel good about it and good about how you handled it. You can also feel good about yourself because you know you'll no longer be used. You now "get it."

Since you now have a good idea of how to finesse situations, you don't have to be immediately in the know of what someone's intentions are, but you've all the faith in the world that if a person is up to no good, you'll know it. How? They'll tell on themselves. You need only listen.

That's right. There's no need to think you have to grill someone to get down to the truth. None of that matters at all. Just let it flow with all the confidence of a positive situation. If and when it turns negative, you'll work it so that they go their way and you yours…all with no hard feelings.

Users will talk about you behind your back. They'll use similar incidents to let others know that you wouldn't help them. They feel you could have assisted them, but you didn't. Most all users do this in order to

SHAKE HANDS WITH YOURSELF

gain the ear and attention of their next potential victim. They live by the art of manipulation and this is their way of feeling out who the next victim will be. Their sob story just added another character (you) and since they couldn't use you at your home without your permission, they found another way to use you: they spin the tale that they were wronged by your selfishness and hope to create an ounce of sympathy from someone that they can parlay into a charity jackpot.

When all the guests of a pity party leave, the host will finally realize it's time to move on and get back to life! Be a true friend and not a facilitator of another's perpetual negativity. Tough love is best for those we care about who find themselves ensnared in the destructive cycle of self-pity. – Charmainism

Again, do not invite the vampires who feed on negative energy into your life!

When you find out you have been talked about disparagingly, just let it go. Really. There's no reason to get anything straight with anyone about it. Users don't pay attention when being chastised. They live for the moment and for their next pigeon. Don't waste a breath or a word. Just let it go. Why? Because, once again, it's in your best interest to do so! Your peace of mind and inner peace are counting on you!

It's like thinking passing new laws will make criminals be more law-abiding. It makes no sense. Criminals, who have no respect at all for themselves or the law, could care less that another law was passed. It couldn't be to thwart them because they don't adhere to the law. They never have! So it's the same way with thinking you can get something straight with a person who uses others. You can't. That person is going to keep the same user mentality they have always had because they have no desire to change it. They have learned to get what they can when they can and care less about whom they hurt in the process.

Let it go. Trust me.

You can most certainly be a loving, kind, and compassionate person without fear of exposing your vulnerabilities and weaknesses. By utilizing the methods you're learning, you'll neutralize such fears and kick worry to the curb. You know that negative energy will never be your friend. Stay positive and surround yourself with optimistic people whenever possible. And until that's possible, let your new skills give you the confidence that you can handle situations deftly and with no anger, animosity, or resentment. Let that alone free your mind from worry and fear. You're being empowered and well on your way up the winding staircase of the Lighthouse of Inner Peace!

You're in control of your destiny! That destiny is one of happiness and inner peace. It's yours for the taking!

Have positive control over your life by first and foremost keeping it peaceful. Steer clear of situations that have the potential to compromise your sense of inner peace and balance within your own household. – Charmainism

Throughout all that led up to meeting my beloved Bill, I remained wholly positive and totally upbeat. I knew no other way to think or be. I couldn't blame anyone for what happened to Gerald and me. The facts are that my father had an affair when he was separated from my mother and he and she were almost a thousand miles apart at that time. When they got back together, many years later, I was the product of that reconciliation. The asterisk, however, was the family secret…except *all* the family didn't know the secret! So who could possibly know that one day Gerald and I would become an item for eight whole months and turn both our families upside down?

Eight months?! That's a long time! Those who *did* know the inside scoop were waiting for my father to tell me. Everyone was waiting on Daddy to tell me before they could utter a word and clean up their own messes. Everyone felt it *should* be him and only him to tell me. So it took eight months and a family meeting called by Gerald's relatives demanding action on my father's part to get the job done to finally get the job done. The relationship was not going to "blow over" as Daddy had thought. Breaking this up and bringing out the truth was not going to be pretty and it could potentially ruin many lives. I'm sure my father knew every possibility and instead had tried to wait it out. Let it "blow over," as he thought. Well, that was not to be. The truth, in this case, had to be set free.

I'll never forget that night. The phone rang at about 2 a.m. and it was Gerald. He never called me quite that late. I'd my own room and my own phone. A pink Princess model, the one that my two older sisters couldn't believe I had! They certainly had nothing like that when they were home at my age…and right next to my bed…sharing a room with no one. Well, in truth, I never shared a bed with anyone because I had Restless Leg Syndrome…just the way I was born. My legs and butt wriggled all the time I was in bed. Sleep was this phantom thing that occasionally came to visit me. Most nights, I was up reading or writing. But this night, 'er, early morning hour, the pink Princess phone was ringing.

"Hello?"

"Hey…"

It was Gerry. He didn't sound right.

"Hey Honey. What's going on?"

He could hardly talk, "I can't. I can't um…oh my God…" He was crying, or so it seemed. Not overtly, but it was obvious to me he was trying to hide the fact that he was distraught.

I talked to him, trying to get out of him what was wrong. I knew someone must have died or something. Something horrible had happened, but he wasn't making sense.

"Gerry, you have to take a breath and stop for a minute. I can't understand you Baby."

"Your Dad is here at my house."

I thought he said my Dad was at his house! Well, that can't be. Dad is out drinking with his buddies. He hasn't come home yet.

I could hear the door downstairs open. My father was home.

"He's not at your house, Gerry. He's here. He just got home. I can hear him downstairs."

"Then he just left," Gerald's says. He continued, very sullenly, as if numb and just going through the motions, "They say he's my father too. I'm your brother."

Oh this was just too much. These fools watch too many dang dumb movies with stupid jokes and childish pranks! Gerry never was like this…must be that it's late and he's just not acting right or something. I'd never joke about something like that. Gotta be that his good pal Jeff or cousin Butch is there in the room with him waiting to bust out laughing or something…I'm not liking this type of humor at all. I got ready to say so, but I heard something. Oh, bet Daddy's wondering just who I'm talking to this time of night.

The downstairs phone extension picked up…

"Mainie?"

"Yes, Daddy, I'm getting off," I said.

"Who are you talking to this time of night?"

"Oh. Well, Gerry, Dad. He's upset about something I think. Not sure."

"Well, I just want you to know you're talking to your brother."

Then that certain "CLICK."

That was it. That's how it was confirmed. I was in a state of shock. Real shock.

Gerry started really crying. Well, sobbing. We both did. We both were crying our eyes out and hadn't talked this over at all. What was there to talk about? How could I've known that this was indeed actually true? I mean TRUE. That means my mother knew… that means everyone knew. That means, oh my. This all means so much and the bottom line equates to it being forgotten. We can't let this kill us. We can't. For surely it could. Surely it could.

For the next fifteen minutes neither of us said a word. We just cried, and cried. And cried some more. I remember hanging up the phone and then regretting it. I should've said goodbye or something but I couldn't. I just wanted to run and run and run. So that's what I did. I got up, put my tennis shoes on, and went outside and ran around the block about four times until I couldn't stand anymore. It's so hard to cry and run at the same time.

But I had to do whatever it took to make sense of this incredible nonsense that happened to be my life! There was no thought of sympathy, and I hardly discussed it at all with anyone. I didn't want to *talk* about it…I needed to *deal* with it!

It was Gerry that I cared about so much. For me, and my deep-seated religious convictions, there was nothing to do but cut the line and get on with my life. Because of that, separating myself from Gerry as a girlfriend was no problem for me. However, I knew it would be a terrible problem for him. To him, whether one was saying "girlfriend" or "sister" meant little difference in this case because it was a total technicality. We didn't grow up together. We simply had the same father. But it wasn't quite that simple to <u>me</u>.

And he was so young at the time. He was actually sixteen when we first met and I was thirteen. We had birthdays soon after that. Even so, we were just youngsters. Kids. Peer pressure at that time, for Gerry, would've been pretty bad over something like this. For me, it wasn't an issue because it wasn't anyone's business. I mean what could anybody say? So no one said much of anything about it to me, unless it was to ask whether it was true or not. And only a very few did that.

I just felt so bad for him. He couldn't get back what he had been cheated out of: what seemed to be the love of his life. And I can't blame him for that. He was a young boy with everything to live for, and suddenly it was ripped away from him. And he also finally got the father that he had always wanted. But it just so happened that it was the wrong father! Wrong father? But without that father, Gerald would've never existed! I wouldn't ever wish for that. I love him tremendously even to this very day. Reminds me of how we must always be so very careful of what we wish for...things have to be thought out and seen for what they really are before we can make the mistake and think that an "undo" button could change our lives for the better. No. In reality, if such a fantasy could be done, it would change *everything*!

There were many who admired that I held no animosity towards my father about any of this. To me, it was a natural response to not blame my father for something that happened long before I was born. It was apparent to me I'd no right at all to act as if it were something that simply happened to *me*. But I most certainly forgave myself first. The rest was relatively easy, except for watching the self-destruction of Gerry.

Thinking that way is how I've remained positive throughout my life. Even when shrouds of depression were nipping at me from time to time, I knew I had to survive it by focusing on keeping my sanity intact. It would've been so very easy to just let go and allow the darkness of self-pity to engulf me.

That's where being a peacemaker at heart really helped me. For I was affable, yes, approachable when my future husband came up and introduced himself to me.

Had I not been affable, I could've missed the opportunity to get to know him altogether. Had I been surly, perhaps he would've had no further interest in me. I would've lost the greatest love of my life! That would've changed the course of history for so many people it's just incredible to think about it.

It just goes to show you that we've got to make things happen for ourselves. We must be READY to make it so.

Facing and dealing with all that's occurred in my life has given me great inner strength and resolve to make each and every day count. Bill has often said that my unwaveringly positive disposition is nothing short of amazing, and that he's learned much by sharing his life with a born peacemaker.

No matter what comes our way, we know we'll find a way to make the best of it and make our lives the better for it! We choose to be happy no matter what. No matter what.

Chapter Nine: The Beacon of Light Becomes the Peacemaker in You

At the Helm of Happiness – Navigating through the perils of negative energy. Your life is your ship. You're the Captain. Whatever scenario arises, it is the Captain who makes the ultimate decisions. The buck stops at the Captain's cabin door. Everything that occurs on that ship, good or bad, the Captain takes full responsibility. – Charmainism

Happiness. Your journey began by exploring your fear and now winds down to end on the upbeat note of real happiness! How poetic! Seriously, as you take these last steps toward your journey's end, it's my hope that by now the thought of happiness brings with it a beacon of enlightenment shining upon it.

We've delved into how everyone knows the kind of happiness that's a natural response when something wonderful occurs. You know that kind of elation one feels that's nothing short of jubilant and positively wonderful. The kind we feel at weddings, or when being informed of the birth of babies, winning in sports, during celebratory parties, or even when the office jokester comes up with another good one! Such things can brighten our day and our spirits.

And we know that when we get too busy or bogged down with details and lose our sense of humor, we fail to take advantage of all the opportunities that pass our way where we could've enjoyed another moment of happiness. When time continues to march on without much infusion of comedic relief, a bit of melancholy has its chance to creep inside our minds, then our hearts.

And when that occurred, we used to wonder what happened because we never really had thought about trying to understand it. All we knew was that we were doing just fine last week, but this week we're feeling rather down. Whenever too much time passed in between our feelings of genuine happiness, we began to believe that perhaps our problem might be that we're unhappy.

Through your journey here, you've learned that you weren't really and truly unhappy, but more accurately, caught up it in the vortex of a zone of the emotional unknown. Before this knowledge, you reacted with fear and worry about it.

You now understand that there resided in you an affinity for misinterpreting those times. When life was not tingling with excitement, you interpreted it as living life dull. You wanted and yearned, but knew not for that which you were searching. You were on a quest to find not only a spark, but also preferably a light so bright it could lead you back to where you left your zest for life.

We expect to be happy. When we're not feeling fully satisfied with ourselves in every way, it's easy for the mind to conclude that since we're not "happy," we therefore are "unhappy."

We have to refrain from the selfish habit of expecting from others, and ourselves, that which we think we deserve. – Charmainism

We can't compare our overall sense of well-being as that of "happiness," until we get the right perspective on what the word means in all reality. Most people associate happiness as a great feeling, one that comes about when good things happen. But if happiness is being

constantly compared to the kind of temporary jubilation one feels when their favorite team wins a major championship . . . well, you see the problem with that. It's not a fair comparison.

Even so, most feel there must be some way to find a deeper, lasting kind of happiness. You'd think, "There has to be a kind of 'true' happiness. A lasting, deep fulfillment with finally being happy!" This is looking for contentment. And now you know that what you yearned for is actually that of having a happy disposition. It means you're happy regardless of what happens. Maybe that's why the two words "happy" and "happen" are so much alike!

When you began to read this book, you were like most people who put too much pressure on themselves thinking that they must make enormous changes in their life in order to rise up from feeling down during this search for 'true' happiness. What you didn't know at the time was that regardless of what notions and perceptions one may have, the path to happiness is always the same. This is why people find it so elusive as they mistakenly take this route or that route, all with no success. They keep trying again and again, but until they get on the right path they'll not attain true happiness and inner peace.

Happiness was there with you, hoping to make it to the surface. It was always standing right before you in your reflection. Happiness has never been that brass ring one grabs while riding the merry-go-round, or any other fleeting type of "feel good" sensation. Rather, happiness is within you!

Happiness is really nothing more than a state of mind. Happiness can therefore be with you each and every day of your life. Happiness is a choice you make. Happiness is a promise you make to yourself. –
Charmainism

Now that you've followed the beacon of light that shines from within yourself, your route to happiness will always be the same. It's simple and straightforward. There's no long list of things "To Do." You're fully aware now that the secret is to simply shake hands with yourself and decide to be happy regardless of what happens on any given day. Happiness is your beacon of light – and the beacon of light becomes you!

Your life is your very own movie script. You write what happens in it and then how you'll react to the scenes that occur. It's your choice to write in, "She was visibly upset, but quickly gained control of her emotions." You're the screenwriter and all the reactions in your life's movie are ones that are completely under your own control. No one can force you to change one direction in that script.

Your emotions are the one thing in life that you can have under your complete control. No one can force you how to think or react. Not unless you allow it. And by now, you know the importance of that all too well.

You have a grasp on the facts about your emotions--that your emotional state is yours to control. No one makes you angry—rather, when angered, you allowed yourself to become angry. No one makes you sad or depressed—rather, you allowed yourself to succumb to it. You've decided to take charge and pull back on the reins of frustration and negativity by opting to keep the gray clouds out! You do this by opening the drapes of enlightenment and letting the sunshine of positivity in!

Control your emotions and you control your inner peace and happiness. It really is that simple. What we feel is more often what we think we should feel, rather than what our own emotions are actually dictating. Start listening to your body and mind...the harmony will drown out the influences of others in this world who have no control of their emotions. You aren't them. – Charmainism

SHAKE HANDS WITH YOURSELF

No more prostrating and wondering! There's no reason to wonder about much of anything. If it's a daydream, go for it! But if your thoughts aren't anything more than a precursor to worry, then leave it at the curb with the last of your baggage. Those days are over!

You've learned that it's human nature to set ourselves up by thinking we've the right to be unhappy during certain times in our life. We've been conditioned to believe it's okay to exploit our emotions, and those of others, during times of what our family, friends, and society has shown us should evoke great pain, worry, and/or intense sorrow.

But now you've graduated to a level where you know your life doesn't have to be programmed this way! You value the alternative to deprogram and neutralize those types of emotions by shaking your own hand and using the beacon of light that your positivity projects. This is how you'll expose and conquer all which looms in the shadows of self-pity. This is how inner turmoil is replaced by inner peace!

Dark skies cannot dampen the light that shines from within...it's <u>always</u> sunny inside the positive heart. – Charmainism

You now understand that all the challenges of life should be embraced; for how else would we truly know the immense joy of triumph! Of course there will be certain events that will cause great pain and sorrow, but now you're fully aware that literally suffering through any of it is simply not necessary.

You understand and embrace the fact that death is as much a part of life as life itself, and knowing this allows you to take an extra deep breath and let the process of mourning and healing take its natural course. You no longer fear it. You know you'll survive it because your love and wonderful memories of those lost will carry you through the hard times. And you'll find them again in your dreams and when you speak to them as if they're still there with you. You refuse to lose them twice! Keeping them in your life is a magical cure!

Our lives take huge blows of pain, suffering, angst and anguish. When those things occur, if we think we should be literally suffering through those trials, then we'll do just that – we'll suffer miserably. We have to remember that it's how we choose to cope with the hard times that will make all the difference being unhappy and being the happiest you can be in the duration.

I'm still incredibly positive and shall remain this way forever and a day, just as my father before me. From my earliest memories of him to my very last as he died, he always remained positive. He died on his own terms and had declared just that to my sisters and me at the time. Mother had passed two years prior and he called us in to his hospital bedside to tell us he was tired. He said it was time for him to move on and that it was all just fine. He calmly stated he liked his private room and that he wouldn't be going home (even though he was only to be in the hospital for a couple of days for a routine procedure). He then told us not to worry, that it was all just fine as he was good with it. Early the next day, his physician said she couldn't understand it but my father's organs were shutting down. We then told her what Daddy declared to us.

That following evening Daddy passed. He always did have a flair of doing things his way. It was a fitting end to his most wonderful earthly life. Even with all the deaths of those near and dear to me that I'd previously faced, little did I know how deeply my father's death would affect me. It was like losing my son and my brother Gerald all over again. They both were so very much like my father. So very much like me. And now they were gone.

We all were around his bed as he slipped into the unknown. I'd left for a couple of hours to get some rest as I'd been up all night with Daddy. My husband said it was too much and that I needed to get some rest. I was exhausted. While I was gone, Daddy left too. I truly believe he wasn't going anywhere until I was no longer in the room. Those in the room at the time said they were all away from the bed for the first time, yet still in the room. They looked over and, well, they knew.

I got back to the hospital in record time and rushed to Daddy's room. You'd think I'd be ready. I wasn't. He truly was gone. My best friend from my earliest days and memories, the man who I could tell anything at anytime, was no more. The one who was my Hero. I'd never hear him say my name again or hear him say, "Stay pretty." The man who always had a twinkle in his eye, and a dimple to accompany every grin, had departed for destinations unknown. He was my greatest mentor and the most magnetic person I've ever known. And he was gone. I thought about my daughter and my grandson, Will. They would be totally devastated.

As my heart grew heavier and my mind raced with all sorts of thoughts about not being able to talk to Daddy again, you know…and all those things that you think about that cut down deep inside your soul. I just couldn't take it. I thought about my daughter when jus two years prior she learned about grandmother passing, and then within the same hour learned her brother had died as well. Those are the type of blows you don't want to take yourself, so you'd do *anything* to keep your children from going through it. But this they would have to endure as well.

Little Will was only seven years old when he found out his father and paternal great-grandmother had passed. The thought of it at that moment as I sat there, having just lost my own father as a grown adult, was something that made my heart feel as if it would literally burst. How can young children endure such things? And then I realize it was not a question. We, as adults, are still the same young children we used to be so long ago. Left on their own, without negative outside influence, children would probably be fine making peace with death. It's our fears that fuel the intense loss that makes it seem we can't recover. Children usually don't have those deep-seeded fears.

And I began to wail at the thought of it all. I loved my father with all my heart. And suddenly, I couldn't quite breathe. My cousin Enyo, my sweet wrestler of my demons, was right there with me. I heard him whisper softly, but firmly, in my ear, "Charmaine, breathe." It was like hearing words spoken by my father for the last time. It was what my father would've said to me. It was what he would've wanted. And I put myself in check and got control of my emotions. It hurt so bad I really was taken off guard. My very first best friend in the world, and my number one hero, was gone from this earth. The thought was hardly bearable.

I remembered, then, to be thankful for the return of my brother Bobby, the spittin' image of my father. Unfortunately, Bobby died a short time thereafter. I'm glad Daddy was not alive to see Bobby die. I'll always be so grateful for the short time my family got to spend with Bobby after forty years of not hearing from him or seeing him. It will always be a miracle for me. I'm sure it was for my father, as he died shortly after the reunion. I think all the hanging threads were back on the spool for him and he had made peace with it all. He had sewn up his life nice and neat...and be at peace before his final sleep.

I had to accept that.

Acceptance is the letter sealed within the envelope of inner peace. –
Charmainism

So just as my father exemplified dignity and grace in his final hours, may we all do the same when we face the deaths of those we love, as well as when it's our turn to face the ultimate transition to destinations unknown. And, so very importantly, may we enjoy the greatness and joy of happiness and inner peace until that time arrives.

Life is full of twists and turns and every wince of strain and strife in between is what makes our lives so challenging. But for those who have learned to make peace with it all and embrace life for all its peaks despite its valleys…we take it all in stride and keep walking on the path called the high road of life. We personify vigor and zest for life! We make peace with ourselves and love every moment. We are peacemakers!

People who have undergone the most horrible of trials can press on and lead wonderfully fulfilling lives. Lives full of happiness and joy despite those horrors and hardships. Even though some may have found themselves temporarily sitting in a pit of darkness and wallowing in their self-imposed prison of self-pity, they eventually can succeed in finding a way out. Those are the people who looked to the light of optimism and the hope that comes from having a positive disposition. My father was a master at it. I'm so proud to have followed in his footsteps throughout my life.

Being positive about the value of being positive is another great lesson. The earlier one learns this lesson, the better life's ride! So hop on the positive train and let your sunny disposition carry you through all of life's rains. – Charmainism

You know there's never a reason for losing control. It doesn't matter what has happened in your life or in the lives of those you love – you realize it makes no sense to use them as an excuse to continue to give in to self-imposed suffering. It's very easy for any fool to make him or herself sick with fear, worry, grief, and/or frustration. But it takes a thinking person to recognize a workable solution will only come about with a clear head and a determination to find a solution! With positive thinking, there's nothing you can't handle.

When we keep these life lessons in the proper perspective, we don't dwell on thoughts that we've been hurt beyond repair, that we can't mend, and that nothing in our lives will ever be the same. You now know better.

When we come to peaceful terms with such things, life flourishes with new experiences, and whether good or bad, each test of our dedication to become a tried and true Peacemaker hones and solidifies our deftness of how to maintain inner peace.

That's why you now must decide to make the changes necessary for you to grasp and put into practice the philosophy learned herein. Because happiness and inner peace are here for you to attain!

You're well aware that when you change your manner of thinking so that your disposition is truly one that's positive in nature, each day builds favorably upon the one that preceded it. The ladder of happiness and contentment can go up as high as you want it. But you have to put your foot on the first rung in order to get there. To find peace with yourself, you must choose the pathway to the Lighthouse of Inner Peace!

Life at times may not seem so sweet...but when staring point-blank at its alternative...life suddenly has the taste of honey, sugar, and Shoo Fly pie! Keep it all in perspective, my darlings. Stay positive! – Charmainism

Putting your happiness and peace of mind first among your priorities means you can handle anything. You understand that no one but you can control your sense of happiness. It simply is that you have to be forever realistic about what happiness actually is. Happiness is a state of mind. I cannot say that enough. This means that happiness can be YOUR state of mind! You'll have to remind yourself of this time and time again. And it's okay! It's worth it.

The light is within you! The task at hand was simply to find a way for you to project that light no matter what circumstances come your way. Life is about circumstances and our choices in dealing with such. It's the choices we make that make the difference in whether we live unhappily or happily.

When our minds are clear of negative energy, we become Peacemakers who exude positive thought and energy. Good things come our way because we're affable and open to new ideas. We are eager to fill our lives with new things and people because we've set aside our fears and put life and all those who cross our path in the proper perspective. We're living life to the fullest and loving each and every moment of it!

The light that we strive to become is one of hope and inspiration to others. It's a beacon of light we all have within us but most haven't learned how to initiate it. So now that we've turned on our beacon of light, we must continue to keep it burning constantly and brightly for all to see and want to emulate.

Through my teachings, you have learned how to think more positively and fully understand that one moment spent entertaining negative energy is a moment too long.

You now are fully cognizant of the negative triggers that lead to unhappiness; and you're armed with the knowledge of what to do to keep those triggers at bay. It's also your understanding that, if not guarded against, the pit of self-pity can turn you back into your own worst enemy once again. But you fear not, for you know that your journey to the Lighthouse of Inner Peace has done exactly what you've needed. You have decided to become a Peacemaker.

You've learned from where many of your reactive negative tendencies emanate and why such behavior is so prevalent in the world of today. But you've also learned the valuable lesson that this type of behavior is counterproductive to your happiness and therefore you employ Positive Indifference to remain calm and collected in the face of confrontation. You know you always have a choice: the light or the dark.

You know that to get what you want in this life, you must choose the light: the beacon of light that shines upon all Peacemakers.

Peacemakers are those who others seek out to be near and eagerly want to get to know. Peacemakers are fascinating to those who'd love to know the secret behind such a pleasant disposition in the face of any and all obstacles. Nothing is an insurmountable obstacle to a Peacemaker. A Peacemaker has what everyone else wants: inner peace. When inside your heart and mind all is well, everything else has a way of falling into place. A Peacemaker is what you become when you're brave enough to love yourself and shake hands with yourself for the rest of the world to take notice and emulate. It really is all about love.

There is no greater power than love. Trust me. – Charmainism

Life and our interactions with others isn't about whom gets in the last word or adds another feather to one's cap. It's not about right or wrong. It's about getting to know another human being and being at peace with whatever the relationship does or does not become. Peacemakers are grateful for everything and everyone.

We win each and every time when we can walk away from any and all confrontation without baggage of any kind. No resentment, no bitterness, no regret, no bad taste, and no worries! We've learned the fine art of Positive Indifference and can truly say, "Always interested in hearing the opinions of others. Nice talking with you!" and mean it.

The burden of rent and taxes on negative energy strains and drains our emotional resources. Balance your emotional budget with strictly positive income. It is up to us which baggage checks we choose to deposit, cash, or discard. – Charmainism

This is how we can feel comfortable talking with anyone. We'll never lose our cool in simple discussion about any subject at any time. There's no reason to do so. For we've learned that once we've lost control of our emotions, our rationale goes right out the door along with it.

Our ways of utilizing a positive disposition has our backs and we treat everything that comes our way as one more experience in life. We're grateful for all experiences because we're here to have them. It is what life is!

If we're alive we can feel it. If we're alive we can handle it!

Children going into high school or off to college, grandbabies being born, friends retiring! The beat goes on. Life is beating like a drum with its perpetual musical score. Take the time to hear and enjoy all of life's rhythms. It's only noise when you perceive it as such. Stay positive! – Charmainism

Every day is day of immense sunshine. No matter what the clouds look like, your day is filled with the heat of the sun and the shine of happiness. Your sun is within you each and every day. That's what real happiness and inner peace are all about. One can't help but smile thinking about it.

You smile when you walk down the street. You say "Hello" to those who pass your way. "Good Morning!" you say, and finally mean it.

I've had people jog by my house while I'm out working in the yard. They hear me say, "Good Morning!" If it is the first time they've ever encountered me, it's not unusual for a person to stop for a moment. The last guy who did this, which happened just a couple of days ago, said, "Can I ask a favor of you?"

I replied, "Anything. What is it?"

He said, "Could you please give me some of your energy!!"

I just love it. I've heard that all my life. Those who want some of my "energy." Those I hug upon meeting all say the same thing, "There's so much energy in your hugs. It feels so wonderful. You should bottle that." Things of that nature are said time and time again.

When I lived aboard my sailboat, s/v September Sea, down in the Florida Keys, the locals' restaurant, "Dockside," quickly became our favorite place for cocktail hour. It got to be that when I arrived, a ritual of those who wanted hugs would line up in the restaurant waiting their turn. It became such a ritual that soon perfect strangers would be in the line and ask if they too could have a hug from me. I was always more than happy to oblige.

I cannot explain just why this is, but I do know that my hugs bring out the best in people. Throughout the decades, there's been only one person who ever asked about what exactly is it that's so special about me, "and those hugs." He actually was skeptical because it was a roomful of youngsters in their 20s and 30s who wanted those hugs. One young man was his own son. Understandable, as the man was new to the area and a parent can't be too careful these days! Instead of offering a verbal explanation, I gave the man a great big hug. It was all the answer he needed.

Perhaps it's because I've always strived to live life to the fullest! My one and only son, Bj, followed in my footsteps. Though his life was prematurely short, his life was living-out-loud tall!! What he did in his thirty-one years, a thousand people never experience even when their lives are combined. People who met Bj only once have told me how he left such an incredibly wonderful and lasting impression on them. He was like that with everyone. He personified LIVING OUT LOUD. He made people smile and feel good about themselves. He truly lived life to the fullest.

Living life to the fullest. To me, it's first about attaining inner peace more than anything else. Reach that and you'll discover your life's cup filled to the brim--no matter how often other factors attempt to deplete from it. When at peace with ourselves we are ever positive and able to refill from within. Living life to the fullest!
− Charmainism

There are people like me in this world who literally love everyone. Fear was never an option for me, so shying away from putting myself out there and embracing people was never given a second thought. I don't have to trust someone in order to show love his or her way; rather, I need only trust myself, and that I do to the nth degree. My father always said I never met a stranger. When others describe him, to this very day, the same is said about him.

When you trust yourself, you've no worry about being taken advantage of or being hurt by others. In my heart, it's instilled in me that being hurt would be my own doing, not what someone else could do to me. My emotions are my own and the controls belong solely to me. When one knows that emotions are totally under one's own control, there's no need for fear. Without fear, there's no frustration. And without frustration there's no disappointment. That very positive mindset serves to extinguish all negative energy from even attempting to inhabit your being!

There are those who may have success with fame or fortune, but if not successful at life by attaining happiness and inner peace, then fame and fortune will not be enough. Happiness is within each and every one of us. It costs not one red cent. Happiness is free of charge.
– Charmainism

Gerald was so much like my father, that for he and I, it was as if we were *meant* to be together…because I *too* was like my father. We could finish each other's sentences. It was like destiny.

But it was not destiny. It was biology. I don't believe Gerald ever recovered from that horrible blow. After his first breakdown at school when he punched the teacher, his visits to the psych ward became an annual event. He was soon diagnosed as manic-depressive. When his episodes would manifest, he used to call and plead with me to leave Bill and go away with him. "We could go to some island where no one knows us," he would say. "We won't have children and no one will be the wiser, they won't know."

And my response was always the same: "But *I'd* know, Gerry. *I'd* know.*"

He died a little more than fifteen years later, still very young and quite tragically at the hand of the police who were sent to pick him up and take him to the hospital. His mother had called them, as she'd done many times before, after the hospital called to let her know his bed on the Psych Ward was ready. This brings up remnants of Robert Jr. and the loss of his eye at the hands of the same police department about fifteen years before that.

Gerald's mother sued the City and received a settlement, just as what happened in my brother Bobby's case with Dad handling it. However, this time, no one would be returning after a forty-year hiatus.

Gerald had called me about three weeks before his death. He apologized for not treating my husband nicer throughout the years. He said that he knew Bill and I were meant for each other and that all those times he accused me of marrying Bill mainly because he couldn't possibly be my brother, was just his anger talking. He said he finally realized that Bill and I were truly in love and were the real deal. I thanked him, but the conversation was very disturbing to me. It felt like he was saying goodbye. Well, the rest is history. Though my heart still aches for him, I keep it simple in my mind. There are things I cannot change. I must accept that.

Life is pain.

The alternative will be here soon enough. – Charmainism

It's up to each and every one of us to find peace within ourselves. Once we learn how to do that, the world becomes a wonderful place. Each day is a blessing and it's an honor to partake in it. This honor has a finite number of days and nights. We know not what number that shall be, but we aren't worried about it at all. When one is at peace, every moment is one in which to relish.

Happiness and inner peace will lead the way for optimal and full development of a better you. Sure, there will be those who won't know whether or not you're the "real deal," and it will be their enlightenment when they discover that you've found the secret to attaining and maintaining true inner peace and happiness.

You have found the harmony that makes your internal choir resonate with the sound of melodies so joyful that others begin to take notice! Share it with them! Let them know where you found it and tell them how they too can attain the same. It isn't difficult; one need only have the desire and follow my philosophy to get where you are now.

We know that situations will arise, and sometimes perhaps in an unpleasant manner, but we have confidence that our peaceful ways will lead us to be kinder and gentler as we work through them. We personify peace and we are lovers of mankind. We are the Peacemakers!

Loving the Olympics. All the participants and spectators remind me as being trees in the forest of humanity. Our forest is so much greener than the news portrays it. When we come together, we flourish! Such is the spirit of the Olympic Games. Such is the spirit of my being. – Charmainism

The pursuit of happiness is very elusive for so many in this world; yet now you know that it's truly attainable. Many have an inkling that they're indeed their own worst enemy; yet have no clue just how to correct this most self-disabling dilemma. You now understand that it's totally within your power to let go of the strangle hold that frustration and disappointment have put upon your attempts at happiness and instead take a strong grip upon the handle of managing your own perspective and seeing things in a more neutralized and positive light. Your reality is what you make it...and you now know it is your choice to choose a happy reality!

Welcome to your new day, your new life, your new way of peacefully handling all that comes your way with the finesse of a fine billiards player. You see what shot needs to be taken and you quickly assess how to make the best of your attempt. In fact, you see it before you've make the attempt. Going through the motions in your mind. You see yourself lining up your cue and with the proper English, you visualize where the stroke's execution will take it to that cushion, then over there, and then, oh yes! You see it all so clearly. You got this and confidently call it out loud:

"Four in the corner, off the three."

I like that call!

Why? Because winners are fearless.

One has to make an attempt to stay in the game in order to make progress. If you don't play, then you can't win. Life is the playground where we can either sit on the benches and watch others have the time of their lives while we wonder why we can't seem to get our motors started, or we can decide to jump start our motors ourselves and get in there and enjoy the light of day with them!

Each day is much akin to that of a Pot Luck. You awake with an invitation to attend. What shall you bring? Let's see...how about ample servings of smiles, joy, and love! When wrapped in a warm embrace of fairness, understanding, and lovingly laced with a positive disposition; you're sure to set your table of life with the best recipes for peace and contentment. – Charmainism

We know it's on us. We know we've been conditioned to think we need to have certain responses and that we're deserving of empathy from others; but now we realize that such types of self-serving behaviors are simply not good for our own well-being. We can change our world by becoming a projector of a positive light, and allowing that light to reflect on others and evoke positive change in them -- one person at a time.

We know that wasting one moment of this precious gift of life is a moment lost for all time. We understand now that we make ourselves either happy or miserable. We've made the decision to let go of the constant wanting and yearning that results from the freefall of a non-purposeful existence. We know that being content and happy is for the taking. Happiness is truly a choice we make.

People haven't come to grips that they're their own itch. They're itching from the inside out; itching for change, but too fearful of failure to try. It's a common problem. It's why there's so much frustration in the world today. Everyone wants change for the better, but until they realize the world won't change until we all make peace with ourselves first – nothing meaningful will change on a global scale. We must change from the inside out. Open your heart so you can be led up the winding staircase and into the door of enlightenment: the Lighthouse of Inner Peace. One Peacemaker at a time, we can indeed change this world.

Somewhere, someone frets over dusting. Elsewhere, there is someone wishing they had something to dust. The smallest things we take for granted are riches to another. Be thankful for every little thing, each and every day. – Charmainism

Reminds me of how Bill and I changed each other's worlds. Bill stabilized my world and I introduced him to a family that was full of life, fun, and comedy. We were nothing like anything that Bill had ever experienced. Bill was inducted into a family that adored him and he loved us back. My younger siblings looked to him like a big brother. My little brothers call him "Brother Bill" to this day.

When we first met, Bill Ladd was a young man of nineteen from a very small, all white community right out of the Spoon River Anthology, and had never had a black acquaintance until he went off to college. Who'd a thunk it? Bill and I were nonetheless totally meant for each other, even if we both had to go through all that transpired to find our way to each other.

Good thing I found him when I did…it was when I was the most vulnerable (though at the time I felt the strongest I'd ever been). When I married Bill, I was sixteen; he was twenty. That was forty-two years ago. Our love has always been with the pedal to the metal and we've never looked back. Our love carried us onto and has kept us on higher ground no matter how low life around us ever got. We've always taken the high road!

We've all been wronged at one time or another in our lives, and when going up against the powers that be, sources with unlimited power and resources, that can be quite a daunting task. So daunting that it becomes prudent to weigh the decision of whether or not righting the injustice, in the big picture, would be worth the toll doing so will take on one's life and all those within and surrounding it.

Such was the battle that Bill and I found ourselves assessing. We made the ultimate decision, after realizing that sometimes it isn't about justice but more about knowing you've done the right thing all along and neutralize destructive power by taking the shortest distance through the storm that would get our lives, and the lives of our children, grandchildren, and all those we love and who love us, back on course the fastest.

Even though it meant enduring hardships and the pain of nearly two years of separation to do it, I kept up a great front so that my beloved husband wouldn't spend one moment worrying about me. He knew his daughter would be fine because I'd make it so, but he didn't think my health could hold up under the stress of it all. My "Shwy" philosophy endured its biggest test to date. We would be strong for him and hold everything together in perfect harmony. And we did.

Once the storm of our lives had passed and my beloved had returned home to me, we were off and running with dates set to chart our course for a new life full of adventure. We made the right decisions and have never looked back. We created a blueprint for a dreamscape few will ever realize.

We went sailing for eleven whole years.

Talk about freedom!

Oh yes we did!

The concept for it actually began at our 25th wedding anniversary party. Many of our closest friends were there, everyone knowing that soon Bill would be gone for a while. I had announced that for our 30th wedding anniversary, we'd be selling everything and buying a sailboat. Bill thought it a joke. But our children knew I was serious.

After the party, I told him I was serious. He still said, "Yeah, right."

About three months later there were packages arriving. Bill comes home and says, "What are all these boxes?"

"Stuff for the boat," I replied.

"What boat?" he asked.

"Our boat. The boat we're buying when we sell the house."

He grinned. Then he looked at me with that, "Are you serious??!!" look. Ha!!

Bill says, "Oh my. You're serious!"

"As a heart attack, Baby. You in?"

Bill smiles wide and says, "With both feet! You mean I get to have a tree house again?"

I affirmed.

Bill has that, this-is-just-too-easy look on his face and questions, "Honey...we don't know how to sail."

This is too easy for me. LOL

"Bill, my love," I responded, "Christopher Columbus didn't have GPS or navigational charts. What's your point?"

The rest is history. If my husband knows anything, it's that I'll find a way to make something happen if it's at all possible. And I went about doing just that.

Bill began working out the details of how to completely run our software development business while living aboard a sailboat. Technology was changing rapidly and it was all in our favor.

Telecommuting was in its infancy in the Caribbean, but we were determined to pull it off. This was the green light we needed to know that we could do it. If we could work aboard while sailing and traversing the waters, then we could live aboard our sailboat full-time and enjoy our new lifestyle to its fullest!

I continued to research and read everything you can imagine (and not imagine!) about the types of boats that would suit us for living aboard yet sailing efficiently in rough seas, sailing in general and detail (including all associated gear), living aboard, buying provisions, planning destination cruises, everyday life, dinghies, outfitting the boat with watermakers, redundant systems, solar panels, wind and diesel generators, etc. etc. etc. It was either a big book propped up in my hands or I was reading while online. Anything I'd read in a book and couldn't figure out, I could find details and schematics online until it was crystal clear to me. And every bit of it was making perfect sense. Bill and I both stayed focused on our new sailing agenda, often sharing new ideas and methods we'd independently discovered.

It was hard while Bill was gone, even though I was pretty used to taking care of a very large home and property mostly by myself long before that, and I did it this time too. I was used to doing all the yard work myself, including the mowing and raking, planting, etc. I even ran the tractor that shoveled the long driveway of snow. My brother, Maurice, and his family lived across the street, so that was a big help for a while. My parents moved in with my daughter and me, as my mother's Alzheimer's was getting pretty bad and it was really nice to have my father with us. Bj would come and visit often, even though he lived in the Chicago area. We were going to be fine. The kids were excited about their parents' plans to buy a sailboat and go on an extended sail when their father returned home.

We were right on schedule to make it all happen.

And when reunited with the love of my life, we were well on our way to making every little thing we'd so perfectly planned a reality. Like what we'd be doing for our 30th wedding anniversary!

We celebrated our 30th wedding anniversary in September of 2002 while aboard our sailboat, which we purchased ten days before that and christened her as September Sea. Bill and I both took to sailing and living board like ducks to water. It was in us all the time. We thoroughly enjoyed sailing and living aboard her for over eleven years.

Our very first year aboard, our anxious children came down to the Keys just a few months after we'd settled into our new lifestyle. That was during the Christmas holiday season of 2002. I'd told Bill that I'd give Bj about three days and he'd announce that he'd return to Joliet, Illinois just long enough to quit his job (as a Corrections Officer) and move down to the Keys. I wasn't off by much. It took him about two days. He asked that we be on the look out for a boat he could buy and live aboard out in Boot Key Harbor. We were delighted to help him through the process. He was a natural born sailor, just like his parents. It was a match made in heaven.

Our daughter, Breighan, loved our new life aboard and coming to visit us. She was in College when we moved aboard and could hardly wait for Christmas vacation to come and see us. She was radiant and so excited about our new adventure. She wasn't at all surprised to know that her brother was going to take the same leap as her parents. I think she expected it just as I did.

But those sailing days, oh, and the hurricanes! The years 2004 and 2005 were incredible. Hurricane Wilma was probably the one that caused all our friends, family, and followers of our website the most concern and dismay. We'd take September Sea up to the Everglades for protection from all manmade objects and other boats and tie her up in the mangroves where she could ride out the storm. The difference with the way we did it, is that we'd be staying aboard her throughout the ordeal.

As we prepared for each hurricane, at our website, I kept a brief accounting of some of the emails sent back and forth from those concerned and those who wished us safety. It's really pretty cool reading to go back there and relive the amazing times we endured with skill, precision, and fearlessness. It was nothing short of amazing. Bill and I were good at this and knew exactly what we were doing, as we'd proved that fact riding out seven hurricanes prior to Wilma. But Wilma was to be a BIG Girl!

All our friends and family had their hearts in their throats on this one because just five months earlier, on Memorial Day, I lost both my son and mother, quite suddenly and totally unexpectedly, about an hour apart. Mother had lost her long battle with Alzheimer's, but was now at peace. Bj succumbed to complications of juvenile diabetes while fighting a bad flu aboard his sailboat in Christenstead, St. Croix, USVI. He had sailed there as First Mate to Captain Dennis Bratton aboard the sailing vessel Coral Sea. Captain Dennis is still heartbroken to this day. He loved Bj with all his heart. We love Captain Dennis with all our hearts. He will always be family to us.

I'll always believe that my mother, knowing that Bj would be leaving this earth, took her grandson by his hand and decided to go with him. That makes it bearable, even though as I type this, I can't stop the flood of rain from my tears.

It's quite understandable that others, without coming out and saying it, were feeling that perhaps Bill and I might be, unknowingly, just a wee bit reckless at this most trying time in our lives when such great heartache had possibly weakened our ability to clearly think things through.

Even though I truly did feel fearless, as the impossible had already occurred in my life, I was ever thinking of daughter Breighan and son Bj's little children. We'd not allow them to have to endure more pain and suffering from loss. We therefore were exceedingly careful but we also loved the challenge that faced us. And we were up to it.

With all I've seen and done throughout my life, I've never spent much time watching soaps because I truly was living my own soap opera! I have been since the day I was born.

When I look back, a flood of fond memories of so many wonderful people who shared with us their love for reading the adventures we had aboard sailing vessel (s/v) September Sea. Our website,

SeptemberSea.com, which began as a way for our families to know where we were and what we were doing, ended up having quite a following of people from around the globe who enjoyed our stories and adventures. I'm sure to this day, many are wondering what happened to us. I just couldn't bear ending the story! So it's sat on the Internet with people coming and going, but with no new updates for quite some time. I'd started writing articles for Claiborne Young's "Salty Southeast Cruisers Net," and had pointed anyone who wanted an update to go to his site.

We decided to go up to the Chesapeake and pay a visit to Bill's brother, Steve, while up there. Steve lives in Ocean City, Maryland. We'd be gone from the Keys about a year for this trip. We'd make it up to South Carolina and spend the winter there, then head up the first of Spring and make it to the Chessie.

But it was not to be. We took the ICW in order to experience something different. Well, we'd previously always sailed on the outside of the "ditch" in open water, but a huge storm cell that hit us around Daytona had us rethinking that strategy. It was the worst storm we'd ever encountered. Fortunately, it only last about an hour. But that was enough for us. For us, it was a no-brainer. This way, we'd not again, while sailing big water, encounter storms appearing out of nowhere that change directions and do what all the forecasters say they never do! Nope! Besides, what's our hurry? We hadn't traveled the ICW along the Florida-Georgia coastline or even farther north, so why not? We're both so glad we did! It was a fascinating glimpse into the backcountry while in waters few people ever get to see up close and personal. We loved every minute of it.

We'd gone to South Carolina and discovered a wonderful marina in Port Royal Landing. The kindest, friendliest owner and staff you'd ever want to meet. It was just the perfect, most pleasurable place when it came to the character of such outstanding people! Close to shopping and groceries, with a courtesy car if needed! And there were tennis courts within biking distance, so Bill and I were in heaven! You guessed it…we stayed in the area with them for quite a while.

So long, in fact, that even when we'd leave for a month just to get out of the marina lifestyle and back to incredible freedom of swinging on the hook invites, we'd miss the people there. At the marina, there's a land-based community as well as a liveaboard community that melds as bread and butter. It's a wonderful and most refreshing union of people who "get it."

Our last outing, we'd been gone for about three weeks and had a wonderful time while out on the hook. When it came time to pull up our hook and get back to the marina, Bill and I couldn't retrieve our anchor.

Our anchor, which is such a great anchor that I've written stories about it, is a 44# Spade. It's the Spade brand, made in Tunisia. Probably the best anchor in the world. It's kept us safe through all types of storms, including a bad on in St. Mary's, Georgia. The boat never moved an inch on two #44 lb. Spade anchors. We were snug as bugs.

After that storm in St. Mary's, our anchor pulled right up as usual. That's the beauty of the Spade anchor. But this time, however, it would not budge.

Our main Spade anchor has our son's name painted on it. He keeps us safe and watches over us. Knowing our Bj was our "anchor," we slept perfectly fine every night while out on the hook and never once set an alarm of any kind for it. It wasn't necessary.

But this time she wouldn't come up. We decided to cut the line to it, note our location on our GPS, and get back to the marina. We'd tried to add a buoy to it but that wasn't working at all. The waters were rough that day and there was obviously something down there below us that succeeded in severing any additional line we tried to add to the detached. Anchor line. We figured we could find it later. Besides, the way the boats went through the area, the additional line and float wouldn't last long on its own.

That was when I told Bill that Bj was saying it was time to leave the sailing life and move ashore. My back wasn't getting any better and my spinal stenosis had been causing me great pain for some time. I just simply learned to grin and bear it, and keep on moving! But it had gotten to the point where it was difficult on the boat, as even a simple task as brushing one's teeth warranted you to brace yourself for movement. If we were at the marina, it wasn't nearly as bad with those types of bracings, but out on the hook, where we loved being, it was not working out anymore.

But even so, we went out and tried to retrieve the anchor. We even had a diver go out there and we went along and showed him right where it was. Though he got close many times, he said there was an incredible amount of seafloor debris that surrounded it. He said it was almost impossible to retrieve it. We decided to leave the anchor there as a permanent mark of it being our last real outing.

It was time to make another lifestyle change. It was time to move on.

I was good with it.

The writing was the ocean floor...and by my own son's hand, it said, "Mom...get off the boat." LOL

So as of April 2013 we moved ashore! And as I sit ashore now in West Central Florida and tend my gardens, I've returned to an old love of mine: writing books.

No regrets. You know me by now to know that's true! Even during the worst of times, I wouldn't have wanted to be anyone else. Every little experience of my life has helped create the fabric that makes up the patchwork sewn into the quilt that blankets my life. I'm good with that!

Think of all the things you've made peace with while reading this book. You're feeling so much better knowing that things need only be put in the proper perspective in order to handle them in a reasonable and calm manner. You think more clearly because you're calm – therefore the best decisions are easier to make! You know that truly, you can have total control over your emotions and therefore your frustrations. You "get it!"

And even that which used to bring us to our darkest times; we realize we can make total peace with that as well. We know that life is death and we're making peace with that. By relying on wonderful memories of the lives that cross our path, we can continue to embrace the love we continue to feel for those who have departed. Our peace has been made to honor those lives by allowing that love to enhance and blossom the appreciation we have for the blessing of having shared that time with them upon this earth. We get it! All facets of life, including death, have their place. When we learn to make peace with that which is as natural as breathing or taking a last and final breath, our hearts can then soar to a fullness that's totally empowering. Life and death are both beautiful – for we can't have one without the other.

Embrace the unknown as if it were a new dance to go to or a new awakening of something especially delightful. For who are we to know if the unknown is any different than that! – Charmainism

When I first began to write this book, my vision didn't include quite so much about my personal life and upbringing. However, the more I got into sharing the benefits of being a peacemaker, the more it felt necessary to illustrate just how my skills were honed as such. There's no doubt I'm a born peacemaker, but it was important that you know it wasn't sheer destiny; rather, it ultimately was a choice. In a household of mixed signals, it was up to me to make sense of just who I preferred myself to be.

The further along I got sharing some of the basic stories, the more the journey to self-discovery truly became a "we" effort. As you began to trust me more with opening your mind and heart to my philosophy, the more the feeling I could trust you with my own thoughts and discoveries along the way. When I said at the book's beginning that we were indeed in this journey together, I truly meant it.

Even though what I've shared is just a fragment of this "soap opera" life of mine, I'm sure it's more than enough for you to recognize there are people who've lost their minds under far less strain than what life has thrown my way. The meat and potatoes of this stew called life is that it's not what has been laid out or prepared for us; rather, it's what we choose to do with the ingredients we've been given and how we use them to make our own preparations – that makes the difference. And what tells the tale as to how good a chef we are is that we know to toss in a potato when we've used too much salt! Being able to adapt is what really matters most.

Making something to sink our teeth into *now* will give us another chance to improve the menu for our tomorrows! Whatever happens in this life becomes that which is part of the glue that promotes our positive growth. No matter what it is. We make it positive. We merely have to make it so.

All tables should be laced

with doilies made of peace. – Charmainism

Sharing parts of my life with you at first had me feeling as if I was making this book all about me...and I didn't want that. But it became apparent that it really was important to divulge just how this true Peacemaker came to be...and that became very much the beating heart that is this book. My Ph.D. in LIFE was hard earned and I'm proud to share with you just how I got it! It was cleansing to me! Good for the soul.

Being positive is what it is all about!! With optimism and positivity, the world is indeed our oyster and nothing can hold us back from happiness and inner peace. Negativity does not intimidate or shake us. The only shaking we do is that of shaking our own hand and thus continuing to renew the pledge to remain our own best friend. We've decided to finesse our life to a new level of contentment as the practice of Positive Indifference keeps us driving our lives safely in the lane of positive growth and comfort. Positive energy remains in abundance, as it's the reward for the effort of maintaining inner peace and happiness.

With a renewed sense of energy and a refreshingly uplifting way of rationalizing the valleys of life, the top of the hill is where you want to be from now on. The low times have been more caused by giving in to the scourge of self-pity. We understand that doing so is no longer an option for good physical or mental health. It's therefore been removed from your life choices menu! Good for you!

And I'm proud of you. With that said, it's time for me to let go of your hand and allow you to fully become the peacemaker you need to be. The door to your peace and happiness is wide open. I've done my part, now it's time for you to do yours.

A peaceful and renewed life awaits you!

Chapter Ten: Welcome to the Lighthouse of Inner Peace

In the garden of inner peace, happiness flourishes. - Charmainism

Hurricane Wilma had raged over s/v September Sea for hours and hours...and then more hours! In between the front side and the backside of the storm was an interim of calmness when the eye of Wilma passed over us. It really was a true calm before the *rest* of the storm. The backside of Wilma was far more powerful than her approach. Though her exit was wicked strong, Bill and I'd done all our preparations and fared through with no injury to us or to our beloved sailing vessel. We'd survived a direct hit from Hurricane Wilma, a category 3 hurricane, as she passed over us in the Everglades with winds clocking 125 knots.

Going up topside, I first climbed through the debris of branches and leaves in the cockpit. It was bright and gorgeous outside. How could a hurricane have just plowed through here? It was mesmerizing.

The sun shone so brightly it appeared as artwork rather than nature. There was a slight buzzing sound coming from somewhere, which was odd, and I looked down just as a hummingbird began to flutter next to me and take a drink of my Diet Pepsi! Holy cow! I yelled down to Bill and he poked his head up the hatch. This was such an amazing sight! I thought if only I'd captured it on camera...what a great commercial that would make for Diet Pepsi or for Nutrasweet: "Even a hummingbird doesn't know Nutrasweet is not sugar!" The closeness with that little hummingbird was a once-in-a-lifetime treat I feel so blessed to have experienced.

And then he (or she) flew off to do whatever after knowing life will continue another day. I certainly felt the same way!

More sounds. What is that? I looked around in time to watch the landings of about five hundred snow-white egrets on the branches of mangrove trees lining the canal where we were. It was a captivating sight. Once they all found a branch, they seemed to eerily look my way. Then it was if they were nodding, as if to say, "Nice to see you. Glad you made it. Well done." Breathtaking and captivating!

There was definitely camaraderie felt between human and animal survivors of this major event that had threatened all of our lives. Bill and I sat topside for hours watching the return of the wildlife to the area. And then the real show began.

As dusk approached and the sky continued to darken, it became readily apparent that Vincent Van Gogh was with us. The sky was a "Starry, Starry Night" of epic proportion. It was incredible. I could see for light years beyond what used to be only a superficial surface eye glimpse of a night of stars. This was like the Twilight Zone. The stars had depth that continued deeper and deeper and deeper until the goose bumps on my arms told me that I'd be approaching infinity at any moment. It was just that riveting. I shall never, ever forget what looked to me being a witness to the scouring of the heavens by God Himself.

I felt refreshed, renewed, and very, very accomplished at what Bill and I had done together. We've always been like that with each other. Together, there was nothing we could not do. To this day, we both feel that way. Our bodies and grey hairs may tell our age, but inside…we're still the star-crossed lovers of yesteryear. And then we had the depths of still being madly in love after all these years together. What about life could be sweeter than that! Our purpose, at that moment, was simply to *be*. And we did just that with the utmost in gratitude for the opportunity.

And so too must you learn to simply *be*. It's that simple. So very, very simple.

Your purpose has been here all along, patiently awaiting your arrival to the realization that it was within you all this time. Your purpose has been to understand the need for genuine gratitude for the gift of life, as all else beyond that is a bonus! We must be grateful to have an invitation to the dance. And then we show up and we do that just: DANCE!

Every moment is a part of that dance called happiness. Happiness becomes you when you're at peace with yourself and others. One who is truly grateful doesn't have time to complain or bicker – they're out enjoying every moment of the blessing of life that flows within their being. With that comes a world that truly is brighter because it's *your* world that is such a wonderful place.

The Fine Art of Aging: Sketch on canvas free of regret; Outline with the glow of gratitude; Draw highlights of fond memories; Shade pain as a confirmation of life; Color with zest for living; Frame in tribute to a golden life; and Display with love for yourself and others. – Charmainism

Happiness is the beacon of light that becomes you! You'll always personify happiness and inner peace when you allow that light to forever shine through you. Keep it fine-tuned by honing your skills to finesse disagreeable situations into agreeable outcomes for you, because you desire to retain your sense of inner peace. Everything else you take with a grain of salt, and a smile on your face. Life becomes a paradisiacal Eden all over again!

Two days after Hurricane Wilma came roaring through the Everglades, it was time to untie s/v September Sea and head back down to our berth at our marina, "Sombrero Dockside," located in Marathon, the "Heart" of the Florida Keys. It's where we'd been since arriving down there three years before. We so loved it there. We'd made a new life and enjoyed the friendship, caring, and love our of "Dockside Family." It was heavenly.

Traversing from our "hurricane hole" and back out towards the open waters of the Gulf of Mexico, we realized there was one major thing we hadn't thought of – what if after a hurricane all the markers were completely destroyed, making finding the way back out to open water difficult? Normally, you'd just look at the chartplotter, which had been uploaded with the charts for this area; but it soon became evident that something more was added to this dilemma: the entire seafloor had changed beneath the normal channel. Where there used to be clear passage and deep enough water, there were tree stumps or entire trees blocking passage. There were also big sand bars where there used to be clear passage. This was a nightmare!

I was at the helm and Bill was watching the water, trying to see his way through the waters to be able to instruct me, "Starboard…. uh, hold it. Keep going straight. Now a little to Port…more. Okay. Yes, that's it. Okay. Straight ahead. Stop."

I could feel that our water was getting shallow. Bill always said I could feel the hairs of weeds hit the bottom of the boat, or some other saying he had to embellish my uncanny ability to notice, when not within eyeshot of the depthsounder, when we were heading into shallower waters. I don't understand it either...but it happens.

"Bill," I said, "we're about to go aground, kiddo."

Sure enough, we slid onto a sand bar that was not there when we'd entered four days ago.

Asking Bill to go up to the bow for helping shift the weight from the stern to the forward section of the boat might allow me to back September Sea off the sand bar, or at the very least, cause a bit of a wriggle that could allow me to manipulate the boat and shimmy her off and back into deeper waters. The biggest problem was that nothing was recognizable anymore. I couldn't tell where deep water was! Nothing looked the same at all and it wasn't the same! That meant my chartplotter, at this point, was doing me not a lick of good! Somehow, I had to find out where the water was in this always very narrow channel. It would be an immense challenge.

As Bill went to the bow, I began to try to wriggle the boat a bit to gain some lift. Sure enough, the bow began to lift as I backed her out the same way I got in there. As I put the engine back into forward, I shouted to Bill that I'd no idea which way to go. The channel was very narrow so we're only talking a matter of feet one way or the other and overshooting it could mean we could be stuck up in the Everglades for weeks. We were sure Marathon got hit very hard and everyone would be scrambling for help. No one was going to come up and get us up in the Everglades. We'd have to wait, perhaps for quite a long time. That was not going to do.

The mosquitoes would eat us alive in short order. Nope. We had to get out of there now.

Just as Bill was telling me he had no clue which way to go, I noticed two dolphins jumping ahead of us. They seemed to be coming our way. How wonderful. They came towards us and then turned around and left the same way, jumping high out of the water and then diving back down. They did this twice in a matter of a minute, and were on their way to do it a third time.

"Bill…honey. They're leading us out of here," I said. Bill has never believed in such things. I always have. To my surprise, Bill said, "When they get next to the boat again, follow them exactly."

And so I did.

The two dolphins, as they led us out, didn't make the short loop they'd been making; instead, they continued jumping up and diving down until we'd followed them all the way out into the open waters of the Gulf. We were free and clear, with plenty of water beneath our keel. And now we were ready to continue the journey back to our homeport. It was upon that realization that we also realized our acrobatic, aquatic guides had quietly disappeared.

Bill and I looked at each other. Our faces were soaked with tears of joy. It was riveting. It was truly and absolutely amazing. Bill says to me, "Honey, that was our son and your mom that lead us out of there." The crying continued, for I felt exactly the same way.

Never in my wildest dreams would I ever have thought I would've heard my Bill say something so spiritual. Spiritual in the sense of it being something that was beyond any thing ever taught to him. Such things were usually outside of his comfort zone and he left them to Rod Serling. But this was something that was unmistakable.

You just can't make this stuff up.

Such is my life and such is my joy of being the person I am. Comfortable in my own skin through it all, through thick and thin! The sense of harmony and inner peace that runs through my very being is who I shall always be. With the heart of a peacemaker, I'll forever choose to make it so.

~In Loving Memory of William Dean "Bj" Ladd II~

Bj's memorial reef is placed approximately one mile offshore Ft. Lauderdale, FL. Coordinates: **25° 57.755' N - 80° 05.875' W**

This incredible sense of inner peace, harmony, and happiness is here for all those who desire a more fulfilling and happier life. Our continued happiness, as Peacemakers, will affect others in a very positive light. This world, theoretically, can change for the better if we allow ourselves to remain a beacon of enlightenment for others to see and follow. We can do it. We are doing it!

It's not over until you let it go...so forget about the fat lady singing! Ha! Make your day positive and productive because that's the way you want it. May you, each and every day, truly enjoy your greatest gift: LIFE. No better time than now to unwrap it! Enjoy! – Charmainism

Shine on, Peacemaker! SHINE ON!

~ End ~

A Word from the Author

Please be so kind as to post a review of my book at the Amazon.com bookstore. Also, you are invited to stay in touch with me via Goodreads.com Your thoughts, experiences, and overall feedback on how my book has affected your life is highly important to me.

With your help, the number of Peacemakers will grow. As each personal world becomes peaceful, so can the entire world – one Peacemaker at a time.

Help keep the wave of happiness and inner peace going by recommending or buying this book for someone you know who needs it. Together, we can do this thing!

May the Peacemaker in you continue to shine forever and a day.

With genuine joy and love,

Charmaine
"Life's a Gift . . . Unwrap It!" – C~

Made in the USA
Lexington, KY
22 July 2015